Preparing Adult English Learners to Write for College and the Workplace

EDITED BY

**Kirsten Schaetzel, Joy Kreeft Peyton,
and Rebeca Fernández**

University of Michigan Press

Ann Arbor

Grateful acknowledgment is given to the following authors, publishers, and individuals for permission to reprint copyrighted material:

The American Council on Education for the sample GED extended responses that appear in Chapter 9. GED® and GED Testing Service® are registered trademarks of the American Council on Education ("ACE"). They may not be used or reproduced without the express written permission of ACE or GED Testing Service. The GED® and GED Testing Service® brands are administered by GED Testing Service LLC under license from the American Council on Education. Used with permission.

Dana Van Bogaert for an adaptation of her figure originally presented at the Conference on Language, Learning, and Culture, Virginia International University, Fairfax, April 8, 2017.

ISBN-13: 978-0-472-03736-0 (print)

2022   2021   2020   2019   4   3   2   1

CONTENTS

Introduction:
Developing the Academic Writing Abilities of Adults Learning English

Joy Kreeft Peyton, Center for Applied Linguistics
Kirsten Schaetzel, Emory University School of Law
Rebeca Fernández, Davidson College

■ The Importance of Academic Writing in Adult Education

The communicative demands of the twenty-first century workplace have led to a fundamental shift in the focus of adult education programs. Whereas basic literacy and life skills were once their sole focus, today's adult education programs must prepare students to understand complex operations, be problem-solvers, have some degree of computer literacy, and attain both oral and written fluency in professional English (Casner-Lotto & Barrington, 2006; Elander, Harrington, Norton, Robinson, & Reddy, 2006; Parrish & Johnson, 2010). Even many minimum wage jobs—such as taking orders in restaurants, parking cars, or providing security in a building—require workers to use computer software, make independent decisions, and find solutions to problems. These tasks involve high-level language skills, critical-thinking skills, computer literacy, and confidence.

To support adult learners' employment and education goals, writing has become more important in the field of adult education. Many adult education practitioners recognize that learners not only need to learn to articulate ideas in a clear and appropriate manner orally but also in writing (Fernández, Peyton, & Schaetzel, 2017). In the past, programs focused primarily on listening, speaking, and reading. Then, learners were interested in improving their listening and speaking skills to get entry-level jobs and be able to converse in their workplaces and neighborhoods. Learners needed to work on their reading skills to get hired for better jobs and to advance in their adult education classes. Teachers, therefore, focused on these two skills, especially reading, because program assessments and funding often depended on them. When writing skills were taught to adult English language learners, teachers typically focused on transactional writing, such as note-taking, writing narratives, and exercises to teach specific language skills (filling in vocabulary words in cloze exercises, correcting grammar and spelling in sentences) (Fernández, Peyton, & Schaetzel, 2017; Reid, 1993; Shanahan, 2015; Zamel, 1982, 1987). Now, however, with changes in the job market and adult learners moving to two- and four-year degree programs, writing instruction needs to extend beyond narrative genres and equip learners to be rhetorically flexible—that is, be able to write for the multiple audiences, purposes, and contexts of college courses and the workplace.

In the United States, the 2013 College and Career Readiness Standards for Adult Education (U.S. Department of Education, 2013) and the 2016 English Language Proficiency Standards for Adult Education (U.S. Department of Education, 2016) were designed to guide teachers as they prepare adult learners for effective participation in academic and workforce settings and ultimately to attain economic self-sufficiency. These standards explicitly describe academic writing skills that learners need to be successful in these contexts. The new focus on writing is also reflected in the high school equivalency tests that were revised and created in 2014: The GED (General Education Development test, revised), HiSET (High School Equivalency Test, created), and TASC (Test Assessing Secondary Completion, created) now contain writing tasks that are more academic in nature. Now, instead of writing an essay on a given topic using their own experience as support, test takers use two readings to support an opinion on a topic that may or may not be different from their own opinion. (See Chapter 9 for a more detailed discussion of the writing tasks on these tests.)

As with any successful change in curricula, changes in teaching methods, approaches, and allocation of class time must follow. However, in federally and privately funded adult education programs, insufficient funding for professional development and instructional materials can limit teachers' ability to teach academic and workplace writing. Furthermore, adult education teachers, unlike their K–12 and post-secondary education counterparts, come from educational and professional backgrounds that may not have prepared them to teach writing to adult English language learners. Crandall, Ingersoll, and Lopez (2008), in their survey of state teaching qualifications, noted that the requirements to teach adult English language learners vary widely, a pattern that continues today (see *Requirements to Teach Adult Education Programs*, https://study.com/how_to_teach_adults. html). Some states require K–12 certification; some require an ESL endorsement; and some do not have any requirements apart from a specific level of education, ranging from an advanced degree to a high school diploma. With respect to writing specifically, Fernández, Peyton, and Schaetzel (2017) found that 29 percent of the adult education teachers they surveyed had participated in workshops and short-term professional development on teaching academic writing within the past year, 39 percent within the past three years, and 33 percent more than three years ago or never. It would seem, then, that more can be done to equip teachers to teach writing skills for academic and workplace contexts.

This volume seeks to address these challenges. It is written for teachers and program managers in adult education and college preparatory programs for English language learners at all levels and for instructors in university programs who are preparing practitioners to work with adults learning English. Although it focuses primarily on adult education programs in the United States, colleagues teaching English to immigrants/migrants in other countries will also find it useful. It provides theory, research, and specific instructional strategies and approaches, including structures for classroom activities and assignments, feedback mechanisms to guide teachers as they help their students develop as writers, and information about writing in different modalities, by hand and on a computer. In this volume, adult education practitioners working with adults learning English will learn about:

- ☐ moving adults into higher education and careers and helping them be college and career ready.
- ☐ enriching and advancing what they are already doing in their classes, based on what they have learned about academic writing.
- ☐ integrating writing into the existing curriculum in adult education programs at all levels, including into content classes.
- ☐ teaching writing in line with national, state, and program educational standards.

■ Academic Writing Skills That Adult Learners Need

In order to help adult learners acquire academic writing skills, it is important to understand what academic writing involves. Most broadly, *academic writing* is situated in the university discourse community, which is "organized around the production and legitimation of particular forms of knowledge and social practices at the expense of others" (Chase, 1988, p. 13). Examples of academic writing include essays, research papers, reports, laboratory write-ups, and exam answers. Although scholars argue that academic writing is neither uniform nor static (Gee, 1989, p. 7), "Only certain ways of constructing knowledge and expressing opinions are recognized and valued within the academic discourse community, and these privileged ways of meaning-making have to be learned" (Tang, 2013, p. 12). These ways of "meaning-making" or knowing, which vary across academic disciplines, are reflected in academic writing (Zhu, 2004). For instance, whereas writing assignments for the humanities (e.g., history, ethics, philosophy) often require close analysis of and textual evidence from a course reading or an archival document, academic paper assignments for the social sciences (e.g., economics, psychology, education) tend to expect writers to demonstrate knowledge of previous research and the scientific method.

Although some learners can acquire the academic literacy needed to write appropriately in different rhetorical situations and disciplines merely through exposure and social practice, many others—especially non-traditional and immigrant students—require a more direct approach. Literacy research in the past two decades has found strong support for the explicit teaching of writing skills, processes, and knowledge (Graham & Perin, 2007). Thus, teachers can and should teach adult English language learners to construct and organize knowledge, state and support opinions, and explicate their ideas according to the conventions of the university discourse community. More specifically, to teach English learners, teachers need to know what the features of academic writing are and what skills this writing entails.

The common features of academic writing are confirmed and amplified in a study by Rosenfeld, Courtney, and Fowles (2004), who examined writing requirements in colleges and universities. They surveyed professors in Master's and PhD programs to learn the literacy practices used and skills needed in their fields and institutions. The survey had a list of 39 tasks, and respondents were asked to rank the tasks from *slightly important* to *extremely important*. Respondents rated 36 of the 39 task statements as *important* or *very important* for students entering their programs to be able to perform competently. The following 12 tasks were rated the highest:

- ☐ Organize ideas and information coherently.
- ☐ Use grammar and syntax that follow the rules of standard written English, avoiding errors that distract the reader or disrupt meaning.
- ☐ Avoid errors in mechanics (e.g., spelling and punctuation).
- ☐ Abstract or summarize essential information (e.g., from speeches, observations, or texts).
- ☐ Analyze and synthesize information from multiple sources.
- ☐ Credit sources appropriately.
- ☐ Integrate quoted and referenced material appropriately.

- ☐ Develop a well-focused, well-supported discussion, using relevant reasons and examples.
- ☐ Write clearly, with smooth transitions from one thought to the next.
- ☐ Write precisely and concisely, avoiding vague or empty phrases.
- ☐ Revise and edit a text to improve its clarity, coherence, and correctness.
- ☐ Work independently to plan and compose a text.

Although not included in this list, vocabulary knowledge is also critical to becoming an effective writer. In recent years, researchers have emphasized the importance of both comprehending written texts and producing the language used in academic and career-focused contexts, orally and in writing (see, e.g., discussion in Friedberg, Mitchell, & Brook, 2016; McKeown, Crosson, Artz, Sandora, & Beck, 2013; Ucelli & Galloway, 2017). These include morphologically complex words, general academic words, and discipline-specific words. In addition to word lists, writing researchers are increasingly studying and promoting the teaching of lexical bundles—phrases, word chunks, and discourse structures characteristic of academic, disciplinary, and workplace discourse (Biber & Barbieri, 2007; Hyland, 2008). McKeown et al. (2013), focusing on middle and high school students, point out that "the vocabulary demand of texts that students are assigned in school is cited [in research reports] as a major contributor to reading problems" (p. 45) and argue that " … we must do more to help students build a deep, flexible understanding of the kinds of words that are used in academic texts" (p. 45). This observation and claim apply to adult education contexts as well.

Discussions about success in the "emerging workplace" point to the importance of the writing skills listed. As outlined in the College and Career Readiness Standards, "Individuals must be able to engage with complex texts, communicate effectively, think critically, and apply what they learn to novel settings" (Haynes, 2012, p. 16). For example, adult learners studying to be nursing assistants need to be able to write answers to problematic scenarios on class exams, stating what course of action they would follow in a specific situation and supporting their choices with reasons. Once employed, they may also be asked to write procedures for co-workers to follow on later shifts. To be able to meet the situational demands of each writing task, they will need to develop the appropriate vocabulary, syntax, and discourse style.

In a survey and follow-up interviews conducted in 2015 by the editors of this book (Fernández, Peyton, & Schaetzel, 2017; Peyton & Schaetzel, 2016), adult ESL educators described the writing needs of adult ESL learners in their classes at community college, community-based, and K–12 adult education programs. They reported that the learners in their classes need to be able to:

- write argumentative, technical, and informative texts.
- create, argue for, and support a thesis statement.
- extract and summarize supporting information.
- write precisely and concisely, using appropriate vocabulary and sentence structure.
- produce a well-edited piece that is easily understood by a native English speaker.
- use and credit sources.

These features, which characterize traditional academic writing, are also present to varying degrees in professional and workplace writing, as shown in Figure I.1 (first identified by Agnew, 1992). By *professional writing*, we mean the kind of conceptual, administrative, and policy writing that office workers, such as program and project managers, sales executives, and directors, engage in (Goins, Rauh, Tarner, & Von Holten, 2016). *Workplace writing*, in contrast, tends to be more transactional and informational (Agnew, 1992), that which general staff and personnel in more physically demanding jobs, such as nurses' aides, mechanics, and hotel and restaurant staff, engage in. For example, hotel staff may be asked to prepare announcements or invitations to special events, reply to customer emails, or monitor the hotel's social media pages.

Figure I.1 Comparing Features of Professional and Workplace Writing

Features of Professional Writing	Features of Workplace Writing (Agnew, 1992)
■ Extended writing tasks are aimed at external and internal audiences and often involve or require feedback and multiple drafts (e.g., white papers, annual reports). ■ Multiple readers may be affected in different ways by the content of the document. ■ Topics vary depending on the specific project and its goals. ■ Writing is often persuasive and goal-oriented (seeking support for a decision, justifying a project, making a case for increased funding, etc.). ■ Tasks may require doing research not only on the topic but also on audience needs and expectations. ■ Writing quality can influence broad outcomes (e.g., receiving or being denied an account).	■ Short, repetitive writing tasks tend to communicate specific information to a limited or internal audience (e.g., short memos, long memos, one-page letters, informal notes to someone, filling out preprinted forms). ■ Readers are primarily supervisors or co-workers who need the information for record-keeping or as a basis for action (e.g., deciding whether a patient needs a particular treatment). ■ Writers focus on well-known and consistent topics, modes, and audiences (e.g., an email message or a note to a supervisor, a patient care log). ■ Writing is transactional or task-based (e.g., providing information about a patient's treatment plan). ■ Research is not usually required, but rather knowledge of the field and context in which the work is taking place. ■ Writing quality can have immediate or specific real-life rewards and consequences (e.g., incomplete or illegible customer records can impact quality of service).

Of course, these features are not exclusive to one work context or the other. Professional writers will often engage in general workplace writing and, on occasion, non-office personnel will produce professional genres, such as a letter of recommendation or a request for increased funding or payment. In any case, writers must use clear language that is appropriately formal, topic-focused, and grammatically correct (Beason, 2001). While thinking beyond specific occupations or professions, we should also prepare students to be rhetorically flexible and capable of adjusting to the writing demands of an increasingly unpredictable job landscape. Thus, teaching the features of academic writing assists all English language learners as they endeavor to participate in higher education, gain employment, and aspire to career advancement.

■ Challenges That Adult Learners Face

Whether seeking a high school diploma or a college-level certificate or degree, few students can avoid writing today. Students learning English who are preparing for, entering, and participating in academic programs, at a community college or a university, experience unique challenges. Eli Hinkel (2004) found that "students may be stumbling during their general education courses, taken during the first years of a higher education program, because of their lack of academic reading and writing skills" (p. 25). Research examining the college and career readiness of English learners has often found them to be the least prepared to meet the challenges of college writing (Kanno & Kangas, 2014). When faced with the need to write an essay or another piece of writing, such students may feel alone and challenged; they are starting with a blank sheet of paper and must put words on it. They need to make a point clearly and turn in a finished product on which they will be judged.

The quality and amount of writing instruction they receive prior to and during college only exacerbate the problem. Referring to postsecondary writing courses, Matsuda (2006) has noted that "in many composition classrooms, … language issues beyond simple 'grammar' correction are not addressed extensively, even when the assessment of student texts is based at least partly on students' proficiency in the privileged variety of English (Standard Written English)" (p. 640). If students do not receive this instruction in credit-granting college composition classes, where teachers may be specifically trained to teach writing, they are unlikely to receive it in courses that only meet general education requirements or in non-credit courses in adult education, where teachers may be less equipped to teach writing and are working with non-traditional native and immigrant student populations.

■ Challenges That Educators Working with This Population Face: Results of a National Survey

Concerns about the quality and amount of writing that non-traditional students in adult education receive guided the vision for this volume and the editors' collaboration. In the survey of adult ESL instructors across the United States previously cited (Fernández, Peyton, & Schaetzel, 2017), we found that while teachers and program administrators recognize that academic writing is important and are shifting their curricula and materials to incorporate academic writing in their instruction, many reported challenges in teaching academic writing to adults learning English and expressed a need for professional development and support. The types of professional development that might be provided (e.g., workshops and longer courses focused on specific knowledge and skills related to instruction and assessment approaches overall, and writing instruction and assessment specifically, through which teachers receive certificates and state-mandated credentials) are described in detail in an article by Schaetzel, Peyton, and Burt (2007), *Professional Development for Adult ESL Practitioners: Building Capacity.*

To provide high-quality academic writing instruction in adult ESL classes that contributes to positive educational and career outcomes, systemic shifts are needed in the field. We can learn from the consequences of a "piecemeal" approach to educational reform (LaVenia, Cohen-Vogel, & Lang, 2015, p. 146) documented at the middle and high school levels, where "second- and third-generation adolescent learners … continue to struggle with the use of language and literacy in secondary-level academic coursework" (Haynes,

2012, p. 3). Regarding this situation, Mariana Haynes (2012) argues:

> The lack of progress [in literacy reforms] at both the federal and state levels can be attributed to the fact that educational policies neither leveraged fundamental shifts in the design of curriculum and instruction nor ensured systemic interventions and supports for English learners. (p. 3)

In other words, to ensure that English learners in adult education programs are college and career ready, policy and mandates alone will not suffice. Quality professional development, sufficient funding, and guidance, such as that provided in this volume, are needed.

■ Organization of This Volume

The chapters are arranged within four parts, each representing different components of and stages in teaching academic writing and considerations unique to the adult education context: **Setting the Stage for Teaching Writing, Supporting the Writing Process, Working with Beginning Writers,** and **Aligning Writing with Accountability Systems.** Chapter contributors are current or former adult educators with experience in community college, university, and adult education programs in the United States and abroad. (Brief author bios are included at the end of the volume.)

The chapters address ten instructional approaches that have emerged from the research related to college and career readiness and standards that guide instruction. Each chapter is designed to help teachers develop a clear understanding of the approach, its research basis, and related policies, as well as to receive specific guidance, tools for implementation, and resources for self-study (Additional Resources). Each chapter opens with questions to guide the reading and closes with reflective questions prompting teachers to think about the relationship between the topic addressed, their current practices, and alternatives they might explore in the classroom.

Part 1: Setting the Stage for Teaching Writing

The two chapters in this section focus on the importance of writing in adult education, ways that writing can be connected with other language skills, and the critical importance of writing in content area classes as adult learners prepare for college courses and work.

1. Connect writing to reading and other skills.

In "Writing as the Basis for Reading and So Much More," Rebeca Fernández (Davidson College) points out that concerns over standardized assessments used to determine program funding often force adult ESL instructors to prioritize reading and speaking skills over writing instruction. This focus is bolstered by a belief that writing takes time away from learning other skills. The chapter provides a theoretical rationale for prioritizing the teaching of writing, presents research on the importance of writing in developing content knowledge and other language modes (speaking, listening, and reading), and proposes writing-centered activities and a sample lesson that incorporate writing at every stage of learning.

2. Build pathways for writing development in content areas.

In "Building Pathways for Writing Development in the Content Areas," Donna M. Brinton (University of California, Los Angeles) and Barry D. Griner (University of Southern California) describe the importance of content-based instruction (CBI), which involves the simultaneous learning of content and language. In this approach, content serves as the point of departure for the selection and sequencing of the language curriculum. An instructional unit from American history (the Lewis and Clark Expedition), with examples of materials that can be used and tasks that can be undertaken, demonstrates how language and content goals can complement each other and how content instruction can be enhanced by a specific focus on language. The chapter describes how the use of academic content material, delivered through the medium of English, provides a firm foundation for literacy skills and how the integrated skills focus of CBI provides the necessary scaffold for students to acquire the organizational and genre-specific skills they require for academic writing.

Part 2: Supporting the Writing Process

The four chapters in this section describe the components of the writing process: tools (including technology) that can be used to facilitate the process and ways that thoughtful, effective feedback can be provided as students write.

3. Use the writing process.

In "The Process of Writing," Dudley Reynolds (Carnegie Mellon University–Qatar) discusses how an understanding of the writing process can inform both pedagogy and learning outcomes when teaching academic and professional writing in adult education programs. After reviewing the research on the behaviors that novice and competent writers engage in when producing a written text and the components of the writing process, specific activities are described that learners can engage in as they write, review, revise, discuss, and edit their own texts and engage in this process with other students in the class. The chapter makes clear how knowledge and use of the writing process help adult students become independent writers.

4. Develop varied options and supports for writing.

In "Scaffolding Writing: Using Interactive Writing and Graphic Organizers," Joy Kreeft Peyton (Center for Applied Linguistics) describes research on the need for and benefits of supports for students engaged in academic writing. Two types of supports that can be provided are described: interactive writing (dialogue journals), through which students articulate their ideas and perspectives in interaction with a more proficient writer (often their teacher) and receive significant feedback and further development of their ideas; and graphic organizers, which provide a framework for shaping the key ideas that will be included in a written piece. The chapter describes these two types of supports and the skills and abilities that they build, including processing of information, sharing of ideas and perspectives, seeing other ways to express ideas, and building a knowledge base and expressive style. It also describes specific ways that the supports can be implemented, with examples of graphic organizers that can be used with learners at different English and writing proficiency levels.

5. Use technology in writing instruction.

In "Leveraging Technology in Writing Instruction," Diana Satin (English for New Bostonians) and Steve Quann (instructional design consultant) describe how teachers can incorporate technology and support learners as they collaborate on a project-based activity. The chapter describes specific methodologies, instructional strategies, and tools to enhance skill building. The authors discuss ways these approaches and technologies can help teachers and learners move through the components of the writing process as they prepare to share their culminating presentations.

6. Provide feedback on students' writing.

In "Providing Feedback on Students' Writing," Dana Ferris (University of California, Davis) describes the importance of thoughtful, supportive feedback from expert mentors for developing students' confidence and competence when writing in a second language (L2). The chapter describes best practices in providing feedback to L2 writers about their texts, with a specific focus on ways to provide three types of feedback: selective and prioritized, clear and specific, and encouraging and empowering. Although mention is made of various sources of feedback (peers, self-evaluation, and tutors), the teacher's critical role in providing feedback is emphasized.

Part 3: Working with Beginning Writers

The two chapters in this section describe processes and provide tools for teaching academic writing to adult learners with limited education and literacy in their home language(s). The processes described lead learners from the knowledge and skills that they have to those that they need to be successful in their future education and employment.

7. Start with writing from the beginning.

In "Getting Started with Writing from the Beginning," Betsy Lindeman Wong (Northern Virginia Community College) describes a particular adult learner population—immigrants and refugees with limited formal schooling and literacy in the language of their home countries who have settled in the United States and are learning English as an additional language. Their literacy backgrounds can present challenges for teachers, who are often unprepared to work with adult students who do not read or write. The chapter reviews research on teaching this learner population and offers standards-aligned instructional approaches and strategies for working with them. The strategies can be used with adult learners who have very limited literacy from the first day of class and over time, as they learn and move to more advanced concepts and skills.

8. Use oral language as a bridge to academic writing.

In "Oral Language as a Bridge to Academic Writing," Patsy Egan and Betsy Parrish (Hamline University) describe how teachers working with adults learning English who have limited prior formal schooling or limited experience with academic literacy can leverage and build on those students' oral language proficiency as a bridge to academic writing. The chapter briefly summarizes differences between oral and written academic discourse and builds the case for harnessing oral language for academic writing development, including ways that teachers can encourage academic conversations as the basis for academic literacy from beginning through advanced levels of

English proficiency. The chapter describes tasks, tools, and scaffolds that generate oral academic discourse that is then used as the bridge to writing in a variety of genres, moving beyond narrative to writing a report, presenting an argument with evidence, or describing a sequence of events. It also invites readers to reflect on how to use the strategies presented with other content and topics, for both general and career-focused purposes.

Part 4: Aligning Writing with Accountability Systems

Writing in adult education occurs within the context of accountability systems, which include assessments and national, state, and program standards that guide instruction. The two chapters in this section describe ways that teachers can adjust instruction so that it is responsive to and helps students to work effectively within these systems.

9. Use test prompts to develop academic writing.

In "Using Writing Test Prompts to Develop Academic Writing," Kirsten Schaetzel (Emory University School of Law) describes sample prompts that are currently being used in the writing portions of high-stakes high school equivalency exams (GED, HiSET, and TASC) in the United States and the ways that these prompts can be used to develop students' academic writing abilities. After offering a rationale for using writing exams consistently to build academic writing skills, an example from the GED is used to show how teachers can identify skills that students must demonstrate in the exam and develop class activities to use with students at all proficiency levels that build their confidence and skills. A learning framework, Habits of Mind, provides the foundation for this work and provides examples of activities that teachers and students can do to build the Habits of Mind needed to perform well on the read-to-write task in high school equivalency exams.

10. **Understand and align writing instruction with national standards.**

In "Teaching Writing in an Age of Standards," Gilda Rubio-Festa (North Carolina Community College System) describes the standards that are driving instruction in K–12 and post-secondary programs in the United States and provides a rationale for and curricular approaches to standards-based writing instruction. The chapter includes examples of tasks and activities aligned with the standards and clearly stated learning outcomes to ensure that students are able to navigate gateway assessments and learning opportunities beyond the classroom.

■ Concluding Thoughts

Although the field of adult education has recognized the importance of writing for some time (e.g., Auerbach, 1992; Barber, Barber, Karner, & Laur 2006), in the past, assessment systems only considered writing skills "in a functional workplace, employability, and life skills context" (CASAS, 2001). The view of academic writing as an essential twenty-first century skill for adult learners—not just for traditional students—gained prominence with the development of adult education standards in 2013 (U.S. Department of Education, 2013) and newly designed high-stakes assessments such as the GED. For English language learners (ELLs), these educational reforms have gone even further, as described by Haynes (2012):

> For ELLs in particular, the academic language competencies embodied in the standards require systemic, district-wide approaches to curriculum design and instructional delivery that intertwine language development and content. The new standards are designed to bridge the gap that has long existed between language acquisition and content proficiency for ELLs. This potential will only be realized if policy leaders and practitioners carefully examine programs and practices and evaluate their impact on ELLs' progress in meeting the standards. (p. 2)

Recognizing that effective writing instruction for adults learning English requires a systemwide commitment that includes robust teacher professional development, the purpose of this volume is to provide the research background and specific approaches and resources that allow programs and classroom teachers to implement these changes.

In addition, we need to find ways to work together as a field to help make the necessary shifts. For example, we might:

- ▣ identify and disseminate promising practices and approaches to academic writing in terms of integration of language and content, time spent writing, types of texts that students write, audiences that students write for, types of feedback given, types of assessments used, ways to use technology, and ways that one type and level of activity can be used to build the next types and levels.

- ▣ coordinate instructional approaches across student proficiency and class levels, so that students build from level to level in a sustained and consistent way.

- ▣ emphasize academic, workplace, and professional writing that is aligned with the national standards at local, state, and national levels.

- ▣ ensure that teachers have opportunities to participate in professional development opportunities, learning communities, and collaborations that have academic writing as a focus.

- ▣ create and make available resource collections of supports for writing at all English proficiency levels (test prompts, graphic organizers, and other types of support).

There is a great deal to be done in the field of adult ESL education to ensure that learners in adult education programs are preparing to succeed in further education and work. Educators are clearly interested in participating in needed changes, but they cannot do it alone. It is time for us to work together as a field to make the needed shifts.

References

Agnew, E. (1992). Basic writers in the workplace. *Journal of Basic Writing, 11*(2), 28–46.

Auerbach, E. (1992). *Making meaning, making change: Participatory curriculum development for adult ESL literacy*. Washington, DC: Center for Applied Linguistics and Delta Systems.

Barber, D. B., Barber, W. D., Karner, N. F., & Laur, D. M. (2006). *Teaching writing: A tool kit for adult basic skills educators.* Boone, NC: Appalachian State University. https://abspd.appstate.edu/sites/abspd.appstate.edu/files/Teaching_Writing_Tool_Kit.pdf

Beason, L. (2001). Ethos and error: How business people react to errors. *College Composition and Communication, 53*(1), 33–64.

Biber, D., & Barbieri, F. (2007). Lexical bundles in university spoken and written registers. *English for Specific Purposes, 26*(3), 263–286.

Casner-Lotto, J., & Barrington, I. (2006). *Are they really ready to work? Employers' perspectives on the basic knowledge and applied skills of new entrants to the 21st century U.S. workforce.* New York: The Conference Board. http://www.scirp.org/reference/ReferencesPapers.aspx?ReferenceID=796672

Chase, G. (1988). Accommodation, resistance and the politics of student writing. *College Composition and Communication, 39*(1), 13–22.

Comprehensive Adult Student Assessment System (CASAS). (2001, February). *CASAS/GED writing skills study. Technical report.* San Diego, CA: CASAS. http://www.casas.org/docs/pagecontents/ia_ged_wrtg_techreportw7_rt.pdf

Crandall, J., Ingersoll, G., & Lopez, J. (2008). *Adult ESL teacher credentialing and certification.* Washington, DC: Center for Applied Linguistics. http://www.cal.org/caela/esl_resources/briefs/tchrcred.html

Elander, J., Harrington, K., Norton, L., Robinson, H., & Reddy, P. (2006). Complex skills and academic writing: A review of evidence about the types of learning required to meet core assessment criteria. *Assessment & Evaluation in Higher Education, 31*(1), 71–90.

Fernández, R., Peyton, J. K., & Schaetzel, K. (2017). A survey of writing instruction in adult ESL programs: Are teaching practices meeting adult learner needs? *Journal of Research and Practice for Adult Literacy, Secondary, and Basic Education, 6*(2), 5–20.

Friedberg, C., Mitchell, A., & Brook, E. (2016). Understanding academic language and its connection to school success. *Lexia Learning.* http://www.lexialearning.com/resources/white-papers/understanding-academic-language

Gee, J. P. (1989). Literacy, discourses, and linguistics: Essays by James Paul Gee. A Special Issue of the *Journal of Education, 171*(1), 5–17.

Goins, A., Rauh, C., Tarner, D., & Von Holten, D. (2016). *Workplace writing: A handbook for common workplace genres and professional writing.* New Prairie Press. http://newprairiepress.org/ebooks/8

Graham, S., & Perin, D. (2007). *Writing next: Effective strategies to improve writing of adolescents in middle and high schools.* A report to Carnegie Corporation of New York. Washington, DC: Alliance for Excellent Education.

Haynes, M. (2012, October). *The role of language and literacy in college- and career-ready standards: Rethinking policy and practice in support of English language learners.* Washington, DC: Alliance for Excellent Education.

Hinkel, E. (2004). *Teaching academic ESL writing: Practical techniques in vocabulary and grammar.* New York: Routledge.

Hyland, K. (2008). As can be seen: Lexical bundles and disciplinary variation. *English for Specific Purposes, 27*(1), 4–21.

Kanno, Y., & Kangas, S. E. (2014). "I'm not going to be, like, for the AP": English language learners' limited access to advanced college-preparatory courses in high school. *American Educational Research Journal, 51*(5), 848–878.

LaVenia, M., Cohen-Vogel, L., & Lang, L. (2015). The Common Core State Standards Initiative: An event history analysis of state adoption. *American Journal of Education, 121*(2), 145–182. doi:10.1086/679389

Matsuda, K. (2006). The myth of linguistic homogeneity in U.S. college composition. *College English, 68*(6), 637–651.

McKeown, M. G., Crosson, A. C., Artz, N. J., Sandora, C., & Beck, I. L. (2013). In the media: Expanding students' experience with academic vocabulary. *The Reading Teacher, 67*(1), 45–53.

Parrish, B., & Johnson, K. (2010). *Promoting learner transitions to postsecondary education and work: Developing academic readiness skills from the beginning.* Washington, DC: Center for Applied Linguistics. http://www.cal.org/caelanetwork/pdfs/TransitionsFinalWeb.pdf

Peyton, J. K., & Schaetzel, K. (2016). Teaching writing to adult English language learners: Lessons from the field. *Journal of Literature and Art Studies, (6)*, 1407–1423. http://www.davidpublisher.com/index.php/Home/Article/index?id=28304.html

Reid, J. (1993). *Teaching ESL writing*. Englewood Cliffs, NJ: Prentice Hall.

Rosenfeld, M., Courtney, R., & Fowles, M. (2004). *Identifying the writing tasks important for academic success at the undergraduate and graduate levels.* (GRE Board Research Report No. 00-04 R). Princeton, NJ: Educational Testing Service. https://www.ets.org/Media/Research/pdf/RR-04-42.pdf

Schaetzel, K., Peyton, J. K., & Burt, M. (2007). *Professional development for adult ESL practitioners: Building capacity.* Washington, DC: Center for Applied Linguistics. http://www.cal.org/caela/esl_resources/briefs/profdev.html

Shanahan, C. (2015). *Disciplinary literacy strategies in content area classrooms.* ILA E-ssentials. Newark, DE: International Literacy Association. https://education.ucf.edu/mirc/docs/Disciplinary-literacy-strategies-in-content-area-classes2015.pdf

Tang, R. (2013). The issues and challenges facing academic writers from ESL/EFL contexts: An overview. In R. Tang (Ed.), *Academic writing in a second or foreign language* (pp. 1–20). New York: Bloomsbury.

Ucelli, P., & Galloway, E. P. (2017). Academic language across content areas: Lessons from an innovative assessment and from students' reflections about language. *Journal of Adolescent & Adult Literacy, 60*(4), 395–404.

U.S. Department of Education. Office of Vocational and Adult Education. (2013). *College and career readiness standards for adult education.* Washington, DC: Author. http://lincs.ed.gov/publications/pdf/CCRStandardsAdultEd.pdf

U.S. Department of Education. Office of Career, Technical and Adult Education. (2016). *English language proficiency standards for adult education.* Washington, DC: American Institutes for Research. https://lincs.ed.gov/publications/pdf/elp-standards-adult-ed.pdf

Zamel, V. (1982). Writing: The process of discovering meaning. *TESOL Quarterly, 16*(2), 195–210.

Zamel, V. (1987). Recent research on writing pedagogy. *TESOL Quarterly, 21*(4), 697–715.

Zhu, W. (2004). Faculty views on the importance of writing, the nature of academic writing, and teaching and responding to writing in the disciplines. *Journal of Second Language Writing, 13*, 29–48.

PART 1

Setting the Stage for Teaching Writing

Chapter 1

Writing as the Basis for Reading and So Much More

Rebeca Fernández, Davidson College

Opening Questions ─────────────────

1. What makes academic writing different from personal or transactional writing (e.g., filling out forms, writing an email, taking class notes, and posting on social media)?
2. What kinds of writing do your students do in class? How do these kinds of writing contribute to their academic literacy?
3. How can you teach so that time spent on writing does not interfere with other program requirements and goals?

In adult literacy education, acknowledgment of the inextricable connection between writing and reading was once commonplace. Paulo Freire, the educator and philosopher whose work with and reflections about "illiterate" adults in his native Brazil has inspired generations of literacy workers to focus on reading and writing's emancipatory potential, famously said, "Reading the word is not preceded merely by reading the world, but by a certain form of writing it, or *re-writing* it, that is, transforming it by means of conscious practical work" (Freire & Macedo, 1987, p. 10, emphasis added).

Many adult educators subscribing to Freire's notion of emancipatory literacy have taught English and life skills (Auerbach, 1992) to new immigrants and routinely asked them to write the proverbial immigration story (Ferlazzo & Schulten, 2010). However, what they have not been able to do consistently is support students in their "re-writing" of the world, emphasizing the skills needed not only to tell their stories and achieve economic self-sufficiency, but also to live personally rich and meaningful lives (Fernández, Peyton, & Schaetzel, 2017).

Personal writing continues to be the primary form of writing in adult ESL classes, but knowing now that critical reading and writing are "centrally important" to college success (Conley, 2007, p. 14), we are preparing to do more. As is noted several times in this volume, adult ESL instructors and program administrators who completed our survey recognized the importance of writing for college and career transitions and success but reported providing limited writing instruction out of concerns about time and performance on reading-focused standardized assessments (Fernández, Peyton, & Schaetzel, 2017). This chapter addresses these concerns by emphasizing the many ways that writing supports other language modes and, above all, student learning. I begin by providing a theoretical rationale for writing instruction from the field of second language acquisition. Then, I present research and teaching ideas for connecting writing, reading, speaking, and listening, as well as grammar and vocabulary. Finally, I provide an example of a writing-centered learning unit that incorporates other skills as well.

■ Theoretical Importance of Writing

Language Input-Interaction-Output

Language teachers often appeal to the notion of "comprehensible input" to justify listening and reading activities (Krashen, 2004) in the classroom. Indeed, the comprehensible input hypothesis, first proposed by Stephen Krashen (1982) along with five other related hypotheses, posits that the optimal conditions for classroom learning require language input, usually spoken or written, that is appropriate to students' language proficiency. Krashen (1985) refers to this notion as *i+1*, a zone in which language input is not so easy that it doesn't challenge students to expand their language skills and also is not so hard that it increases their affective filter, or levels of anxiety that interfere with learning. For beginners, a language learning context that consists primarily of receiving language input and does not require production of language (output) avoids direct correction and does not force production.

Other theorists, believing that input alone does not explain the underlying mechanisms for second language acquisition, have expanded on Krashen's perspective by emphasizing the role of interaction in language learning. Michael Long, who first proposed the interaction hypothesis (1983), reasoned that, during communicative exchanges, interlocutors negotiate for meaning by adjusting and modifying their language (output), which produces comprehensible input and facilitates language acquisition.

Writing as Comprehensible Output

Merrill Swain (1985), who was concerned with grammatical development, further refined the notion of comprehensible input and interaction. She argued that comprehensible input and low-pressure interactions in which linguistic accuracy is not emphasized may aid fluency, but they do not facilitate grammatical competence. Proposing an analogous comprehensible *output* hypothesis, Swain writes: "Negotiating meaning needs to incorporate the notion of being pushed toward the delivery of a message that is not only conveyed, but that is conveyed precisely, coherently, and appropriately" (p. 249).

Several years later, Merrill Swain and Sharon Lapkin (1995) made an even stronger case for emphasis on linguistic output: "Sometimes, under some conditions, output facilitates second language learning in ways that are different from, or enhance, those of input" (p. 371). The act of *noticing*, the mechanism whereby learners tap into the potential of output, was subsequently introduced by Richard Schmidt (1990) as the Noticing Hypothesis. Schmidt asserts that conscious awareness of grammar through the act of noticing is important to language competence.

More recently, David Block (2003) and others (Canagarajah, 1999) have sought to further extend the Input-Interaction-Output model by drawing new attention to sociocultural factors in second language acquisition and the need to reframe traditional conceptions of language learning that, while beyond the scope of this chapter, deserve mention and consideration in adult education.

◼ Research and Teaching Ideas for Connecting Writing to Language Skills and Modes: Writing to Learn

In the late 1970s, James Britton (1975) and Janet Emig (1977) proposed writing-to-learn pedagogy as a way of integrating writing into all subject areas to help students explore and process new ideas (see discussion in Bazerman et al., 2005, p. 57). Writing-to-learn practitioners assigned various writing tasks, including note-taking, short-answer responses, analytical essays, summary writing, and journaling. They reported that students who engaged in such tasks spent more time thinking about the subject matter, which improved their content knowledge as well as their ability to articulate their own ideas more clearly (p. 63).

In the field of instructed second language acquisition, *writing-to-learn* also includes a belief that writing can play a facilitative role in language learning (Manchón, 2011; Williams, 2012). Whether we are concerned with subject knowledge or language acquisition, few activities compare to writing in their ability to encourage noticing of meaning and form (Qi & Lapkin, 2001) and acquisition of vocabulary (Kim, 2008; Webb, 2005). Speaking and oral interaction certainly provide opportunities to practice and negotiate meaning with others, but it is difficult to pay *attention*, which is critical to learning (Schmidt, 1995), to both meaning and grammatical features, unless one can record, revisit, and study those interactions. Writing is distinctive precisely because it is a visible and permanent modality through which language can be slowed down and analyzed, a process with strong potential for second language acquisition.

In her examination of research on writing's role in supporting second language (L2) development, Jessica Williams (2012) points to several writing-centered instructional tasks, including collaborative writing, reformulation, and corrective feedback. Collaborative tasks involving writing are most effective in advancing language proficiency when learners actively engage in *languaging*, the use of language to negotiate meaning. Swain (2006), who coined the term, explains that, through languaging, learners work out communicative problems: "Whether the problem is about which word to use, or how best to structure a sentence so it means what you want it to mean, or how to explain the results of an experiment, or how to make sense of the action to another" (p. 97). Ruiying Niu (2009), who also found evidence for the language learning potential of collaborative writing—and writing in general—explains its benefits in terms of linguistic processing, a claim that Kathleen M. Arnold and her colleagues (2017) have explored recently in their experimental research on the cognitive processes involved in writing-to-learn. Bolstering prominent models of communicative language competence in a second language (Alcón, 2000; Bachman, 1990; Canale, 1983; Canale & Swain, 1980; Celce-Murcia, Dörnyei, & Thurrell, 1995), Arnold's work suggests that the potential of writing to facilitate language acquisition depends, in part, on students' ability to deploy appropriate learning strategies. For practitioners, this means that it is not simply enough to assign writing and assume that students will naturally attend to and negotiate for meaning, notice gaps in meaning, and self-correct. These skills also have to be taught (O'Malley & Chamot, 1990), as the activities in the following sections demonstrate.

Writing to Support Grammar and Vocabulary Development

Much of the writing-to-learn research focuses on ways that writing activities can improve grammar, syntax, and vocabulary overall. The practice of reformulation, in which instructors produce more precise and grammatically accurate versions of individual students' sentences, can be most effective when learners use it as an opportunity to notice and learn from their errors, rather than simply copying down the teacher's improved form and moving on to the next sentence (Santos, López-Serrano, & Manchón, 2010, p. 138). Williams (2012) asserts that "the act of writing, which prompts learners to reflect on holes in their knowledge and primes them to focus on specific aspects of future input, combined with the pedagogical technique of reformulation, promotes noticing and at least short-term changes in language production" (p. 324).

Responding to doubts raised about the long-term benefits of certain writing practices on language acquisition in general, Ferris (2011) states that "it certainly may be argued that long-term development is unlikely without observable short-term improvement" (p. 12). Ferris was referring specifically to written corrective feedback, which she and others consider superior to reformulation in its language learning potential (Ferris, 2011; Santos, López-Serrano, & Manchón, 2010). Corrective feedback involves direct or indirect correction of grammar and vocabulary errors (see Chapter 6, this volume). Presumably, its long-term effects on language acquisition rely on students' ability to reflect on and make deliberate attempts to avoid these errors in the future.

Focus-on-form activities, which draw students' attention toward language elements at any point in the writing process, can ensure that students also benefit from the full potential of writing-to-learn (Coxhead & Byrd, 2007; Doughty & Varela, 1998; Ellis, 2002). Diane Larsen-Freeman (2003) recommends some teacher-led activities that use writing to help students focus on language and notice gaps in meaning during writing. In one activity, the teacher takes on the role of writing coach by engaging in an "instructional conversation or prolepsis" (p. 95) that helps students resolve difficulties while writing. Instead of offering up the correct form, she may ask students to recall and apply their prior knowledge of vocabulary or grammar rules. In another technique, the language experience approach, teachers act as scribes while students dictate what they would like to express in writing. The teacher may encourage noticing by writing down the correct form or by asking students to compare their original to a corrected version (p. 101).

Williams (2012) cites evidence that written production can also support vocabulary acquisition and is superior to reading alone in aiding short-term word recall, especially at the early stages of second language acquisition (p. 324). In his research study comparing traditional fill-in-the-blank writing exercises and original sentence writing, Keith Folse (2006) found that multiple opportunities to practice target words through fill-in-the blank exercises supported retention of target words better than writing original sentences. Research by Eli Hinkel (2006) and Siok Lee and James Muncie (2006) underscores the value of contextualized vocabulary instruction. Instead of teaching lists of vocabulary words that students may or may not use in the future, Lee and Muncie found that an "integrated skills approach, integrating reading, writing, and vocabulary, makes vocabulary learning durable and improves writing quality" (p. 314). In their study, intermediate-level English learners showed significant improvement in their lexical profiles (a measure of vocabulary richness in students' writings) through an instructional procedure that adult ESL teachers could easily incorporate into their intermediate or advanced classes. Here is a simplified version:

1. Students view a film.

2. The teacher develops a list of vocabulary words to be discussed and learned based on the film and readings about the film. These words include Tier 2 academic words and Tier 3 words specific to the subject of the film (Beck, McKeown, & Kucan, 2013).

3. Students complete a teacher-made handout in which they fill in the missing vocabulary words in a passage about the film.

4. After filling in the missing vocabulary words, students and the teacher read and discuss a short passage about the topic of the film from an authentic source, such as an online news or movie review site, and discuss the target words. As they discuss the target words, students write down the dictionary definition of the word, its use in context, and any metaphorical meanings it may have.

5. Each student then takes turns reading the passage, either to the class or in pairs.

6. Afterward, students answer reading comprehension questions that require using the target words in writing.

7. The teacher scores the reading comprehension assignment, reviews answers in class, and requires that students re-submit the assignment with corrections.

8. The teacher prepares an extended writing assignment about the film that includes question frames prompting students to produce the target words often and appropriately.

9. As students write, the teacher uses instructional conversations (Larsen-Freeman, 2003) as needed to scaffold students' writing and offers written corrective feedback (see discussion in Chapter 6) after development of the first draft. The teacher may also ask students to exchange papers and review each other's use of the target words after they have completed their first drafts.

10. Before students submit their final, corrected assignments, the teacher asks them to share what they wrote about each of the target words. During this exchange, students can settle any questions they have about the meaning or usage of the word.

Lee and Muncie (2006) credit their intermediate-level students' ability to productively use advanced vocabulary words, in part, to encountering the words in multiple modes (reading, writing, listening, and speaking), practicing the words across time (i.e., distributed practice), using the words in a variety of writing tasks (depth of processing), and having to revise the same composition in multiple drafts (p. 312). Other researchers have added that the level of cognitive engagement (i.e., higher involvement load) required to complete the various writing tasks that they assigned over time might also explain the vocabulary growth in their students (Harklau, 2002; Hulstijn & Laufer, 2001). Ultimately, Lee and Muncie (2006) conclude with a nod to Eli Hinkel's (2006) call for integrated skills instruction, stating that "integrating reading, writing, and vocabulary makes vocabulary learning durable and improves writing quality" (p. 314).

Writing to Support Speaking and Listening

Teacher- and student-mediated writing activities naturally involve active listening and speaking. Depending on their L2 background, students may be asked to talk their way into writing (Rubin & Dodd, 1987), or vice versa, to write before speaking (Vrchota & Russell, 2013, p. 54). Though this activity is backed by limited research, some language teachers and mainstream instructors interested in fostering greater confidence and encouraging oral participation assign short writing tasks before class discussions. Adam Mendelson (2010) observed and analyzed how a language teacher used online forum posts to scaffold students' oral discussions in class (p. 16). The day before class, the teacher posed questions in the online forum on topics she would be covering in class. During class, she carefully incorporated those questions into their discussion and gave students the opportunity to repeat orally what they had written. He posits that her techniques were a form of "expansive framing" that facilitated noticing and the transfer of their written content in the classroom speaking situation.

Writing accompanied by oral practice and repetition were also the subject of Lynch and Maclean's (2001) study of a "poster carousel" activity. Students at various levels of language proficiency were paired up to prepare posters based on a research article. A member of the pair was then assigned the role of the host and answered impromptu questions from classmates who visited their posters. Whereas the higher-level learners improved their language use through their repeated performance alone, the researchers found that the lower-level learners' improvement was directly influenced by their interactions with different listeners.

While relatively scarce, research on the relationship between writing and listening suggests that collaborative activities and opportunities to notice language gaps can also facilitate listening, grammar, and overall language skills. Kiany and Shiramiry (2002) conducted a study with lower-level language learners in which the experimental group who completed frequent dictation exercises made greater improvements in listening comprehension than the comparison group. To improve the reputation of dictation exercises as "boring," Richard

Kidd (1992) proposed several variations. Among them, *dictogloss* has been the most researched. Maria Kowal and Merrill Swain (1997) found that dictogloss was effective at getting foreign language students to notice, talk about, and work on their language errors. Instead of transcribing what the teacher says verbatim, as per traditional dictation exercises, in dictogloss activities, students produce their own written version of an orally read text and then work in groups to refine and make corrections, as needed. A summary of the steps for dictogloss, as described by Wajnryb (1990), is provided:

1. **Preparation:** The teacher first has a discussion with students to activate prior knowledge and raise awareness of key vocabulary. To conclude, the teacher lets students explain the activity and what they are expected to do.

2. **Dictation:** The teacher reads a selected text at a normal speed, as students listen and take notes. Depending on students' levels, the teacher may re-read the text, but she should avoid isolating words and phrases and keep a natural, continuous pace.

3. **Reconstruction:** Students work individually or in small groups to produce their version of the text with as much detail as they can remember and in the most grammatically correct way possible.

4. **Analysis and correction:** Students provide peer feedback to help each other fill in missing information in their versions of the text and correct language forms.

The Mutually Supportive Roles of Reading and Writing

Steve Graham and Dolores Perin (2007), authors of several articles and books on writing research and instruction, point out that "reading and writing often draw from the same pool of background knowledge—for example, a general understanding of the attributes of texts" (p. 8). Integrated-skills approaches to language teaching, such as content-based instruction (CBI), are more effective at facilitating college and career readiness when teachers incorporate both reading and writing (Oxford, 2001). (See Chapter 2.) Yet, as our survey revealed, many adult ESL teachers focus entirely on reading to motivate speaking, vocabulary, and grammar instruction without ever working on extended writing assignments (Fernández, Peyton, & Schaetzel, 2017). Moreover, as mentioned previously, when they do assign writing, it tends to be reflective and about personal topics.

By definition, however, academic writing is source-based writing. As Gerald Graff and Cathy Birkenstein (2018) mention in *They Say/I Say: The Moves That Matter in Academic Writing*, regardless of discipline, academic writing "[requires] writers to frame their own claims as a response to what others before them have said" (p. xviii). Most often, what "they say" is derived from texts. Combining reading and writing not only provides motivating content about which students can speak and write, but it also improves reading comprehension (Carr, 2002). Put another way, Gina Biancarosa and Catherine Snow (2006) state that "students who are given the opportunity to write in conjunction with reading show more evidence of critical thinking about reading" (p. 19).

Alan Hirvela's (2004, 2016) *Connecting Reading & Writing in Second Language Writing Instruction* provides research on and teaching suggestions for using writing as the basis for reading, and vice versa. He describes reading-for-writing activities, which use reading to stimulate or prepare for writing in some way. These activities include *writerly reading*, through which readers study both the structural features and rhetorical effects of a text. Teachers guide students as they examine a text both for its message and as an object of study. A related approach, *rhetorical reading*, teaches students to identify the parts of an argument (e.g., thesis, examples, supporting evidence, counterarguments) as well as the rhetorical situation. (See discussion in Chapter 3.) Both writerly reading and rhetorical reading can be used to develop writing models that students can imitate to improve their academic writing skills (Hirvela, 2016, p. 58). Teachers can also refer to Graff and Birkenstein's (2018) ready-made models of rhetorical moves that are common in academic writing, such as disagreeing, refuting counterarguments, and establishing the significance of an argument.

These reading-for-writing approaches are premised, at least in part, on the assumption that good readers make good writers. However, research complicates this assumption. Virginia Berninger and her colleagues (2002) found that, at the earliest literacy levels, reading had a direct effect on writing, but that as students' literacy skills improve, the relationship between reading and writing is bidirectional. That is, starting at intermediate literacy levels, the quality of written compositions is associated with reading comprehension, and vice-versa (p. 46). Belief of such a relationship undergirds Alan Hirvela's discussions about writing-for-reading activities, which assume that "writing before, during, or after reading enables a reader to make sense of his or her reading, which in turns strengthens the quality of the reading and contributes to the L2 reading ability" (Hirvela, 2016, p. 69). *Writing-for-reading* (also known as writing-to-read or writing while reading) can be used to motivate students to read, to activate prior knowledge before reading, to engage with a text during reading, and to make sense of the text after reading. Writing produced in writing-to-read can become the foundation for extended essays. Students' writing about a topic prior to reading can become the basis for an opening paragraph in an academic essay: for example, "I used to think that_____." Their annotations while reading can help them summarize what they have read, as well as identify points of convergence and tension with the author's perspective, from which they can develop a thesis statement.

The next section combines reading-for-writing, writing-for-reading, and integrated skills activities to demonstrate what a writing-centered lesson in an adult ESL class might include.

■ A Writing-Centered Learning Unit

In this learning unit, I describe a series of writing activities that scaffold students' learning during the writing process while facilitating their speaking, listening, reading, vocabulary, and grammar skills.

These activities are part of a broader writing project that culminates in an academic essay. Each of the major sections constitutes one phase in the writing process. The types of activities undertaken are described, and sample materials are provided.

Writing Project

This first section provides a context for and a detailed description of the primary writing assignment that students receive at the beginning of the learning unit and on which subsequent activities are based. Combined, these can be referred to as a writing project (Kuh, 2008).

Assignment Description for Students

So far in our course, you have improved your English language and college- and career-readiness skills through the topic of immigration. In the previous unit, we focused on the "American Dream." We now turn to a challenge everyone experiences—maintaining good health. We begin by reading Sabrina Tabernise's *New York Times* article "The Health Toll of Immigration," about health problems among foreign-born and American-born Hispanic individuals living in the United States. Tabernise writes for a general audience and presents information from interviews with scientists and immigrants in Brownsville, Texas.

After you have read Tabernise's article, you will begin to write a short response paper. We will practice the writing process again in this assignment. We will do pre-writing activities, drafting, peer reviews, teacher conferences, revision, and editing. Your final paper will be three pages long (about 500 words, double-spaced, typewritten) and must include quotations, in-text citations, and a references section.

To help you get started, follow the structure and answer the questions.

- ☐ Context: Who is interested in this topic? What background does the reader need?

- ☐ Summary: What is Tabernise's central message about the effects of immigration on health? What supporting evidence does she use? What does she conclude?

- ☐ Response: What aspect of Tabernise's article interests you? What specific problem, question, or issue does it ignore or raise for you? How will you address this problem/question/issue in your essay?

- ☐ Body paragraphs: Develop your topic and perspective by adding examples from your own experience.

- ▪ <u>Advanced assignment option:</u> For this writing project, you will use Tabernise's article as an example (a model) as you write a new article of similar length that reflects your interests and perspectives on the topic. If you use any information from Tabernise's article, make sure to include quotations and/or citations. To add new and current information to your article, you will complete <u>one</u> of the activities here:

1. Read and add evidence from a research article by Gopal K. Singh and his colleagues, "Immigrant Health Inequalities in the United States: Use of Eight Major National Data Systems" (Singh, Rodriguez-Lainz, & Kogan, 2013).

2. Interview two or three classmates about their health habits since moving to the United States.

3. Read the Singh article and conduct one interview with a classmate or a worker at a community health center.

Before Reading

Collaborative Writing (Jiang & Grabe, 2007; Yarrow & Topping, 2001)

The teacher pairs up students at complimentary or different language proficiency levels to answer the questions: What are the components of a healthy lifestyle? How have your health habits changed since moving to the United States?

Option: If needed, the teacher can scaffold the activity by providing sentence frames. To help students practice and internalize the sentence form, she may write out each sentence fully instead of merely filling in the blanks.

In your opinion, what are the components of a healthy lifestyle?

    1. I believe that a healthy lifestyle should include _____,

    _____, _____, and _____.

    2. To be healthy, I think that a person should _____.

    3. They should also_____.

    4. They should avoid_____.

How have your health habits changed since moving to the

United States? Explain.

    1. Since moving to the United States, my health habits have

    [improved/worsened/not changed].

    2. In my country, I used to_____, but now, I

    _____.

    3. I _____ every day in my country, and I do the

    same now.

    4. My health habits have [improved/worsened/not changed]

    because_____.

Class Concept Mapping (Nesbit & Adesope, 2006)

Students share the sentences they wrote collaboratively with the teacher, who uses their answers to construct a concept map on the board. If students have previous experience with concept mapping, the teacher may provide a concept map template that students fill out in small groups first and refer to while participating orally to complete the whole-class concept map.

During Reading

Annotating (Porter-O'Donnell, 2004; Starkey, 2015)

The teacher reads aloud and models annotating the first page of Sabrina Tabernise's *New York Times* article, "The Health Toll of Immigration" on GoogleDocs. Annotating can also be done on a transparency sheet or regular paper copies of the article through a literature circles method (Okura, 2001).

In literature circles, students are assigned different roles while reading a text. Some students are responsible for looking up vocabulary, others may ask questions about the text, and others may discuss personal connections to the reading. The teacher can annotate the text using these categories. Afterward, each student can annotate the GoogleDoc for vocabulary, personal connections, questions, etc. If, for example, another student has already tagged the same word or asked the same question, the student can simply add his or her initials to the annotation.

After Reading

Modified Literature Circles (Okura, 2001)

Before discussing the text as a whole class, the teacher can group students according to each category (a vocabulary group, a questioning group, a personal connections group, etc.). Students in each group are responsible for looking up vocabulary definitions, listing and (if possible) answering questions, and summarizing personal reactions. All of this information should involve writing. It can be written as a PowerPoint presentation or made into a handout.

Thick and Thin Questions (Harvey & Goudvis, 2007, pp. 115–116)

The teacher can do further work on reading comprehension by sorting, discussing, and writing down answers to questions raised by students during reading and any others you think are important. Questions that can be answered directly by searching the text (yes/no and clarifying questions, steps in a process, definitions) will be put in the "thin questions" category and addressed first. Those that require thinking beyond the text (*Why? How come? I wonder . . .*) will be put in the "thick questions" category and addressed second.

Drafting

Summary (Friend, 2001)

After students have discussed the parts of the article and its implications, they will consolidate their understanding of the text by drafting a summary. The value of summary writing for improving reading comprehension is well-known (e.g., Graham & Hebert, 2010). Rosalie Friend (2001) provides several tips and procedures for writing a summary, as do Rinehart, Stahl, and Erickson (1986) and Taylor and Beach (1984).

In general, summaries capture ideas in the whole text and do not include specific examples or details unless these are important to the writer's agenda or response. Graff and Birkenstein (2018) capture the paradoxical nature of summaries: "A good summary ... has a focus or spin that allows the summary to fit with your own agenda while still being true to the text you are summarizing" (p. 34). Striking this balance not only makes summarizing a challenge for most students but also makes each person's summary unique. Although different students' summaries of the same text will share certain elements, they should not be identical, because not all students will build from the same ideas in the source text that they are summarizing in their essays.

Response (Graff & Birkenstein, 2018)

According to Graff and Birkenstein (2018), the main ways of responding to texts include agreeing, disagreeing, and being of two minds. The first two are the most straightforward for novice writers. To get students started on their responses, teachers can model how to build a paragraph from one of Graff and Birkenstein's templates.

Sample Templates for Disagreeing (p. 225)

■ I think X is mistaken because she overlooks _____.

■ In light of recent research showing _____, I disagree with X that _____.

Sample Templates for Agreeing (p. 226)

■ I agree with X that _____ because my own experience with _____ confirms it.

■ Recent studies about _____ support X's point that _____.

Written Feedback (Ferris, 2011; Rollinson, 2005)

During the writing process, both peers (Liu & Hansen, 2018) and teachers (Ferris, 2011) should offer feedback on intermediate drafts. (See Chapter 6 for a discussion of teacher corrective feedback.) Peer feedback offers several benefits. From a language learning perspective, givers of feedback seem to benefit more than receivers (Rouhi & Azizian 2013). From an affective and pedagogical standpoint, written feedback "gives both readers and writers more time for collaboration, consideration, and reflection than is normally possible in the cut and thrust of oral negotiation and debate … it gives students further practice in being explicit, detailed, persuasive, and audience-focused in their writing" (Rollinson, 2005, p. 27).

Modeling and explicit instruction is important for developing effective peer feedback (Rollinson, 2005, p. 28), not only because it helps students understand what to look for and how to respond to the work of others, but also because it teaches students metalanguage for talking about and interpreting feedback from teachers and peers (Hyland, 2003). To prepare students to offer and interpret feedback, the teacher introduces key words (Brittenham & Hoeller, 2004) in the assignment rubric (see Appendix 1A). Next, she randomly selects an anonymous student draft, projects it on the board, or distributes paper copies. Students read and rate the draft in pairs and then discuss their ratings with the teacher, who offers her own assessment of the paper to help students internalize her standards for quality. After the teacher and students finish rating the paper, they compose their written feedback. The acronym R.A.R.E. can help students remember what to include in a written peer review statement. Appendix 1B can be copied and made into a handout to scaffold students' oral and written peer reviews.

────────── **Questions for Reflection and Application** ──────────

1. In addition to research and practices from the adult ESL field, this chapter draws from K-12, academic ESL, composition studies, and applied linguistics. What challenges and possibilities do you anticipate when applying this work in your classes?

2. Review the College and Career Readiness Standards for Adult ESL (U. S. Department of Education, 2013). In what ways do they align with or diverge from the research and best practices recommended in this chapter for integrating writing with other skills?

3. What additional training and resources will you need to design a writing-centered adult ESL classroom? Keep in mind that, while on-site professional development opportunities are limited in adult ESL, online resources and communities of practice (CoP) groups provide opportunities for teachers to engage in self-directed professional learning. Visit the LINCS Community (https:// community.lincs.ed.gov), Center for Adult English Language Acquisition (CAELA, http://www.cal.org/caela), and World Education (www.worlded.org) websites to learn more about research and training opportunities in adult ESL.

References

Alcón, E. (2000). Desarrollo de la competencia discursiva oral en el aula de lenguas extranjeras: Perspectivas metodológicas y de investigación. In Muñoz, C. (Ed.), *Segundas lenguas: Adquisición en el aula* (pp. 259–276). Barcelona, Spain: Ariel Lingüística.

Arnold, K. M., Umanath, S., Thio, K., Reilly, W. B., McDaniel, M. A., & Marsh, E. J. (2017). Understanding the cognitive processes involved in writing to learn. *Journal of Experimental Psychology: Applied, 23*(2), 115–127.

Auerbach, E. (1992). *Making meaning, making change: Participatory curriculum development for adult ESL literacy.* Washington, DC: Center for Applied Linguistics and Delta Systems.

Bachman, L.F. (1990). *Fundamental considerations in language testing.* Oxford, England: Oxford University Press.

Bazerman, C., Little, J., Bethel, L., Chavkin, T., Fouquette, D., & Garufis, J. (2005). *Reference guide to writing across the curriculum.* West Lafayette, IN: Parlor Press.

Beck, I. L. McKeown, M., & Kucan, L. (2013). Choosing words to teach. In *Bringing words to life: Robust vocabulary instruction* (2nd ed., pp. 19–39). New York: Guilford Press.

Berninger, V.W., Abbott, R. D., Abbott, S. P., Graham, S., & Richards, T. (2002). Writing and reading: Connections between language by hand and language by eye. *Journal of Learning Disabilities, 35,* 39–56.

Biancarosa, C., & Snow, C. E. (2006). *Reading next—A vision for action and research in middle and high school literacy: A report to Carnegie Corporation of New York* (2nd ed.). Washington, DC: Alliance for Excellent Education.

Block, D. (2003). *The social turn in second language acquisition.* Washington, DC: Georgetown University Press.

Brittenham, R., & Hoeller, H. (2004). *Key words for academic writers.* Harlow, England: Pearson Longman.

Britton, J. N. (1975). *The development of writing abilities* (pp. 11–18). London: Macmillan Education.

Canagarajah, S. (1999). Interrogating the 'native speaker fallacy': Non-linguistic roots, non-pedagogical results. In G. Braine (Ed.), *Non-native educators in English language teaching* (pp. 77–92). Mahwah, NJ: Lawrence Erlbaum.

Canale, M. (1983). From communicative competence to communicative language pedagogy. In J. C. Richards & R. W. Schmidt (Eds.), *Language and communication* (pp. 2–27). London: Longman.

Canale, M., & Swain, M. (1980). Theoretical bases of communicative approaches to second language teaching and testing. *Applied Linguistics, 1,* 1–47

Carr, S. (2002). Assessing learning processes: Useful information for teachers and students. *Intervention in School and Clinic, 37,* 156–162.

Celce-Murcia, M., Dörnyei, Z., & Thurrell, S. (1995). Communicative competence: A pedagogically motivated model with content specifications. *Issues in Applied Linguistics 6,* 5–35.

Conley, D. T. (2007). Redefining College Readiness. Eugene, OR: Educational Policy Improvement Center. Available: https://www.inflexion.org/redefining-college-readiness/

Coxhead, A., & Byrd, P. (2007). Preparing writing teachers to teach vocabulary and grammar of academic prose. *Journal of Second Language Writing, 16,* 129–147.

Doughty, C., & Varela, E. (1998). Communicative focus on form. In C. Doughty & J. Williams (Eds.), *Focus on form in classroom second language acquisition* (pp. 114–138). Cambridge, England: Cambridge University Press.

Ellis, R. (2002). Does form-focused instruction affect the acquisition of implicit knowledge? A review of the research. *Studies in Second Language Acquisition, 24*(2), 223–236.

Emig, J. (1977). Writing as a mode of learning. *College Composition and Communication, 28*, 122–128.

Ferlazzo, L., & Schulten, K. (2010, June 10). English language learners and the power of personal stories. *New York Times*. https://learning.blogs.nytimes.com/2010/06/10/english-language-learners-and-the-power-of-personal-stories/?_r=0).

Fernández, R., Peyton, J. K., & Schaetzel, K. (2017). A survey of writing instruction in adult ESL programs: Are teaching practices meeting adult learner needs? *Journal of Research and Practice for Adult Literacy, Secondary, and Basic Education, 6*(2), 5–20.

Ferris, D. (2011). *Treatment of error in second language student writing* (2nd ed.). Ann Arbor: University of Michigan Press.

Folse, K. (2006). The effect of type of written exercise on L2 vocabulary retention. *TESOL Quarterly, 40*(2), 273–293.

Freire, P., & Macedo, D. (1987). *Literacy: Reading the word and the world*. Westport, CT: Bergin & Garvey.

Friend, R. (2001). Teaching summarization as a content-area reading strategy. *Journal of Adolescent & Adult Literacy, 44*(4), 320–329.

Gee, J.P. (1989). Literacy, discourses, and linguistics: Essays by James Paul Gee. A Special Issue of the *Journal of Education, 171*, 5–17.

Graff, G., & Birkenstein, C. (2018). *"They say/I say": The moves that matter in academic writing* (4th Ed.). New York: W. W. Norton.

Graham, S., & Hebert, M. (2010). *Writing to read: Evidence for how writing can improve reading. A report from Carnegie Corporation of New York*. Washington, DC: Alliance for Excellent Education.

Graham, S., & Perin, D. (2007). *Writing next: Effective strategies to improve writing of adolescents in middle and high schools*. New York: Carnegie Corporation of New York.

Harklau, L. (2002). The role of writing in classroom second language acquisition. *Journal of Second Language Writing, 11*(4), 329–350.

Harvey, S., & Goudvis, A. (2007). *Strategies that work: Teaching comprehension for understanding and engagement.* Portland, ME: Stenhouse Publishers.

Hinkel, E. (2006). Current perspectives on teaching the four skills. *TESOL Quarterly, 40,* 109–131.

Hirvela, A. (2004). *Connecting reading & writing in second language writing instruction.* Ann Arbor: University of Michigan Press.

Hirvela, A. (2016). *Connecting reading & writing in second language writing instruction* (2nd ed.). Ann Arbor: University of Michigan Press.

Hulstijn, J., & Laufer, B. (2001). Some empirical evidence for the involvement load hypothesis in vocabulary acquisition. *Language Learning, 51,* 539–558.

Hyland, K. (2003). Genre-based pedagogies: A social response to process. *Journal of Second Language Writing, 12*(1),17–29.

Jiang, X., & Grabe, W. (2007). Graphic organizers in reading instruction: Research findings and issues. *Reading in a Foreign Language, 19*(1), 34–55.

Kiany, G. R., & Shiramiry, E. (2002). The effect of frequent dictation on the listening comprehension ability of elementary EFL learners. *TESL Canada Journal, 20*(1), 57–63.

Kidd, R. (1992). Teaching grammar through dictation. *TESL Canada Journal, 10,* 49–61.

Kim, Y. (2008). The role of task-induced involvement and learner proficiency in L2 vocabulary acquisition. *Language Learning, 58,* 285–325.

Kowal, M., & Swain, M. (1997). From semantic to syntactic processing: How can we promote it in the immersion classroom? In R. Johnson & M. Swain (Eds.), *Immersion education: International perspectives* (pp. 284–309). New York: Cambridge University Press.

Krashen, S. D. (1982). *Principles and practice in second language acquisition.* Oxford, England: Pergamon Press.

Krashen, S.D. (1985). *The input hypothesis: Issues and implications.* Harlow, England: Longman Group.

Krashen, S. D. (2004). *The power of reading.* Portsmouth, NH: Heinemann.

Kuh, G.D. (2008). *High-impact educational practices: What are they, who has access to them, and why they matter.* Washington, DC: Association of American Colleges and Universities.

Larsen-Freeman, D. (2003). *Teaching language: From grammar to grammaring.* Boston: Thomson Heinle.

Lee, S. H., & Muncie, J. (2006). From receptive to productive: Improving ESL learners' use of vocabulary in a postreading composition task. *TESOL Quarterly, 40*(2), 295–320.

Liu, J., & Hansen, J. G. (2018). *Peer response in second language writing classrooms* (2nd ed.). Ann Arbor: University of Michigan Press.

Long, M. H. (1983). Native speaker/non-native speaker conversation and the negotiation of comprehensible input. *Applied Linguistics, 4*(2), 126–141.

Lynch, T., & Maclean, J. (2001). "A case of exercising:" Effects of immediate task repetition on learner's performance. In M. Bygate, P. Skehan, & M. Swain (Eds.), *Researching pedagogical tasks: Second language learning, teaching, and testing* (pp. 141–162). London: Longman.

Manchón, R. M. (Ed.). (2011). *Learning-to-write and writing-to-learn in an additional language.* Philadelphia: John Benjamins.

Mendelson, A. (2010). Using online forums to scaffold oral participation in foreign language instruction. *L2 Journal, 2*(1), 23–44. https://escholarship.org/uc/item/8xs1r2tq

Nation, P. (1984). *Vocabulary lists: Words, affixes, and stems* (Occasional Publication No. 12). Wellington, New Zealand: English Language Institute, Victoria University of Wellington

Nesbit, J. C., & Adesope, O. O. (2006). Learning with concept and knowledge maps: A meta-analysis. *Review of Educational Research, 76*(3), 413–448.

Niu, R. (2009). Effect of task-inherent production modes on EFL learners' focus on form. *Language Awareness, 18*(3–4), 384–402.

Okura, D. S. (2001). Students become real readers: Literature circles in high school English classes. In B. Graham (Ed.), *Teaching reading in high school English classes* (pp. 84–100). Urbana, IL: National Council of Teacher of English.

O'Malley, M. J., & Chamot, A.U. (1990). *Learning strategies in second language acquisition.* New York: Cambridge University Press.

Oxford, R. (2001). *Integrated skills in the ESL/EFL classroom.* ERIC Digest ED456670. Washington, DC: ERIC Clearinghouse for ESL Literacy Education. http://www.ericdigests.org/2002-2/esl.htm

Porter-O'Donnell, C. (2004). Beyond the yellow highlighter: Teaching annotation skills to improve reading comprehension. *English Journal, 93*(5), 82–89.

Qi, D., & Lapkin, S. (2001). Exploring the role of noticing in a three-stage second language writing task. *Journal of Second Language Writing, 10,* 277–303.

Rinehart, S. D., Stahl, S.A., & Erickson, L. G. (1986). Some effects of summarization training on reading and studying. *Reading Research Quarterly, 21,* 422–438.

Rollinson, P. (2005). Using peer feedback in the ESL writing class. *ELT Journal, 59,* 23–30.

Rouhi, A., & Azizian, E. (2013). Peer review: Is giving corrective feedback better than receiving it in L2 writing? *Procedia-Social and Behavioral Sciences, 93,* 1349–1354.

Rubin, D. L., & Dodd, W. M. (1987). *Talking into writing—Exercises for basic writers.* Urbana, IL: National Council of Teachers of English.

Santos, M., López-Serrano, S., & Manchón, R. M. (2010). The differential effect of two types of direct written corrective feedback on noticing and uptake: Reformulation vs. error correction. *International Journal of English Studies,* 131–154.

Schmidt, R. W. (1990). The role of consciousness in second language learning. *Applied Linguistics, 11,* 129–158.

Schmidt, R. W. (1995). Consciousness in foreign language learning: A tutorial on the role of attention and awareness in learning. In R. W. Schmidt (Ed.), *Attention and awareness in foreign language learning* (pp. 1–67). Honolulu: University of Hawaii Second Language Teaching and Curriculum Center.

Singh, G. K., Rodriguez-Lainz, A., & Kogan, M. D. (2013). Immigrant health inequalities in the United States: Use of eight major national data systems. *The Scientific World Journal.*http://dx.doi.org/10.1155/2013/512313

Starkey, D. (2015). *Academic reading: A brief guide for busy students.* Tonawanda, NY: Broadview Press.

Swain, M. (1985). Communicative competence: Some roles of comprehensible input and comprehensible output in its development. In S. Gass, & C. Madden (Eds.), *Input in second language acquisition* (pp. 235–253). Rowley, MA: Newbury House.

Swain, M. (2006). Languaging, agency, and collaboration in advanced second language proficiency. In H. Byrnes (Ed.), *Advanced language learning: The contribution of Halliday and Vygotsky* (pp. 95–108). London: Continuum.

Swain, M., & Lapkin, S. (1995). Problems in output and the cognitive processes they generate: A step toward second language learning. *Applied Linguistics, 16,* 371–391.

Tabernise, S. (2013, May 18). The health toll of immigration. *New York Times.* http://www.nytimes.com/2013/05/19/health/the-health-toll-of-immigration.html

Taylor, B. M., & Beach, R.W. (1984). The effects of text structure instruction on middle-grade students' comprehension and production of expository text. *Reading Research Quarterly, 19,* 134–146.

U.S. Department of Education. Office of Vocational and Adult Education. (2013). *College and career readiness standards for adult education.* Washington, DC: Author. http://lincs.ed.gov/publications/pdf/CCRStandards AdultEd.pdf

Vrchota, D. A., & Russell, D. R. (2013). WAC/WID meets CXC/CID: A dialogue between writing studies and communication studies. *English Publications, 15.* https://lib.dr.iastate.edu/engl_pubs/15

Wajnryb, R. (1990). *Grammar dictation.* Oxford, England: Oxford University Press.

Webb, S. (2005). Receptive and productive vocabulary learning: The effects of reading and writing on word knowledge. *Studies in Second Language Acquisition, 27*(1), 33–52.

Williams, J. (2012). The potential role(s) of writing in second language acquisition. *Journal of Second Language Writing, 21,* 321–331.

Yarrow, F., & Topping, K. J. (2001). Collaborative writing: The effects of metacognitive prompting and structured peer interaction. *British Journal of Educational Psychology, 71,* 261–282.

Appendix 1A: Sample Rubric for Teaching Metalanguage for Writing Feedback

Tasks	★	★ ★	★ ★ ★	★ ★ ★ ★	★ ★ ★ ★ ★
Context for the Paper **(Key words: *context, background, audience*)**	The writer does not attempt to provide a background or context for the audience.	The writer attempts to provide a context for the audience, but it is mechanical and incomplete.	The writer attempts to engage the audience by providing a context, though its accuracy and relevance to the texts or his own project may be unclear.	The writer offers a context with possibly some inaccuracies that nonetheless engages the interest of the audience and hints at broader issues.	The writer creates a strong context or background that captures the audience's attention and clearly puts his/her work within the context of a broader issue or debate.
Summary of the Article **(Key words: *fair, generous, gist, summarize, motivated, purpose*)**	The writer does not summarize the reading.	The writer mentions the reading but does not provide enough information for an unfamiliar reader to understand the gist.	The writer's summary reads like a retelling or a list of ideas; may include significant inaccuracies, and/or shows no sign of the writer's purpose.	The writer presents the gist of the source text's ideas but may need to represent the writer's purpose.	The writer presents a fair and generous summary of the source text that is clearly motivated by the writer's purpose for the paper.
Response to the Article **(Key words/ phrases: *central claim, support/-ing evidence, detail-/s/-ed, substan/-ce/-tial/-tive, superficial*)**	The writer does not respond to the reading; may misunderstand assignment.	The writer's response is not connected to the article and/or is supported with disconnected and superficial evidence.	The writer's response is focused but is mostly summary and does not include enough of the writer's ideas.	The writer responds with a clear central claim and supporting evidence. Some points could be supported better and with more detail.	The writer responds to specific parts of the reading in a detailed and substantive way with a strong central claim and supporting evidence.

Framing, Citing, and Quotations (Key words/ phrases: fram/ -e/-ing/, cit/-e/-ing/, quot/-e/ -ing/-ations)	The writer does not use quotations or overwhelms the paper with quotations; no citations	The writer does not frame quoted terms, phrases, or passages; the quotations may seem random and not related to topic; some citations may be missing.	Generally, it is unclear exactly what the writer wants readers to notice about a quoted term, phrase, or passage; some citations may be incomplete or unclear.	Writer attempts to frame quoted terms, phrases, or passages, but these guiding remarks are uneven or at times unhelpful; citations may be incomplete.	The writer frames quotations with an introductory phrase, uses appropriate citations, and comments on quotations in a way that connects with and supports the central claim.
Grammar, Mechanics, and Style (Key words/ phrases: clear/ clarity, appl/ -y/-ies, grammar, mechanics, punctuation, style)	The essay has too many errors to be readable.	The essay lacks clarity and does not show understanding of the grammar and punctuation topics taught in class.	The essay lacks clarity in a few places and does not always apply grammar and punctuation topics taught in class.	The essay is mostly clear and correctly applies grammar and punctuation topics taught in class.	The essay is clear and correctly applies all grammar and punctuation discussed in class; may contain only errors that the teacher can identify.

NOTE: This appendix was developed for adult ESL students from several first-year composition rubrics and used by the Writing Program at Davidson College. Changes include key words, star ratings, and simplified language.

Appendix 1B: RARE! Written Peer Review Template

Directions: In a peer review, classmates read and give feedback to one another about their work. Follow the RARE! procedure to write a peer review of a classmate's essay with a partner.

R: Recap, or summarize, the essay. First, write down separately the main idea of the text. Next, compare your versions and decide what you will write for your classmate.

- Your essay focuses on_____.
- You write about_____.

A: Applaud, or compliment, your classmate's work. Each person writes down one positive aspect of the essay. Combine each comment and decide what you will write for your classmate.

- We think it does a good job of _____.
- We enjoyed the part where you_____.

R: Recommend, or suggest, changes. Discuss ways to improve the content (e.g., examples, details, use of evidence). Write down the two most important recommendations that you will give your classmate.

- To improve your essay, we recommend_____.
- You might consider_____.

E: Encourage your classmate. For example: "This is a solid first draft!" "We look forward to reading the next version!"

- This is a strong start!
- We look forward to learning more about_____.

Building Pathways for Writing Development in the Content Areas

Donna M. Brinton, University of California, Los Angeles
Barry D. Griner, University of Southern California

Opening Questions ─────────────────────

1. Which models of integrated content and language instruction are you already familiar with?

2. How can the use of academic content as a source enrich language instruction?

3. What are the challenges of using academic content in language instruction?

Many volumes have been written about underprepared students entering university. These students come from all walks of life. They are both native and non-native speakers of the language of the institution; they are international students, citizens, and legal or undocumented residents; they are recent high school graduates, transfer students from community colleges, or "returning students" who have left the workplace to pursue a higher education; they are from cultures that are similar to their adopted country or cultures that are vastly different; they live in intact family structures or alone, having left behind or lost all of their family members. Perhaps the most fragile of all of the populations of aspiring university students are those enrolled in adult basic education (ABE) programs. Burns and Ollerhead (2017) and Eyring (2014) remind us that, in addition to students who work in low-skilled environments (and hence require life and vocational skills, which are becoming increasingly complex), the adult learner population consists of students who aspire to opportunities that they did not have in their home countries, such as study at an institution of higher education. It also consists of those who left behind a professional career in their home countries and possess academic literacy in the first language but now require additional certification to pursue this career in their new country of residence.

Upon entering the university, these students face multiple challenges, caused primarily by their lack of familiarity with the conventions and expectations of academia. Included in the hurdles they encounter are time management; unfamiliar academic vocabulary (both sub-technical and technical); complex grammatical structures; lack of knowledge concerning the various genres and text types in assigned readings and subject matter lectures; lack of familiarity with written requirements, such as the need to paraphrase source material and cite sources; and difficulty organizing and supporting ideas in both oral and written assignments, to name just a few. According to Murray and Christison (2011), it is critical that ABE programs provide explicit instruction in the use of learning strategies and inform students of learning expectations. Also essential are selecting learning experiences that are relevant to learners' experiences and providing learning-oriented feedback (Burns & Ollerhead, 2017). Finally, as noted by Weigle (2014), students need to be initiated into the socially and culturally situated literacy practices required of university-level writers.

We examine the relevance of *content-based instruction* (CBI) to preparing college-bound ABE students, where the ultimate goal of the preparatory program is to build students' comprehension, academic writing, and overall communication skills. Specifically, we show how use of a content-based syllabus can help *scaffold*, or guide, students' mastery of advanced literacy skills and academic conventions and help forge pathways to writing development in the content areas as students read, write, listen, and speak about challenging and relevant university-level content.

■ Theoretical and Research Background

Content- and language-integrated instruction is a global trend at virtually all educational levels. It takes many forms, depending on whether the main instructional focus is language instruction, content instruction, or both. (See Brinton & Snow, 2017, for an updated overview.) In today's second/foreign/world language classrooms, one of the major paradigms of content- and language-integrated instruction is that of CBI.

CBI entails the concurrent learning of content and related language use skills, with content serving as the point of departure for decisions regarding the selection and sequencing of language in the curriculum (Brinton, Snow, & Wesche, 2003). It is an integrated skills approach, where all four skills are seen as supporting each other (i.e., work on reading skills helps to develop students' writing skills, work on listening helps to develop speaking skills, etc.) and where an overt focus on language issues (vocabulary, grammar, pronunciation) occurs through focused, content-related tasks.

By far the most widely used form of CBI is *theme-based instruction*, where the language course revolves around specific themes of interest and relevance to the learners. These themes provide the foundation for skill- and language-based instruction and create the organizing principle for the language syllabus. Typically, each theme extends over one or more weeks and provides the rich input necessary for learners to acquire new language (Brinton, 2007). In a theme-based curriculum, themes may be geared toward issues of general interest (e.g., smartphones, social networking, "voluntourism") or more academic issues (e.g., ancestral pueblo culture, origins of sirocco winds, the great Dust Bowl migration), depending on the background and needs of the student population for whom the course is designed.

In the latter case, theme-based instruction often takes the form of *sustained content instruction* (Murphy & Stoller, 2001), wherein the theme-based unit is extended (i.e., with the entire course exploring only one or two themes). At the core of the unit are *authentic materials* (e.g., academic readings, lectures, online sites) that form the basis for language development activities and that "require students not only to understand information but to interpret and evaluate it as well" (Brinton, Snow, & Wesche, 2003, p. 2). According to Murphy and Stoller (2001), sustained content instruction offers a unique advantage for students in academic preparatory programs (including Career Pathways and College- and Career-Readiness [CCR] programs), because it simulates the conditions and demands of the content area course, thus causing students to engage with the content material more deeply. At the same time, it carefully scaffolds students' language development along with their critical-thinking skills and their higher-order *cognitive and metacognitive strategies* (e.g., inferencing, summarizing readings and lectures, using advance organizers, along with a personal awareness of the cognitive processes they employ in learning).

For these reasons, sustained content instruction is ideally suited to academic preparation or pathway programs seeking to provide underprepared students with *higher-order cognitive* and *academic language skills*. Simply put, academic language is the language that students need to know to succeed in their content-area classes, whether in elementary school, middle school, high school, or higher education settings. It involves a range of features, including general academic (sub-technical) as well as content area–specific vocabulary; academic *genre/text types* (e.g., an abstract, a lab report, a research proposal); complex grammatical structures; and language functions and discourse devices (Snow, McCormick, & Osipova, 2017). Each content area can be said to be appropriate for its own specific *discourse community*, where the members of a community (e.g., nurses, computer programmers) use discipline-specific lexicon and genres. The goal of programs that prepare students to transition into academic or vocational education, then, is to assess students' current knowledge of academic language and to then, via scaffolded, skill-enhancement activities, increase their knowledge of this language in all four skill areas. As Frodesen (2017) notes, authentic content-based units provide an invaluable opportunity for us to guide students in analyzing and discussing these academic language features, the organizational structures of texts, and the various genres that occur in both the written and oral discourse of subject matter disciplines. She notes also that content-based units can provide a forum for fostering students' *critical literacy* skills, where students are guided to question or challenge assumptions (or discover contradictions and controversies) that they encounter in the authentic content area sources to which they are exposed.

Next, we highlight a sustained content unit that focuses on a seminal episode in American History—the Lewis and Clark Corps of Discovery (1803–1806)—also known as the Lewis and Clark Expedition.

■ Classroom Application: The Lewis and Clark Expedition

We have selected the Lewis and Clark Expedition as an example of possible course content for several reasons:

1. The Expedition is an essential part of U.S. history; it is, therefore, appropriate for adult L2 learners, who will find the information interesting and relevant.
2. Given its historical focus, the unit fits squarely within traditional adult ESL civics objectives as well as the history sections of many high school equivalence exams.

3. It is part of every elementary school curriculum. As such, it is helpful for adult immigrant parents with children in school to be familiar with this historic event; and, for those wishing to naturalize, familiarity will acculturate them to the topic on the U.S. citizenship test.

4. Historical topics (unlike current events) are far less affected by time, and they do not require changing or updating every year. This helps to ensure the relevance of the unit over time.

5. Because of the importance of the Lewis and Clark Expedition in the growth of the United States, there is a wide range of authentic visual, audio, and print materials available, such as school textbooks, academic literature, authentic journals from the Expedition, and video documentaries.

Unit Activities

The activities in this unit follow the "into, through, and beyond" organization of many CBI curricula (see, for example, Brinton & Holten, 1997), where students: (1) build background schemata through reading and listening; (2) commandeer newly acquired language and concepts to discuss and analyze the content; and (3) apply critical-thinking skills to support their content-related ideas and opinions in writing. Table 2.1 provides a summary of the unit's activities with a description of the content and language goals of and the skills practiced with each activity. Activities 1–3 are more content focused, while Activities 4–6 are more language focused. The earlier "into" activities give students the vocabulary and content they need to do more advanced language production activities later in the unit.

Table 2.1   Summary of Unit Activities

Activity	Content Goal	Language Goal	Skills Practiced
1. Warm Up: Recalling details of the Lewis and Clark Expedition	Review assigned reading; elicit student knowledge	Build necessary content vocabulary	Speaking; vocabulary reinforcement and use
2. Jigsaw Reading: Learning more about Lewis, Clark, and Jefferson	Provide details about key players of the Expedition	Effectively compile an oral summary of a reading passage	Reading, critical thinking, paraphrasing, summarizing, and clarifying
3. Critical Listening: Understanding the historical significance of the Expedition	Explain the important place of the Expedition in U.S. history	Develop comprehension of an academic lecture and discrimination between major and supporting points	Listening, note-taking, critical thinking
4. Answering the Call: Writing a persuasive personal statement	Learn about the expertise of other members of the Corps	Review verb tenses; write a persuasive summary about the background and expertise of individuals	Reading, critical thinking, paraphrasing, summarizing, and persuasive writing
5. Solving Problems: Using supplies to address unexpected hardships	Familiarize students with hardships encountered on the Expedition	Brainstorm, negotiate, articulate, and write up a process to solve a problem	Vocabulary, speaking, listening, problem-solving, critical thinking, logical sequencing, and process writing
6. Descriptive Writing (and Presentation): Describing discoveries from the Expedition	Familiarize students with the Expedition findings	Develop descriptive language skills and use of sources	Reading, spelling, finding sources, critical thinking, paraphrasing and citing sources; descriptive writing (and presentation)

Table 2.2 provides more detail on the execution of the activities and the materials needed for each activity. The procedures may need to be altered depending on factors such as the number of students and their proficiency levels.

Table 2.2 Description of Unit Activities

1. **Warm Up:**	Recalling details of the Expedition
Materials	Authentic reading assignment at students' comprehension level; word chart of key terms from the reading (e.g., on a slide, blackboard, or chart paper)
Procedures	Teacher posts a word chart or word wall at the front of the class as a prompt for the warm-up activity. Students can refer to the chart to volunteer information that they recall from the reading. Additional key terms or ideas from students can be added to the chart by the teacher or students. If necessary, the teacher can point to a term and elicit what students remember from the reading.
2. **Jigsaw Reading:**	Learning more about Lewis, Clark, and Jefferson
Materials	Jigsaw passages of brief authentic biographies of Lewis, Clark, and Jefferson; expert group guide questions; collaborative comprehension grid (see Appendix 2A for sample materials)
Procedures	After explaining the task, the teacher divides students into three "expert" groups and gives each group one of the jigsaw "pieces." (The jigsaw reading passages should be selected with the students' proficiency levels in mind. Depending on the content of the passages, the comprehension grid will need to be slightly altered. To expand the activity into a four-part jigsaw, an additional biography of Sacagawea could be added.) Students silently read their passage, then in a group discuss their biography, collaborating to answer the group guide questions. When students are finished with this task, the teacher regroups students into groups of three or more, with at least one expert from each biography group. Experts then summarize (preferably in their own words) and clarify what they learned from their biography, with each group completing the collaborative information grid. The teacher can then follow up with a whole-class activity in which students report their results and receive feedback.

Table 2.2 (Continued)   Description of Unit Activities

3. Critical Listening:	Understanding the historical significance of the Expedition
Materials	Excerpts from an authentic video documentary or a teacher-prepared lecture; student notebooks (An excellent source of video footage, including free short video previews of appropriate viewable length, is Ken Burns's detailed documentary "Lewis & Clark: The Journey of the Corps of Discovery," available at http://www.pbs.org/lewisandclark.)
Procedures	The teacher asks students to take notes on a film or lecture (chosen to be appropriate to the proficiency levels of the students). Following the viewing or the lecture, students compare their notes and discuss what they did or did not understand. This can be followed by either a whole-class share or a comprehension quiz. Teachers should make sure that students understand not only what transpired during the Expedition but also its significance.
4. Answering the Call:	Writing a persuasive personal statement
Materials	Example of Clark's application letter to Lewis, tense grid, list of other members of the Corps (see Appendix 2B)
Procedures	See detailed procedures in *6: Descriptive Writing.*
5. Solving Problems:	Using supplies and provisions to address unexpected hardships
Materials	Index cards describing authentic problem situations encountered on the Expedition (see Appendix 2C); supply and provision cards
Procedures	See detailed procedures in *6: Descriptive Writing.*

Table 2.2 (Continued) Description of Unit Activities

6. Descriptive Writing:	Describing discoveries
Materials	Handout containing authentic journal entries describing Expedition discoveries (Jones, 2002; see Appendix 2D); photos of Native Americans, animals, and landscapes typical of what would have been encountered by members of the Corps
Procedures	The teacher begins by explaining the descriptive writing task and dividing the class into three groups, each with a set of photos and a journal extract with the accompanying worksheet. Students read the extract and collaboratively complete the worksheet. Then students choose a photo from one of the three categories (animal, landscape, Native Americans) and brainstorm descriptive language. As a group they write a short descriptive paragraph, which they read to the class. More advanced students could be asked to search for 2-3 outside sources about the subject chosen (e.g., prairie dog, Sioux medicine man) and write a one-page description with sources properly paraphrased and cited.

Each of the activities in this unit will require different degrees of scaffolding, depending on the levels of the students. Activities 4 and 5 are next described in depth to illustrate the type of scaffolding provided to prepare students for each activity's final written product.

Writing a Persuasive Personal Statement (Activity 4)

Many adult learners may be interested not only in academic preparation but also in professional preparation. One such professional skill is to be able to write a letter of application in response to a call for employment; this activity can help students prepare for the real-life experience.

In this guided activity, the finished product is a short persuasive letter (from a potential Corps member to Lewis and Clark) responding to the call for recruits to the Corps. Students will need to know the names of various members of the Corps and their backgrounds. They will also need to be able to write about the person's background and experience using appropriate tense and aspect (e.g., simple present, simple past, present perfect). The letter will not only need to provide the background qualifications but also contain persuasive language.

Task 1—Analyzing a letter. The teacher provides a handout with a letter to Lewis from Clark, in which Clark affirms to Lewis that he is the perfect partner to accompany Clark on the Expedition (see Appendix 2B). (This is not an authentic letter, but it provides students with an example for the guided writing activity.) After a review of the use of present and past tenses to show relationships in time, students discuss and answer the questions on the handout, working in small groups. This task helps students focus on persuasive language as well as on the grammar used in discussing personal qualifications.

Task 2—Researching other Corps members. Students are provided a list of other Corps members along with some possible internet sources. (See, for example, http://www.pbs.org/lewisandclark/inside/idx_corp.html.) After they have had a chance to familiarize themselves with several Corps members, they select one (with even the option of Seaman, the Corps dog) and imagine characteristics, abilities, and experiences the member may have had before joining the Corps.

Task 3—Writing a letter. This task can be done in small groups, in which each student composes a letter of application to become a Corps member; then, they exchange letters and give each other feedback on both content and language. A revised version is then assigned for homework.

Task 4—Role-playing. As an additional option, students could take turns playing Lewis and Clark as they read the letters and discuss why they want the particular candidates to join the Corps.

Writing a Solution to an Unexpected Hardship (Activity 5)

The problem-solution paper is another genre of academic writing that teachers may want to introduce to adult students. In this genre, a problem is introduced, a solution is presented, and the presented solution is evaluated. This genre often includes a process description.

In this activity, students will need to negotiate the best solution to a problem that occurred during the Expedition. Their solution will likely involve the use of a limited tool supply (see Task 3) and include a process description using time adverbials (e.g., *first, then, next, finally*). The solution is presented to the class for evaluation, and then a Corps journal posting is written up about the event.

Task 1—Vocabulary building. The class is divided into multiple groups (each with 4 or 5 members). Each group is given a set of cards: half with pictures of tools and half with the names of the tools. For our activity, we selected these tools: *surveyor's compass, telescope, rope, lead weight, chisel, hatchet, handsaw, hammer, silk ribbons, pocket mirror, tobacco, kettle, sewing needle, scissors, sewing thread, buffalo skin, tourniquet, forceps, knife,* and *whiskey*. After the students have had a chance to match the names with the pictures (e.g., *hatchet* with the picture of the hatchet), they are given the opportunity to explain how each tool is typically used.

Task 2—Understanding the problem. Each group is then presented with a problem on a card (see Appendix 2C). Students first discuss the meaning of the problem (with help from the teacher if necessary) and then come up with possible solutions. While the groups are discussing solutions, the teacher posts the pictures of the various tools around the room.

Task 3—Gathering tools. Students are told that there are limited supplies, so each group is allowed no more than four tools. They are then given limited time (e.g., five minutes) to "gather" the tools they think they need—even bartering with other groups if necessary—and adequate class time to devise a solution to the problem, using the tools they have at their disposal. It is likely that a few groups will not have all the tools they had hoped for, so they may need to make adjustments to their solution. Students should be encouraged in their solutions to use adverbs that are commonly used in process descriptions (e.g., *first, next, before/after, finally*). <u>Note</u>: If necessary, a supplementary scaffolding activity could be created to precede this task. In this activity, an example procedure could be cut into strips of paper, which the students then have to order correctly.

Task 4—Presenting the solution. Each group chooses a spokesperson to present the problem and their solution to the problem to the rest of the "Expedition," and the teacher (as Lewis or Clark) evaluates the quality of the solutions presented.

Task 5—Making a journal entry. For homework, students are asked to write individual journal entries as Corps members of the event, detailing the problem and their solution as well as the evaluation of the "Corps leader."

◼ Concluding Thoughts

According to Snow (2014), much of the research support for CBI is drawn from work on second language acquisition (SLA). As evidence, she notes that the authentic materials used in content-based units provide the necessary comprehensible input that assists learners in acquiring the second language (L2), while the unit's interactional tasks provide the critical opportunity for learners to engage in negotiation of meaning and to be guided to produce comprehensible output (i.e., in the content-related oral and written assignments). She further explains that by incorporating tasks that draw attention to both form-function relationships and meaning, CBI assists learners in focusing on genre/discourse structure, meaning, and grammatical aspects of the L2.

In addition to the support from SLA, CBI is also supported by research in educational and cognitive psychology (Fitzsimmons-Doolan, Grabe, & Stoller, 2017). Specifically, research in these fields shows that learning processes, prior to becoming autonomous, begin with explicit experiences and become autonomous only through repeated practice and content exposure. Such exposure leads to greater depth of processing and recall. Exposure to discourse structures and discourse awareness tasks also helps students to better understand the nature of academic writing. Finally, research into motivation underscores the need for high-interest content and interactional tasks that promote social collaboration among students (Dörnyei, 2014; Fitzsimmons-Doolan, Grabe, & Stoller, 2017). All of these elements are central to a content-based approach.

Our goal in this chapter is to provide an example of ways in which the content-based syllabus can help prepare ABE students for the rigorous writing demands of college or university study. Our selection of history as a discipline and the Lewis and Clark Expedition for the content reflect a choice calculated to appeal to immigrants and refugees. The Expedition itself is filled with fascinating events, which lend themselves to the construction of language-focused and critical thinking–oriented tasks. Not only does familiarization with the Lewis and Clark Expedition help students acculturate to their new country (the United States), but it also brings with it closer ties between these adult learners and their children, who are studying similar content in their school curriculum. Ultimately, one of the greatest strengths of CBI is its flexibility as an approach (Brinton & Snow, 2017) and the many ways in which it can be molded to fit the many unique parameters of educational settings in which students are learning English (Fitzsimmons-Doolan, Grabe, & Stoller, 2017). We believe that CBI's "two for one" claim—increased content knowledge and increased language proficiency—holds great promise for ABE populations aspiring to a higher education.

———— Questions for Reflection and Application ————

1. The sample unit in this article, the Lewis and Clark Corps of Discovery, is drawn from U.S. history. As a rationale, we note that the unit's content is both motivational and relevant to students learning about and becoming acculturated in their new country (with a possible view toward becoming citizens).

   a. Do you agree with this rationale? Why or why not?

   b. Can you think of other historical events that would be of interest and relevant to students in your setting?

2. Scaffolding is defined as "the support provided to learners to enable them to perform tasks which are beyond their capacity" (Richards & Schmidt, 2010, p. 507).

    a. Where in the unit's activities do you see evidence of scaffolding occurring? Be specific.

    b. Given the activities described, can you suggest any additional scaffolds that the teacher might employ?

3. As one of its core principles, CBI employs authentic materials, defined as "[materials] created for some real-world purpose other than language learning, and often, but not always, provided by native speakers for native speakers" (Zyzik & Polio, 2017, p. 1).

    a. Which of the materials used in the Lewis and Clark unit fit this definition of authentic materials?

    b. What are the challenges and benefits of using authentic materials with ABE students?

References

Brinton, D. M. (2007). Two for one? Language enhanced content instruction in English for academic purposes. In *Teaching English for specific purposes: Meeting our learners' needs* (pp. 1–16). Alexandria, VA: Teachers of English to Speakers of Other Languages. Retrieved from http://www.tesol.org/docs/default-source/new-resource-library/symposium-on-teaching-english-for-specific-purpose.pdf?sfvrsn=0

Brinton, D. M., & Holten, C. (1997). Into, through, and beyond: A framework to develop content-based material. *English Teaching Forum, 35*(4), 10–21.

Brinton, D. M., & Snow, M. A. (2017). The evolving architecture of content-based instruction. In M. A. Snow & D. M. Brinton (Eds.), *The content-based classroom: New perspectives on integrating language and content* (2nd ed., pp. 2–20). Ann Arbor: University of Michigan Press.

Brinton, D. M., Snow, M. A., & Wesche, M. (2003). *Content-based second language instruction* (Mich. Classics ed.). Ann Arbor: University of Michigan Press.

Burns, A., & Ollerhead, S. (2017). "Bringing the outside in": Content-based instruction and English language adult continuing education. In M. A. Snow & D. M. Brinton (Eds.), *The content-based classroom: New perspectives on integrating language and content* (2nd ed., pp. 204–215). Ann Arbor: University of Michigan Press.

Dörnyei, Z. (2014). Motivation in second language learning. In M. Celce-Murcia, D. M. Brinton, & M. A. Snow (Eds.), *Teaching English as a second or foreign language* (4th ed., pp. 518–531). Boston: National Geographic Learning/ Heinle Cengage.

Eyring, J. (2014). Adult learners in English as a second/foreign language settings. In M. Celce-Murcia, D. M. Brinton, & M. A. Snow (Eds.), *Teaching English as a second or foreign language* (4th ed., pp. 568–585). Boston: National Geographic Learning/Heinle Cengage.

Fitzsimmons-Doolan, S., Grabe, W., & Stoller, F. L. (2017). Research support for content-based instruction. In M. A. Snow & D. M. Brinton (Eds.), *The content-based classroom: New perspectives on integrating language and content* (2nd ed., pp. 21–35). Ann Arbor: University of Michigan Press.

Frodesen, J. (2017). English for academic purposes in content-based instruction. In M. A. Snow & D. M. Brinton (Eds.), *The content-based classroom: New perspectives on integrating language and content* (2nd ed., pp. 253–269). Ann Arbor: University of Michigan Press.

Jones, L. Y. (Ed.). (2002). *The essential Lewis and Clark.* New York: Harper Collins.

Murphy, J. M., & Stoller, F. L. (Eds.). (2001, Summer/Autumn). Sustained-content language teaching: An emerging definition. *TESOL Journal, 10*(2/3), 3–5.

Murray, D. E., & Christison, M. A. (2011). *What English language teachers need to know* (Vol. II). New York: Routledge.

Richards, J. C., & Schmidt, R. (2010). *Longman dictionary of teaching and applied linguistics* (4th ed.). Harlow, England: Longman.

Snow, M. A. (2014). Content-based and immersion models of second/foreign language teaching. In M. Celce-Murcia, D. M. Brinton, & M. A. Snow (Eds.), *Teaching English as a second or foreign language* (4th ed., pp. 438–454). Boston: National Geographic Learning/Heinle Cengage.

Snow, M. A., McCormick, J., & Osipova, A. (2017). Academic language across educational levels in content-based instruction. In M. A. Snow & D. M. Brinton (Eds.), *The content-based classroom: New perspectives on integrating language and content* (2nd ed., pp. 270–283). Ann Arbor: University of Michigan Press.

Weigle, S. C. (2014). Considerations for teaching second language writing. In M. Celce-Murcia, D. M. Brinton, & M. A. Snow (Eds.), *Teaching English as a second or foreign language* (4th ed., pp. 222–237). Boston: National Geographic Learning/Heinle Cengage.

Zyzik, E., & Polio, C. (2017). *Authentic materials myths: Applying second language research to classroom teaching.* Ann Arbor: University of Michigan Press.

— **ADDITIONAL RESOURCES**

- Parrish, B. (2004). *Teaching adult ESL: A practical introduction.* New York: McGraw Hill.

- Snow, M. A. (2017). Content-based language teaching and academic language development. In E. Hinkel (Ed.), *Handbook of research in second language teaching and learning* (Vol. III, pp. 159–172). New York: Routledge.

- Snow, M. A., & Brinton, D. M. (Eds.). (2017). *The content-based classroom: New perspectives on integrating language and content* (2nd ed.). Ann Arbor: University of Michigan Press.

- Teachthought. (n.d.). *28 critical thinking question stems for any content area.* Retrieved from http://www.teachthought.com/critical-thinking/28-critical-thinking-question-stems-content-area

Appendix 2A: Jigsaw Reading Activity

Part 1: Sample Expert Group Guiding Questions for Meriwether Lewis

Task: In your groups, answer the questions.

1. How old was Meriwether Lewis when he began the Expedition up the Missouri River?

2. How old was Lewis when he died?

3. What are three adjectives that you could use to describe Lewis?

4. What was Lewis's role in the Expedition?

5. What is one fact about Lewis that you found interesting?

6. In the context of the reading passage, what do you think the following vocabulary means?

   a. to run something

   b. naturalist

   c. ambiguous

   d. to drive someone to do something

Part 2: Sample Collaborative Comprehension Grid

Task: In your groups, fill in the missing key events from your readings on Jefferson, Lewis, and Clark.

	Jefferson (1743–1826)	Lewis (1774–1809)	Clark (1770–1838)
1776	is the principal author of the Declaration of Independence.		
1784			
1794			
1800			
1803			
1804			
1805			
1806			
1807			
1809			

Appendix 2B: Answering the Call

Clark's Application to Join the Corps of Discovery

When Lewis asked Clark to join him on the Expedition, he knew much of
what Clark had already accomplished, but President Jefferson may not have. If
Clark had written a letter to Lewis about his accomplishments to present to the
President, it may have looked something like this:

Task 1: Read the letter and complete the questions.

Dear Captain Lewis,

I am honored to accept your invitation to join the Expedition to explore the
Louisiana Purchase. I believe that I (am) highly qualified for the Expedition,
since I (come) from a family of honor; all of my brothers fought in the
Revolutionary War. I have lived much of my life in the wilderness of
Kentucky, and I joined the Kentucky Militia when I was 19 years old. In
the regular army, I was eventually promoted to captain. During my time
in the army, I learned many important skills that will be helpful during the
expedition; for example, I have built forts and led pack trains. I even spied on
Spanish settlers building forts along the Mississippi River.

I am a tall, rugged frontiersman, and while I do not have a formal
education, I have strong communication and drawing skills, as I have
communicated with the native inhabitants and have sketched many of the
plants and animals that I have seen in the wilderness. I am also an accurate
cartographer. All of these skills will be very useful as we explore unknown
lands.

Respectfully yours,

William Clark

*a. Complete the list of characteristics, abilities, and experiences that make Clark an ideal
Expedition co-leader.*

Characteristics	Abilities	Experiences
honorable family	fort building	has lived in the wilderness joined the Kentucky Militia

b. Now, read the letter again. Circle simple present verbs; underline simple past verbs; double underline present perfect verbs. Some examples have been done for you. When you are finished, compare your answers with a partner and discuss why the different tenses were used.

Task 2: Research some other members of the Corps (see http://www.pbs.org/ lewisandclark/inside/idx_corp.html). *Choose a member and use your imagination to list characteristics, abilities, and experiences of the member <u>before</u> they joined the Expedition.*

Characteristics	Abilities	Experiences

Task 3: Now write a letter to Lewis and Clark from the member of the Corps that you chose. The letter has been started for you.

Dear Commanders Lewis and Clark,

I am writing this letter because I heard that you are interested in recruiting strong, able-bodied men for an Expedition to the Pacific Ocean. I believe I am an ideal recruit.

Appendix 2C: Sample Problem Situation Card

Problem 1

On a hunting expedition, one of the team accidentally shot Lewis in the leg, thinking he was a deer. As experienced soldiers and explorers you have dealt with this kind of problem before. Save the life of Lewis by removing the bullet and dressing the wound.

Task: With your group members, complete the steps.

1. Find the names of the tools posted around the room that you will need to complete your job.

2. Describe the tools.

3. Explain how the tools are used to do your job in fixing the problem.

4. Choose a spokesperson to relate your solution to the rest of the "expedition" (your classmates).

Appendix 2D: Descriptive Writing

Descriptive Paragraphs: Animals—Group 1

Task 1: Read the descriptive paragraph extracted from the Expedition journal kept by Meriwether Lewis.

> February 15, 1806
>
> Their horses appear to be of an excellent race; they are lofty, elegantly formed, active and durable. In short, many of them look like the fine English coarsers and would make a figure in any country. Some of those horses are pied with large spots of white irregularly scattered and intermixed with the black brown bey or some other dark colour, but much the larger portion are of an uniform colour with stars, snips and white feet, or in this respect marked much like our best blooded horses in Virginia, which they resemble as well in fleetness and bottom as in form and colours. An elegant horse may be purchased of the native in this country for a few beads ... Among the Sosones of the upper part of the S.E. fork of the Columbia we saw several horses with Spanish brands on them which we supposed had been stolen from the inhabitants of Mexeco.

Task 2: Since the first dictionary of American English was not published by Noah Webster until half a century after the Lewis and Clark Expedition, the spelling used by both Lewis and Clark is often erratic. Underline at least three words in the extract that are not correctly spelled by today's standards. Then write the correct spelling.

_____   _____   _____

Task 3: The account of Lewis's encounter with the Sosone or Snake tribes' horses is made colorful by its use of descriptive adjectives, active or colorful verbs, and prepositional phrases. Reread the passage to locate examples of these and provide them in the word chart.

Descriptive Adjectives	Active Verbs	Prepositional Phrases
lofty	mark	of an excellent race

PART 2

Supporting the Writing Process

Chapter 3

The Process of Writing

Dudley Reynolds, Carnegie Mellon University–Qatar

Opening Questions

1. How were you taught to write? Based on those experiences, what generalizations did you make about processes for writing?
2. What other experiences have you had learning a process for writing? What made the experiences helpful, or not?
3. What might distinguish a more effective writing process from a less effective process?

Placement exams introduce many adult learners of English to writing as a focus for study. Prospective students are shown a topic, a question, or possibly a quotation and asked to quickly fill a blank space on a paper or screen with an "essay." Because they will have to take a similar test at the end of the course to gauge their readiness for the next course, their teachers may ask them to repeat this task multiple times during the course. This experience may not seem strange to them because it often replicates their experiences learning to write in their first language. If they generalize from this experience, they probably view writing as an individual performance that deals with generic topics, has no clear communicative goals, allows little time for planning, and most important, is something for which you only get one attempt.

Anyone who has ever worked with colleagues on a report, drafted a request for a rule exception, or worked with an editor to get something published, however, can tell you that writing is not always a timed, one-shot performance by an individual. We frequently discover what we want or need to write while we are writing; we negotiate content and form with other people; and we might have multiple drafts on our computer before we arrive at a document on which we are willing to put our name. If we are preparing adult English learners for the workplace or for a higher education system where their learning will be assessed through writing, we must therefore broaden their understanding of effective writing processes.

This chapter examines research on how people write in general, what adult English learners need specifically, and principles of effective writing instruction. It then focuses on how teachers can build metacognitive awareness about writing and scaffold students' writing processes.

■ How We Write

When the ancient Greeks recognized the need to analyze the rhetorical arts of persuasion for the purposes of teaching those arts, they began identifying components of a process. They realized that the effectiveness of an appeal would depend in part on the characteristics of the audience as well as the nature of the appeal. They developed techniques for generating content, categorized structures to arrange the content, and critiqued the role that language plays in the delivery of the content (cf. Rhetoricae, 2007, *The Forest of Rhetoric*). As Faigley (1986) shows, contemporary scholars have seen in the writing process a way to help students discover and express their own ideas instead of mimicking those of others (Elbow, 1973), study the cognitive strategies that differentiate expert writers from novices (Flower & Hayes, 1980), and understand the social conditioning that goes into both the production and interpretation of texts (Bartholomae, 1986).

Interest in the writing process stands in contrast with research that describes finished texts and the features that make them more or less effective. In the 1960s, as higher education began to serve larger and more diverse populations, learning to write became a central issue for applied research. Drawing support from the fields of behavioral psychology, structural linguistics, and literary criticism, some teachers asked students to study and emulate model texts as a path to improving their writing. This models approach was seen as particularly effective for multilingual students learning to write in English (Susser, 1994). As cognitive psychology, generative linguistics, and writing and composition programs began to have more influence on university campuses, a new instructional approach, "process writing," became firmly entrenched from kindergarten to first-year college composition in both first and second language writing classes (Berlin, 1987; Matsuda, 2003; Susser, 1994). These differences came to be known as *product versus process approaches*. Many writing teachers today, however, recognize the importance of working with students to understand both the goals for a piece of writing and the means for achieving them (Atkinson, 2003; Casanave, 2017; Cumming, 2013; Kalan, 2014; Yancey, 2009).

The metaphor of a "process" suggests a series of steps or stages. However, empirical researchers, interviewing individual writers and asking them to "think-aloud" while writing, have shown, however, that writing is anything but linear (e.g., Bereiter & Scardamalia, 1987; Emig, 1977; Flower & Hayes, 1981). Writers think about different things while writing and employ different cognitive strategies to manage their process, but the sequence is highly recursive and varies from individual to individual and task to task (Torrance, Thomas, & Robinson, 2000). For this reason, it is probably better to think of the writing process as having distinct components, including:

- **Analysis of the rhetorical situation:** Who is the audience? What effects should the finished product achieve? What, if any, are the specifications for the task?

- **Generation and refinement of content:** What knowledge, ideas, or arguments already exist that would be useful? What new knowledge, ideas, or arguments can be contributed?

- ☐ **Planning and revising organization of the text:** What patterns for sections and their sequence can be appropriated from the writer's experience with other texts? What effects do different sections of the text create? What effects does the sequence of sections create?

- ☐ **Selection and editing of language forms:** What patterns for the use of words and connecting ideas can be drawn upon? Do the words and patterns conform to conventions for usage?

- ☐ **Physical production:** How are technologies and different media used to produce and contribute to the meaning of a text?

■ What Adult English Language Learners Need

Anchors 1–3 of the Writing Standards for the College and Career Readiness Standards for Adult Education (U. S. Department of Education, 2013) establish argumentative, informative/explanatory, and narrative texts as types of writing that adult students need to be able to produce. Anchors 4–6 clearly indicate the centrality of the writing process in enabling adult students to produce these types of texts. Students need understanding of what makes a piece of writing "appropriate to task, purpose, and audience" (Anchor 4, p. 26), the ability to "develop and strengthen writing as needed by planning, revising, editing, rewriting, or trying a new approach" (Anchor 5, p. 26), and knowledge of ways to use technology "to produce and publish writing and to interact and collaborate with others" (Anchor 6, p. 27). The English Language Proficiency Standards for Adult Education further indicate that English language learners will develop the ability to "adapt language choices to purpose, task, and audience" (U.S. Department of Education, 2016, p. 50). Through the refinement of goals, trial use of different forms of writing, and listening to reactions that are part of an opened-up writing process, students will come to see writing, not as matching a fixed form, but as a fluid balancing of their own identity, the linguistic tools they command, and a desired end with respect to a specific audience.

■ Effective Instruction

Susser argues that "process writing pedagogies have two essential components: *awareness* and *intervention*" (1994, p. 34, emphasis in original). One way to gloss his distinction would be to say that instruction should lead to students having metacognitive knowledge of writing as well as affective and cognitive strategies for producing it. This means having explicit conversations about writing and its component tasks, not just learning by doing. Susser concludes, "Students who are aware of writing processes can then choose the process that suits their writing style and the particular writing task they face" (1994, p. 35). As argued earlier, students' experiences in particular with writing assessment may communicate false understandings of writing as an automated process leading to a fixed target. Effective instruction, therefore, needs to dispel myths while also building knowledge of writing as a complex task with a range of subcomponents.

In *Fundamental Principles of Effective Adult Language Education*, it is argued that effective instruction "creates and maintains a supportive learning environment" and "encourages learners to take responsibility for their own ongoing learning" (Center for Applied Linguistics, 2015). The ultimate goal of any pedagogy is learner independence and autonomy. When teachers *intervene* in students' writing process, to use Susser's term, they adopt a different approach from teaching through corrections on a final, never-to-be-repeated product. Instead, they acknowledge the challenges that writers face: formulating the task, figuring out what readers already know and how they think, evaluating how different uses and forms of language will be perceived, and ensuring that forms on the page match intentions in the mind. They also have a chance to model and suggest strategies that can facilitate future independence. Finally, as evidenced in many of the suggested activities in the next section, intervention in a student's writing process frequently opens that process not only to teacher input but also to peer input. Through peer and teacher interventions, students come to learn that writing is not necessarily a solitary act and that one of the most important skills for their future is the ability to collaborate (Yancey, 2009).

■ Classroom Applications

When it comes to writing, metacognitive awareness refers to "the ability to know when and how knowledge and strategies should be applied" (Negretti, 2012, p. 144). This section describes how we can help students develop awareness of components of writing processes and intervene in their use of strategies to address writing challenges. While some interventions address specific components, others can be used to explore any or all of the components at once.

Multicomponent Interventions

Two of the most common strategies in this regard are *writing conferences* and *rubrics*. Writing conferences may be between a teacher and a student or between two or more students, often referred to as *peer conferences*. The topic of the conference is something that the student has drafted. It may be a draft of a paragraph or an introduction to a text; it may be a draft of the whole assignment. In addition to the draft, students may be asked to prepare explanations of their goals or strategies in the writing or, alternatively, to identify problems they are having. By labeling the work under discussion a "draft," the conference scaffolds revision. Conferences may help students understand the task, clarify their own thinking, envision readers' perceptions, or pull together a strategy for managing the process.

Rubrics are usually thought of as tools for grading assignments. They identify specific traits of a written product such as organization or language use, desirable characteristics for each trait (e.g., clear organization, standard language use), and an algorithm for turning assessments of each trait into an overall judgment. Beyond generating a teacher's grade, however, they can also be used as a heuristic for self-assessment or a way to provide written feedback analogous to what is provided during a conference. (See suggestions in Chapter 6 for scaffolding peer feedback.) One way to support understanding of writing as a process is to frame the traits as components of the process (e.g., understanding the assignment, generating original ideas, organizing in a way that meets readers' expectations, attending to presentation). (See Chapter 4 for discussion of ways that graphic organizers can be used to guide student writing.) Judgments of the traits may in turn be framed as reader reactions (e.g., confusing; sometimes yes/sometimes no; clear) with narrative comments being added for each trait as well. Although rubrics do not allow students to pursue their own questions or seek clarification the way that conferences do, they can still be a way to make different components of writing processes salient for students while also providing a modicum of individualized feedback. By making the components explicit, they also help students develop the vocabulary and metalanguage they need to talk about writing (Thonus, 2003).

Analysis of the Rhetorical Situation

The *rhetorical situation* is a cover term for understanding one's audience, purpose, and task. Students' initial understanding of the rhetorical situation is often limited to what is in the assignment, which may mean that they do not distinguish among audience, purpose, and task when deciding what to write. Thinking about audience helps a writer make decisions about which concepts need explaining, how much explanation to provide, and what might be perceived as persuasive or entertaining. Decisions about purpose (e.g., persuade, inform, or entertain) influence overall organization, techniques for introducing a text, and language style. Similarly, recognizing the exact nature of the task helps writers link a piece of writing to conventions for genre, length, and format as well as formulate a timeline for reaching a final product.

One of the most important intervention strategies, therefore, often is helping students to analyze the assignment, asking questions that use the words *audience, purpose,* and *task.* Where the assignment does not specifically identify one of the dimensions, ask students to make an educated guess. For example, many teachers view the audience for a response on an "essay exam" to be the teacher, but the audience for a "paper" is often individuals who have no knowledge that the text was produced as an assignment. That means that if writing an essay exam for a philosophy class, we can say things like "when

Galston discusses the three social facts, he is showing . . ." In a paper for the same class, however, the claim would require an introduction to who Galston was and what the three facts were. Students may fail to elaborate, because they think the teacher is their audience and the teacher already knows who Galston is. Teachers, on the other hand, may perceive this lack of elaboration as a failure to demonstrate knowledge (Roen & Willey, 1988). Once students have identified a specific audience, they can then be asked specific questions about what those readers would know and need to know.

Discussions of audience help scaffold discussions of purpose. Students can be asked what readers of their text should be thinking at different points in the text and how their thinking should be different when they have finished the text. Persuasive texts typically begin by establishing the importance of the topic. Persuasive introductions present readers with a problem, which sets up the readers' expectation that the problem will be solved. Explanatory texts, on the other hand, begin by characterizing the topic for explanation and establishing a framework for further characterization. Texts meant to entertain rely heavily on stylized language to evoke affective reactions and questions in the reader. If students have a hard time imagining what a reader might be thinking at a given point in a text, they can work in groups, where the author reads a paragraph, for example, and then stops so that the other members of the group can voice their reactions.

To help students realize the constraints of a specific writing task, it is often helpful to ask them to imagine how the writing would change if something about the task were changed. For example, students might be asked to prepare an email message justifying a new policy on what employees can do during a break. Before they start writing, the teacher might ask them how the task would be different if they had to deliver the content through a memo that would be placed in employee breakrooms. Alternatively, they could be asked what more they could do to prepare the assignment if they were given a full week to produce it instead of having to submit it for the next class meeting. Having such discussions as a class both encourages students to think of writing as "something that will be read" and exposes them to a range of possibilities for accomplishing a task.

Generation and Refinement of Content

For many students, one of the most difficult challenges is coming up with topics to write about. Traditionally referred to as *invention*, writing teachers often take either a bottom-up or a top-down approach to scaffolding this part of a student's process (Spack, 1984). The bottom-up approach, called *freewriting*, encourages students to take a topic and just write, usually for a certain amount of time. They write without worrying about grammar, organization, or anyone else reading it. Because the focus is on generating ideas, it does not matter what language they write in. Once finished, they go back and analyze what they have written on their paper. The method for analysis will depend on the kind of content they need. If generating ideas for a persuasive assignment, for example, they might sort what they have written into ideas that focus on the problem, ideas that identify wrong solutions to the problem, and ideas that suggest better solutions to the problem. Alternatively, they might try to pull out claims and examples that could be useful. If generating ideas for an informational task, they might look for ways to categorize (e.g., core/peripheral, positive/negative, causes/results) or sequence what they wrote about.

Top-down approaches to invention, on the other hand, begin by providing an analytic framework as a way of inspiring students. (See Chapter 4 for a discussion of graphic organizers.) If the task is to write a character sketch about an inspirational person, for example, students could be given a chart with two or three columns, each corresponding to a different person. Then the rows would ask specific questions about the people. An example is shown in Figure 3.1.

The teacher could provide these questions or, even better, might ask the class as a whole to discuss characteristics that can make a person inspirational. In addition, the chart could have some empty rows that are filled in with questions the students generate. The rationale for asking students to fill in the chart for more than one person is so that they can then make a choice about which one they have the best material to use when writing. They might also use the ideas about different people as material for a comparison piece.

Figure 3.1 Plan for Writing a Character Sketch

	Person 1 (Name)	Person 2 (Name)
When has this person helped someone else?		
What has this person accomplished?		
What do people say about this person?		

Some students may find it easier to generate ideas through conversation (Ciccone, 2001). For a persuasive task, students might be put in pairs, where one member is the proponent of an idea and the other is an opposing voice. Alternatively, the other student could be instructed to ask *why?* every time a claim is made.

One task that can be fun is to involve the whole class in generating content for a far-fetched response. The teacher can model an analytic framework by asking questions, and students can be encouraged to respond with outlandish or hypothetical answers. For example, the teacher might ask students to suggest reasons that ice cream should be provided free of charge by grocery stores. Some students might talk about how customers would be happy. Others might talk about the people who would be employed in ice cream factories. Finally, some students might point out that customers who come for the ice cream would buy other things at the same time. The teacher can write all of the responses on the board. After the suggestions have been made, the teacher can then ask students to group suggestions that are similar. Students might realize that free ice cream benefits the customer, the store, and the larger economy. The teacher can then point out that these groupings provide the basis for several paragraphs. Focusing on a hypothetical question, such as reasons for providing free ice cream, has the advantage of showing students how an argument can be generated and supported rather than asking students to come up with their own arguments and support, at least initially. Using this type of example shows students the form for presenting and supporting ideas before they become engaged in writing about complicated or confusing content.

Another task can help them support ideas with both old and new information. Since students often see their writing in isolation, they do not see how it is influenced by what they have already read or heard. In this task, students describe texts as if they are turns in a conversation. Taking turns, they repeat or refer to what the previous speaker said and anticipate what may follow. By repeating and anticipating, students learn to link ideas and information. These conversations can be written as they are spoken to help learners focus on ways to link and develop ideas in writing.

English language learners frequently also need help not only with systems for citing sources but also with the difference between using source material to support their claims and simply *patchwriting* a string of material from other writers (Howard, 1993; Li & Casanave, 2012; Mott-Smith, Tomaš, & Kostka, 2017; Pecorari & Petrić, 2014; Wette, 2017). Many writing courses explicitly address information literacy skills, covering topics such as search techniques, databases, and how to recognize and reference quality sources.

Planning and Revising Organization of the Text

Many students expect teachers to "teach" organization by providing them with a structural template. One of the most common templates, the five-paragraph essay format, calls for an introduction, three body paragraphs, and a conclusion. Often students are also provided with instructions on how to write the opening sentence of the introduction (e.g., a broad generalization about the topic), the thesis statement at the end of the introduction (e.g., a compound-complex sentence), the topic sentences for the three body paragraphs (e.g., repeat part of the thesis statement), and an opening sentence for the conclusion (e.g., *In conclusion,* . . .). Unfortunately, these kinds of templates contribute to students' notion that writing is an automated attempt to match a fixed product. The challenge for teachers, therefore, is how to introduce conventions for text structure while also encouraging students to control the process.

One way to address this challenge is to build students' awareness of options for text structure by having them analyze other texts. This can be done by asking them to outline texts that they read. Outlines encourage students to see natural groupings within a text as well as hierarchical relations between main and supporting points. If students outline multiple texts, they will quickly realize that published texts rarely follow the convention embedded in the five-paragraph essay of providing three reasons, advantages, or characteristics for everything. They will also realize that expert writers generate infinite variations on common patterns. (See discussion in Caplan & Johns, 2019.)

One problem with using outlining to teach students how to organize is that outlines capture the sequence and hierarchy of what the writer says, but they do not prompt students to think about the rationale for the sequence or hierarchy. Instead of asking students what the first claim is in a text, it may be helpful instead to talk about the text as a series of strategic "moves" (Graff & Birkenstein, 2018; Swales & Feak, 2012). Beginning with the first sentence or segment of an introduction, ask students what a reader will be thinking after just reading that section. Then ask them how the next section will change what the reader is thinking. When the introduction is finished, ask students what expectations the reader should have. If the writer seems to be explaining something that they later show they disagree with, ask them why the writer started by appearing to agree. If the writer provides an example, ask them why readers might have needed an example. Like outlining, this kind of discussion generates a map of content and logical relations between segments, but it frames them as attempts to produce an effect on a reader.

Once students have developed awareness of how texts can be organized, they will apply this knowledge to their own writing process. If the curriculum allows, it may be helpful to include some assignments where strategic thinking becomes very important, such as writing a memo that delivers bad news or a job application cover letter. With a bad news memo, there is a clear choice between delivering the bad news first or starting with something positive before delivering it. For the job application cover letter, the greatest challenge is being noticed in a crowd, which is why following a template can be especially disadvantageous. Writers have to select their top selling points and present them as meeting the employer's needs. Highly strategic writing tasks like these help students see organization as a response to the rhetorical situation. Seeing organization as a series of choices further frees students from the notion that they are trying to approximate a pre-determined structure and opens them up to the possibility of moving, deleting, or inserting entire sections while producing a draft, and as they move from one draft to another.

Selection and Editing of Language Forms

One of the results of teaching writing through making corrections on a final product is many students' tendency to associate "good" writing with "correct" use of linguistic forms. The easiest thing for teachers to correct is language use, and the sheer number of words, phrases, and sentences in a student-produced text is likely to generate a large number of possibilities for correction. As a result, many language learners will stick to language that they believe they command; they will avoid risking errors and end up sounding simplistic. It is important to realize that what students need if they are to develop as effective writers is not only individual words, but rather strings of language: phrases that identify something as a cause or result (e.g., *one of the artefacts of* [cause] *is that* [result]), signal contrast (e.g., *on the other hand*), or introduce a categorization (e.g., *this is based on* [number] *types of* . . .). Such phrases are sometimes called *formulaic language* (Wray, 2008), because they work like an algorithm to connect ideas and signal the writer's intentions. A useful book for writing teachers that analyzes such patterns in detail is Graff and Birkenstein's *They Say/I Say* (2018). Once students have been introduced to the notion of formulaic language, they can begin identifying such phrases in texts they read as well as in their own writing. (See also Chapters 1 and 8.)

The second challenge that students face with respect to linguistic forms is editing. For language learners, editing may be perceived as a type of second-guessing because their tendency is to go with their first instinct and they hesitate to go back and change what they have already written. Furthermore, if the focus of a class is "writing" as opposed to "English," then it is likely that class time will be dominated by topics such as invention and organization, not grammar (Ferris, 1999). Nevertheless, language learners need to attend to language forms, and there are time-efficient ways to help students understand that their first instinct is not always right.

When students begin to see writing as a complex, multilayered process, it may be easier for them to understand that their brain's attention is constantly juggling the need to invent content, create a desired effect on a reader, and encode ideas in constructed linguistic forms. The complexity of the mental task often means that something has to give, and it is often the construction of forms (Kasiri & Fazilatfar, 2016; Kellogg, 1988). Once a draft has been produced, however, and writers revisit their use of language, they often see things that they missed during production. This simple message can be communicated by creating worksheets with excerpts from student drafts where students indicate whether the excerpt is grammatically correct, and if not, suggest changes. This can also be done as a whole-class task, where teachers provide immediate feedback on suggested revisions. Another approach, suggested by Merrill Swain (2010), involves *languaging*, or providing pairs of students with a text that has had problem areas marked and asking them to use language to talk about how to edit the text. Swain and colleagues (e.g., Brooks, Swain, Lapkin, & Knouzi, 2010) have provided convincing evidence that talking through language use in this way leads to improved performance.

Physical Production

The final dimension of the writing process to consider is the physical production of texts. This includes using word processing software and visual design tools, formulating a production schedule to manage the overall task, and possibly even sharing a publication with prospective readers to evaluate and aid revision. For many teachers, these tasks may extend beyond the scope of what they think of as writing and writing instruction. As educators are increasingly asked to connect learning to real-world tasks, we must acknowledge and prepare students for forms of communication that are multimodal and embedded in business contexts that include focus on operations and design (Edwards-Groves, 2011). This suggests that educators engage students in ethnographic research to discover how and why people write the ways they do in their jobs and social lives. Many students going into STEM fields (Science, Technology, Engineering, and Math) may not realize, for example, the importance of writing as a means for assessing learning in STEM classes or the need to generate visually effective reports, proposals, and brochures in STEM jobs. If there is not time to ask students to conduct interviews and observations about how writing functions in a particular context, teachers can invite classroom guests who students can interview about their writing processes and products.

Beyond researching how writing is used as part of professional fields, teachers can also encourage attention to the physical production of texts by considering alternatives to the traditional word-processed paper when students submit their work. For example, they may ask students to create a blog where they can "publish" their work. They might also require photo illustrations that would involve attention to layout and design. Students might also be asked for a series of related works (e.g., a proposal, a final report, and an oral presentation).

■ Concluding Thoughts

This chapter argues that there is a fundamental need to explore with adult learners the processes that make written products different and unique and to move them beyond notions of writing as correct or incorrect. The challenge involves both raising students' awareness of these processes and actually intervening in the various processes to support students' strategic competencies. As a way of concluding this discussion, consider the potential learning outcomes of taking on this challenge:

1. Students will know the difference between a draft and a final product. They will understand that we sign our names to final products and invite the world to critique them. We can be held accountable for a final product, even sued for libel. But a draft is an invitation for feedback, an intermediary stage that is but a moment in time in an ongoing process. It commits us to very little, while giving us the chance to take risks.

2. Students will be able to collaborate with others, whether they are producing a single-authored report or working on a corporate sales pitch. They will realize that by involving others in our writing process, we gain appreciation for how forms, structures, and ideas are perceived. We learn that meaning is jointly constructed among writers, readers, and social situations and that negotiation improves the results for everyone.

3. Students will be able to distinguish idea from expression, the signified from the signifiers (Johnson, 2004), and realize that both are essential for effective communication. They will have strategies not only for generating original thoughts, but also for organizing them in a stable, meaningful form. They will care about spelling, punctuation, and margins, because readers use those features of writing to form first impressions.

4. Perhaps most important, they will believe that writing is an opportunity not only to demonstrate what they know and can do, but also to explore, learn, and think. It is an activity that pushes them to new places and encourages them to make sense of the jumbled and ill-defined ideas that they may encounter or develop. It is as much about the process as it is about the product.

——————— Questions for Reflection and Application ———————

1. The chapter opening suggests that assessment practices are a major reason for notions of writing as an attempt to approximate a fixed-form product. What types of formative assessments might encourage different, more flexible notions of effective writing?

2. In the discussion of physical production of texts, it is suggested that students might engage in ethnographic research to study how people use writing in their professional and social lives. What other kinds of research projects could students engage in to develop a deeper understanding of writing processes?

3. If you could add a learning outcome to the list in the Conclusion, what would you add?

References

Atkinson, D. (2003). L2 writing in the post-process era: Introduction. *Journal of Second Language Writing, 12*, 3–15.

Bartholomae, D. (1986). Inventing the university. *Journal of Basic Writing, 5*(1), 4–23.

Bereiter, C., & Scardamalia, M. (1987). *The psychology of written composition.* Hillsdale, NJ: Lawrence Erlbaum.

Berlin, J. A. (1987). *Rhetoric and reality: Writing instruction in American colleges, 1900–1985.* Carbondale: Southern Illinois University Press.

Brooks, L., Swain, M., Lapkin, S., & Knouzi, I. (2010). Mediating between scientific and spontaneous concepts through languaging. *Language Awareness, 19*(2), 89–110.

Caplan, N. A., & Johns, A. M. (Eds.). (2019). *Changing practices in the L2 writing classroom: Moving beyond the five-paragraph essay.* Ann Arbor: University of Michigan Press.

Casanave, C. P. (2017). *Controversies in second language writing: Dilemmas and decisions in research and instruction* (2nd ed.). Ann Arbor: University of Michigan Press.

Center for Applied Linguistics. (2015). *Fundamental principles of effective adult language education.* Washington, DC: CAL. http://www.cal.org/adultesl/resources/fundamental-principles.php

Ciccone, E. (2001). A place for talk in a writers' workshop. *The Quarterly, 23*(4), 25–27.

Cumming, A. (2013). Multiple dimensions of academic language and literacy development. *Language Learning, 63*, 130–152.

Edwards-Groves, C. J. (2011). The multimodal writing process: changing practices in contemporary classrooms. *Language and Education, 25*(1), 49–64.

Elbow, P. (1973). *Writing without teachers.* New York: Oxford University Press.

Emig, J. (1977). Writing as a mode of learning. *College Composition and Communication, 28*, 122–128.

Faigley, L. (1986). Competing theories of process: A critique and a proposal. *College English, 48*(6), 527–542.

Ferris, D. (1999). The case for grammar correction in L2 writing classes: A response to Truscott (1996). *Journal of Second Language Writing, 8*(1), 1–11.

Flower, L., & Hayes, J. R. (1980). The cognition of discovery: Defining a rhetorical problem. *College Composition and Communication, 31*(1), 21–32.

Flower, L., & Hayes, J. R. (1981). A cognitive process theory of writing. *College Composition and Communication, 32*(4), 365–387.

Graff, G., & Birkenstein, C. (2018). *"They say/I say": The moves that matter in academic writing* (4th ed.). New York: W. W. Norton & Company.

Howard, R.M. (1993). A plagiarism pentimento. *Journal of Teaching Writing, 11* (3), 233–46.

Johnson, B. (2004). Writing. In J. Rivkin & M. Ryan (Eds.), *Literary theory: An anthology* (2nd ed., pp. 340–347). Oxford, England: Blackwell Publishers.

Kalan, A. (2014). A practice-oriented definition of post-process second language writing theory. *TESL Canada Journal/Revue TESL Du Canada, 32*(1), 1–18.

Kasiri, F., & Fazilatfar, A. M. (2016). The impact of task complexity on cognitive processes of L2 writers and writing quality: The case of writing expertise, L1, and lexical retrieval. *Procedia—Social and Behavioral Sciences, 232*, 561–568.

Kellogg, R. T. (1988). Attentional overload and writing performance: Effects of rough draft and outline strategies. *Journal of Experimental Psychology: Learning, Memory, and Cognition, 14*(2), 355–365.

Li, Y., & Casanave, C. P. (2012). Two first-year students' strategies for writing from sources: Patchwriting or plagiarism? *Journal of Second Language Writing, 21*(2), 165–180.

Matsuda, P. K. (2003). Process and post-process: A discursive history. *Journal of Second Language Writing, 12*(1), 65–83.

Mott-Smith, J. A., Tomaš, Z., & Kostka, I. (2017). *Teaching effective source use: Classroom approaches that work.* Ann Arbor: University of Michigan Press.

Negretti, R. (2012). Metacognition in student academic writing: A longitudinal study of metacognitive awareness and its relation to task perception, self-regulation, and evaluation of performance. *Written Communication, 29*(2), 142–179.

Pecorari, D., & Petrić, B. (2014). Plagiarism in second-language writing. *Language Teaching, 47*(3), 269–302.

Rhetoricae, S. (2007). *The forest of rhetoric.* http://rhetoric.byu.edu

Roen, D. H., & Willey, R. J. (1988). The effects of audience awareness on drafting and revising. *Research in the Teaching of English, 22*(1), 75–88.

Spack, R. (1984). Invention strategies and the ESL college composition student. *TESOL Quarterly, 18*(4), 649–670.

Susser, B. (1994). Process approaches in ESL/EFL writing instruction. *Journal of Second Language Writing, 3*(1), 31–47.

Swain, M. (2010). Talking it through: Languaging as a source of learning. In R. Batstone (Ed.), *Sociocognitive perspectives on language use and learning* (pp. 112–130). Oxford, England: Oxford University Press.

Swales, J. M., & Feak, C. B. (2012). *Academic writing for graduate students: Essential tasks and skills* (3rd ed.). Ann Arbor: University of Michigan Press.

Thonus, T. (2003). Serving generation 1.5 learners in the university writing center. *TESOL Journal, 12*(1), 17–24.

Torrance, M., Thomas, G. V., & Robinson, E. J. (2000). Individual differences in undergraduate essay-writing strategies: A longitudinal study. *Higher Education, 39*(2), 181–200.

U.S. Department of Education. Office of Vocational and Adult Education. (2013). *College and career readiness standards for adult education.* Washington, DC: Author. http://lincs.ed.gov/publications/pdf/CCRStandardsAdultEd.pdf

U. S. Department of Education. Office of Career, Technical and Adult Education. (2016). *English language proficiency standards for adult education.* Washington, DC: Author. https://lincs.ed.gov/publications/pdf/elp-standards-adult-ed.pdf

Wette, R. (2017). Source text use by undergraduate post-novice L2 writers in disciplinary assignments: Progress and ongoing challenges. *Journal of Second Language Writing, 37,* 46–58.

Wray, A. (2008). *Formulaic language: Pushing the boundaries.* New York: Oxford University Press.

Yancey, K. B. (2009). *Writing in the 21st century.* Urbana, IL: National Council of Teachers of English. http://www.ncte.org/library/NCTEFiles/Press/Yancey_final.pdf

──────────────────────────────────── **ADDITIONAL RESOURCES**

- Center for Adult English Language Acquisition. (2007). *The CAELA guide for adult ESL trainers.* Washington, DC: Center for Applied Linguistics. http://www.cal.org/caela/scb/CAELAGuide.pdf. (Section III-E deals with Teaching Writing to Adult English Language Learners)

- Pritchard, R. J., & Honeycutt, R. L. (2005). The process approach to writing instruction: Examining its effectiveness. In C. A. MacArthur, S. Graham, & J. Fitzgerald (Eds.), *Handbook of writing research* (pp. 275–290). New York: Guilford Press. https://www.nwp.org/cs/public/print/resource/2384

- Reynolds, D. (2009). *One on one with second language writers: A guide for writing tutors, teachers, and consultants.* Ann Arbor: University of Michigan Press.

- Stanley, G. (2003). *Approaches to process writing.* British Council. https://www.teachingenglish.org.uk/article/approaches-process-writing

Chapter 4

Scaffolding Writing: Using Interactive Writing and Graphic Organizers

Joy Kreeft Peyton, Center for Applied Linguistics

Opening Questions ——————————————————

1. How do the students in your classes feel about being and becoming writers who can write academic texts?

2. What supports do you or other individuals or sources provide to help them develop their academic writing?

3. Do the supports that you use promote the types and levels of writing that students need to be able to do?

As described in the introduction to this volume, adult learners of English as a second or additional language (ESL/EAL) need to master a variety of forms of writing, in English, to be successful in their academic and professional endeavors. To accomplish this, they need opportunities to write, time to write, and guidance and support for the writing that they do. The opportunities that they have, and the guidance and support that they need, can vary greatly depending on their academic, work, and life goals and on their level of English language proficiency (oral and written). Teachers working with these students in adult education, community college, and university programs need to know how to provide the needed guidance and support for the students they are working with that are appropriate to the type of writing that students need to learn, at the language and literacy levels of the students. After reviewing the challenges that adult English language learners face as they learn to write academic texts, this chapter describes supports that teachers can provide for learners at all levels, with a specific focus on two types of support—interactive writing and graphic organizers.

■ Academic Writing Skills That Adult English Language Learners Need

The introduction to this volume describes in detail the academic writing skills that adult English learners need to be prepared for future academic opportunities and work/professional opportunities. These include the ability to analyze and synthesize information from multiple sources; based on this information, write argumentative, technical, and informative texts that clearly argue for and support a well-focused thesis statement; discuss the topic of focus, using relevant reasons, supporting information, and examples; organize ideas and information coherently, with smooth transitions from one thought to the next; write precisely and concisely, avoiding vague or empty phrases and using appropriate vocabulary, sentence structure, grammar, and syntax; use and credit sources appropriately; revise and edit the text to improve its clarity, coherence, and correctness; and submit a well-edited piece that is easily understood by a native English-speaking professor, supervisor, or co-worker.

The need for these skills has been described by researchers since the 1980s (e.g., Scheiber, 1987; Spack, 1988) and confirmed and amplified by surveys of professors who teach writing in colleges and universities (e.g., Rosenfeld, Courtney, & Fowles, 2004) and in the survey of and follow-up interviews with adult education teachers, conducted in 2015 by the volume editors (Fernández, Peyton, & Schaetzel, 2017; Peyton & Schaetzel, 2016).

■ Challenges That Learners Face

The list of the skills needed is long, mastering these skills is not easy, and research in programs for adults learning English (e.g., Matsuda, 2006) has found that students receive differing amounts of instruction in these skills in writing courses, even those that focus on academic writing. In addition, students often feel anxious, alone, and unsupported as they seek to fulfill writing assignments. Martinez, Kock, and Cass (2011), in a study of factors predicting university students' writing anxiety and sense of self-efficacy with writing, describe the situation this way:

> Anxiety is prevalent among university students (Baez, 2005). While many factors contribute to college students' anxiety, high expectations for writing across the curriculum are likely to contribute to increased writing anxiety, which can affect students' motivation and willingness to take writing courses. Writing anxiety is also related to students' poor performance on English writing exams and in jobs requiring writing (Cheng, 2004). Therefore, writing anxiety is a central concern for university faculty. (p. 352)

Minahan and Schultz (2015) found that what may be perceived by teachers as "troubling behaviors" and "problem behaviors" of students can, in many cases, be linked to the students' anxiety about the tasks they need to perform, including completing a specific type of writing.

As Kirsten Schaetzel (personal communication) has seen in her courses for students learning English: "Students entering and participating in academic programs, when faced with the need to write an essay or another piece of writing, often feel alone and challenged. They start with a blank sheet of paper or screen and must work alone to put words on it. Writing is often the most difficult academic activity for them, because they do it alone, without receiving immediate or ongoing feedback about clarity, meaningfulness, and correctness." As one student explained, "You're putting your product out there, and it will be judged based on how it looks, how correct it is. Outside the classroom, there is no opportunity to redo it."

Providing many opportunities for students to engage in academic and professional writing and clear, specific, visible supports for developing this type of writing is critical. Ferlazzo (2017) describes the importance of providing scaffolds to help students learning English write argumentative essays that meet the requirements of the Common Core State Standards (2007). Lee (2017) argues that the ability to engage in the argumentative process and produce written products is achievable when students are provided with appropriate supports of teacher guidance and scaffold-rich curricula.

■ Developing Academic Writing Ability: Supports for Teachers and Learners

It is clear from the literature, and from responses to our survey and interviews with teachers (described in the Introduction), that both teachers and students need supports to think about and implement different approaches to writing; engage in activities that connect oral language, reading, and writing; develop topics and structure for the writing being done; and align this with the writing standards that are being followed in the program. Stephen Krashen (1984; Krashen & Terrell, 1983) has written extensively about ways to promote student self-engagement in oral interaction, reading, and writing, including leisure writing, to move students from where they are to a new place in their proficiency (*i+1*). Lev Vygotsky (1962, 1968), has described the fact that learning takes place in the space, or "zone," in which the learner is working to solve a problem or accomplish a task. When the teacher or a more competent peer "scaffolds" the learning by working collaboratively with the learner and demonstrating ways to move forward, proficiency develops in the context of interaction and guidance. James Gee (1989, p. 7) claims that *discourses*—social practices that involve appropriate ways of speaking, writing, talking, and valuing associated with particular social roles—are mastered by enculturation (apprenticeship) into social practices "through scaffolded and supported interaction with people who have already mastered the discourse" (citing Cazden, 1988; Heath, 1983). Cotterall and Cohen (2003) describe how scaffolding can be used specifically with students learning English in university programs to develop their writing proficiency.

■ Two Specific Types of Support for Learners: Interactive Writing and Graphic Organizers

A number of resources (shown in Additional Resources, Support for Developing Learners' Writing) are available for teachers and students when the specific focus of learner engagement and scaffolding is developing writing and overcoming writer's block. They are particularly helpful for teachers and for adults learning English.

This section focuses specifically on two types of scaffolds and supports that can be provided to help students develop proficiency with academic writing: (1) interactive writing (in "dialogue journals"), in which students articulate their ideas and perspectives in interaction with a more proficient writer (often their teacher) and receive significant feedback and further development of their ideas; and (2) graphic organizers, which provide a framework for shaping key ideas in a written piece. In these supportive contexts, students have the opportunity to process information with the support of a more proficient language user/writer, share ideas and perspectives, see other ways to express ideas, build a knowledge base and expressive writing style, and lessen their anxiety about writing.

Interactive Writing

We are seeing a shift in education away from a complete focus on independent thinking and writing to an understanding that, in order to think and express themselves effectively, students (and we, as writers who are teachers, managers, and researchers) need to have opportunities to interact and collaborate with others. Lee (2017) describes the research that is guiding this shift, with a focus on argumentative writing:

> A growing body of research shifts attention from what an individual student can do in isolation to how to establish a classroom community in which students experience an authentic need to engage in argumentation. Members of such classroom communities work together and make decisions about what counts as argument and what is required to support a new knowledge claim. (p. 92)

The approaches that she describes include partner discussions, in which each person makes their argument. The speaker relies on facial expressions to determine whether they are being understood; their partner questions them to help them clarify their positions.

Considerable research has been done on the role of interaction in writing development, which helps to scaffold the writing and transforms writing from a solitary to a collaborative activity (described in Englert, Raphael, Anderson, Anthony, & Stevens, 1991). The focus in this research (and in Lee's observations) is on oral interaction throughout the writing process.

A different approach to working collaboratively, and scaffolding student writing, is interactive writing, in what has been called a *dialogue journal*. Initially, when dialogue journal writing was discovered in a teacher's practice and studied, the teacher was writing with her students in small, individual composition books. (See Peyton & Staton, 1993; Staton, Shuy, Peyton, & Reed, 1988, for a description of the practice and of patterns found in the writing.) Today, however, the writing can also be done in email exchanges, in text or WhatsApp messages, through exchanges of Word files, by sharing a Google document, or by other means. A recent entry for *dialogue journal* on Wikipedia, describes it as "an ongoing written interaction between two people to exchange experiences, ideas, or reflections. It is used most often in education as a means of sustained written interaction between students and teachers at all education levels. It can be used to promote second language learning (English and other languages) and learning in all areas."

Dialogue journal interactions can be between a student and a teacher or with a mentor or coach who is more proficient in English than the student; at the level of the student, beginning to advanced writers, with the goal that the writing will become more complex over time and that it will focus on topics determined by the teacher or by the teacher and students together. Some teachers think about having students write with each other, but many report that this is not as effective and that writing proficiency does not develop as it does with a more proficient writer who is working as a teacher, a mentor, or a coach and who takes seriously the plan to interact with focus and to build the language proficiency of the student (and possibly their own as well).

Advantages of Writing with Another Person

Writing collaboratively with another person has a number of advantages over writing alone:

1. **The writer is motivated to write because there is interaction with someone else who cares what the writer has to say and writes back.** Also, the writing is not judged by a formal assessment or graded. This can bring a sense of freedom and boldness. As Jana Staton (1988) said in the early days of studying dialogue journal writing, "While personal journal writing has a long history in education settings as a way to promote reflective thinking, interactive writing in a dialogue journal promotes not only personal reflection but also reflection with another person, who is often more knowledgeable about the topics under consideration" (p. 5).

2. **The writer can experience a sense of community.** As Ferlazzo (2017) and Lee (2017) describe, current research is finding that building a sense of community is beneficial to student learning and can relieve students of the sense of isolation. Through writing to and with a more experienced writer, students' anxiety when faced with a blank page or computer screen can be significantly lessened. The student can imagine the audience and "rest" in the knowledge that the writing is not yet a final product, but part of an ongoing conversation on a topic of interest.

3. **The writer has the opportunity to develop a sense of self-authorship in an interpersonal context.** Leslie Bohon (2017), who works with Chinese undergraduate university students, learned over time about the value of harmony and relationship in their lives and learning. During interactions with them and review of their writing assignments, she started thinking about the conceptual framework of self-authorship, which was developed by Robert Kegan (1982, 1994) and then fleshed out by Marcia Baxter Magolda (2001, 2009). The framework includes three integrated domains of psychological development:

- *Cognitive—knowledge, beliefs*: What to believe, what to value, and assumptions about how knowledge is acquired.
- *Intrapersonal—identity*: How we view ourselves as learners and as writers.
- *Interpersonal—relationships:* How we choose to interact with others and what we want from those relationships.

Bohon asked, "Are we making use of the interpersonal domain (which she saw was so important to her students)? How can we develop it and support it?" Dialogue journal writing is one way to develop the interpersonal domain in learning and writing, the mutually supportive and scaffolded interaction that was described as critical by Gee (1989).

4. **The writing partner receives feedback, in an interactive style.** The writing is not corrected, so there is a strong sense of personal self-expression and of building thought and expression over time.

When I was in the graduate program in Linguistics at Georgetown University, my professor, Dr. Roger Shuy, kept dialogue journals with the students in the class. Recently, I reviewed my own dialogue journal writing with him, and what I discovered is shown in Figure 4.1. We were discussing the research I was doing, presentations I was

---

Figure 4.1 Writing Focus of a Learner and a Mentor/Professor

Learner	Mentor/Professor
<ul><li>Exploring and trying out ideas; taking risks with ideas and expression</li><li>Expanding on ideas expressed earlier</li><li>Asking questions</li><li>Acknowledging my confusion about specific concepts and directions</li><li>Seeking feedback and suggestions for next steps and ways to express myself</li><li>Expressing the idea again in a different way after receiving feedback</li></ul>	<ul><li>Reading what I had written, understanding, and reflecting back</li><li>Explaining and expanding my concepts and expressions, and saying them in a new way</li><li>Asking questions about some of my ideas and declarations</li><li>Giving me feedback on some of my ideas and concepts, and a sense of future directions and next steps</li><li>Providing resources that were relevant to the concepts and questions that we were discussing</li></ul>

planning to make, and publications I wanted to write, and when I reviewed what we were doing in our dialogue journals, it appeared to me that we were using writing to "choose and define problems; develop and test multimodal inquiry methods; examine findings; build, critique, and review theories and models; and make a persuasive case for claims" (described as critical by Prain & Hand, 2016, p. 432, who were focusing on scientific writing). Ashbury, Fletcher, and Birtwhistle (1993, writing with first-year medical students), Lucas (1990, writing in a graduate linguistics course for deaf university students), and Walworth (1985, 1990, writing with deaf high school and university students) describe similar patterns in their writing with students. Ashbury, Fletcher, and Birtwhistle (1993) found that the interactive journal writing that they did "provided a safe place for students to describe their experiences and relationships and to question their own values and beliefs" (p. 200). It eliminated barriers between them through a mutual sharing of thoughts and feelings, which led to enhanced rapport and communication, and thus facilitated the students' personal and reflective perspectives and initiated and encouraged self-awareness. A similar dynamic was found by Kim (2005), with adult ESL learners in a community-based adult literacy program. Kim (2005) found that the writing gave the learners the opportunity to learn about themselves, appreciate their knowledge, and feel more confident and comfortable expressing themselves. It also developed critical literacy, and engagement in active learning and thinking, rather than simple mastery of functional literacy skills.

Teachers often ask how much work dialogue writing is for the teacher. It does take time. Teachers have developed ways that work for them, which might include writing with different groups of students for different periods of time. Peer-to-peer journaling is also possible, and some people use that. The teacher wouldn't necessarily need to continually monitor the writing, but some agreements would need to be made about possible issues such as the focus of the writing, the ways the writing would be done, the forms of the writing, and how to respond if the interaction becomes challenging or frightening.

The teacher would want to ensure that the goals for the writing were being achieved.

Whether the teacher is writing with students or students are engaged in writing with peers, the teacher and the writers will want to consider these questions:

- What are we seeking to accomplish with the writing that we are doing?
- How much writing are the students doing?
- About what topics?
- At what level of thinking and written complexity do these interactions occur? At what level do we want them to occur?
- How engaged are both parties in the interactions?
- How can I manage these interactions in the contexts in which I work, with the students I work with?

In summary, interactive writing creates a sense of community and personal engagement as students express themselves in writing, over time, with a more proficient writer. This can diminish the sense of anxiety that students experience when their writing must meet certain requirements, reduce the sense of being "alone" in this endeavor, and create a sense of self-efficacy, described in the research as critical to learning overall. The teacher is not simply a judge who determines if the students' writing meets certain criteria but is also a collaborator, thinking through ideas and ways to express them and scaffolding expression in writing. The teacher can also see areas of strength and weakness in the students' writing and teach more strategically, making better use of limited class time.

Graphic Organizers

Graphic organizers are another scaffold or writing support used often in education, from K–12 to college and university classes. A graphic organizer—also known as a knowledge map, concept map, story map, cognitive organizer, advance organizer, or concept diagram—uses visual symbols to represent knowledge, concepts, thoughts, or ideas in a text and show the relationships among them. Jiang and Grabe (2007) conducted research on the use of graphic organizers in reading instruction and concluded that they are an effective way to facilitate text comprehension because they make the structure of texts visible. Here we focus on the use of graphic organizers to develop ideas for and approaches to writing an academic text.

One graphic organizer that is commonly used to promote thinking and learning, especially for informational and argumentative assignments, is a KWL table or chart, which helps students, with their teachers (or teachers, in a teacher learning community), consider what we **know**, what we **want to know,** and what we have **learned** about a specific topic. Individuals, small groups, or a class together can think about a topic (e.g., causes of climate change) and fill in the chart (together or individually) with information about what they know and what they would like to know about the topic. After discussing, reading, writing, and engaging in other activities about the topic, they can fill in the last section, what they have learned. If a group or class fills it out together, many questions, perspectives, and learnings will be shared and available. The first line in Figure 4.2 gives an example if the topic were causes of climate change.

Figure 4.2 Sample KWL Chart

Know	Want to Know	Learned
Earth's temperatures are getting warmer.	What are all of the causes of climate change?	Climate change is caused by both natural changes to the earth and oceans and by human activity.

Another commonly used graphic organizer is the Venn diagram, in which participants think about a topic and write, in the outer parts of overlapping circles, ideas or features that are different and in the inner section, ideas/features that are the same, similar, or overlap. For example, if the topic of a piece of writing is the key features of the countries of origin of the students in the class, students might work in pairs and complete the Venn diagram in Figure 4.3, each focusing on their country. They would write the name of one country at the top of one of the circles and the other country at the top of the other circle. Working together, they would list features of their countries that are different, in the outer part of the circles, and features that are the same in the center section. This activity could lead to a considerable amount of discussion, reading, and writing. If the entire class then came together to consider the countries of origin of all of the students in the class, the Venn diagram would have as many overlapping circles as the countries involved. The result could be writing informational pieces (writing about one's own or another person's country), comparative writing (describing how the two countries are similar or different), or argumentative writing (making a statement about the key features of two or more countries and defending it with data). (Additional Resources, Graphic Organizers, has examples of many different Venn diagrams that can be used, with many degrees of complexity.)

Figure 4.3 Sample Venn Diagram

Heide Wrigley and Janet Isserlis (n.d.) have created a webpage with a discussion and examples of graphic organizers that can be used in adult ESL literacy classes at many different levels (www.centreforliteracy.qc.ca/sites/default/files/GridsSurveys.pdf). They argue that:

> using grids as graphic organizers provides opportunities for basic-level literacy learners (in any language) to contribute content and information and to raise topics and questions of interest as part of the process of developing oral and written language (e.g., getting to know one another, listing languages that they speak, listing favorite activities). Use of grids can accommodate multiple levels of ability, fluency, and comfort with reading and writing.

Other graphic organizers can be used with adult English learners at different levels, from low-beginning and beginning ESL to advanced. Some of the examples come from our interviews with adult ESL teachers and their descriptions of how they teach writing. (See Peyton & Schaetzel, 2016, for discussion.)

Beginning ESL Literacy and Low-Beginning ESL Levels

One teacher who works with adult beginning writers scaffolds their writing as they move from writing a single sentence to a paragraph. The writing support that she provided (which could be considered a graphic organizer) was a simple statement on the board each day with the date, which the learners copied in their notebooks (e.g., "Today is Thursday, September 28, 2017."). After a few weeks, she added a second sentence (e.g., "Today is President's Day." or "The weather today is cold."), and the students copied both sentences. Later, she stopped adding sentences to the board but still required students to write two sentences in their notebooks each day (they had their previous writing in their notebooks to consult). It is easy to see how this simple writing support could develop over time until the students are writing topic-focused paragraphs about the content on the board or in their notebooks. (These additional opportunities are described in Peyton & Schaetzel, 2016, p. 1418.)

Another writing support is to give students a sheet of paper, a conversation grid, with four student names across the top and four questions in a column down the left of the page. Each student goes to four different students, asks one of the four questions of the student, and writes the answer in the appropriate space in the grid (as shown in Figure 4.4). Again, this simple exercise can build over time to more and more complex writing. Students might start by writing a few words and gradually move to writing phrases and then sentences. They might also advance to the point of asking each student all four questions, writing the answers in the spaces in the grid, writing summaries of the responses, comparing the responses, and sharing with others (orally or in writing) a summary of what they have learned. Like other organizer examples, this can lead to informative/descriptive writing, comparative writing, and argumentative writing. (See Peyton & Schaetzel, 2016, pp. 1418–1419, for a discussion of ways that writing opportunities can grow using this grid.)

Figure 4.4   Sample Conversation Grid

	Name 1 Juan Morales	**Name 2**	**Name 3**	**Name 4**
Question 1 What country are you from?	Juan is from Venezuela.			
Question 2				
Question 3				
Question 4				

Intermediate Levels and Multilevel Classes

It is clear from our interviews with teachers that multilevel classes can present challenges for teachers seeking to facilitate the writing of students at different levels, all with different knowledge and language proficiencies. One writing graphic organizer that students can use alone or in groups, at their proficiency level, is RAFT (which stands for Role, Audience, Format, and Topic) , in which students think about a piece of writing from different perspectives, fill in a chart, and answer questions before they begin to write a paper.

Role: Who am I as a writer?

Audience: To whom am I writing?

Format: What form will the writing take?

Topic: What is the subject or focus of the piece of writing?

Calderón, Carreón, Slakk, and Peyton (2015) give an example of what these components might look like in different writing activities (see Figure 4.5) since they would be adjusted by the teacher and the students, depending on students' interests and levels and the focus of the class, unit, or lesson. Completing the RAFT chart for different writing pieces gives students opportunities to explore different genres, styles, and tones and to consider different points of view on a topic. It also helps students to frame what may seem like an overwhelming assignment, to begin thinking about what they will write, and to lessen their anxiety in completing the assignment. (More resources for using RAFT to guide writing can be found in Additional Resources, Graphic Organizers.)

Figure 4.5 Examples of RAFT Components in Different Pieces of Writing

Role	Audience	Format	Topic
News reporter	College-educated adults	News article	Global warming
Astronomer	First graders	Travel guide	Journey through the solar system
Acute triangle	Obtuse triangle	Letter	Differences among triangles
Jackie Robinson	Hall of Fame audience	Acceptance speech	My life in baseball
Tornado tracker	Weather reporter	Interview	Facts about tornados
Hermione Granger	Harry Potter	Dialogue	Why are you so suspicious?
Rosa Parks	Historians	Diary entry	The boycott

Advanced Levels

Students at advanced levels need to be able to enter fully into the endeavor of writing academic texts. Although advanced learners bring a considerable amount of language proficiency and personal resources to the task of writing, they now have to complete more high-stakes writing assignments.

One graphic organizer for doing this that has been adapted and used by an adult EFL educator (Van Bogaert, 2017) is *force field analysis*. Its use in writing instruction was inspired by the work of social psychologist Kurt Lewin, who introduced the concept in the 1940s (Lewin, 1951). Later, it was further developed by Hurt (1998) as a guide for individuals to make a decision or a change in their lives by analyzing the forces for and against a particular topic or proposed change and considering or communicating the reasons behind the decision. Using this type of graphic, individuals or groups consider both "driving" forces (that would promote change) and "restraining" forces (that would inhibit change). In life generally, this can be a helpful way for students to think through personal decisions, life goals, and responsibilities. When used to support writing development, this graphic can help "unstick thinking"; visually represent different views about or approaches to a topic; organize those views in a systematic way; generate ideas and develop a thesis or opening statement (particularly for developing an argument or problem/solution piece); support the ideas generated; explore perceptions or opinions of opposing parties (what we know and what we don't know about the topic) and clarify which perceptions have a basis in fact and which do not; and develop a piece of writing or a presentation using this as the basis (Van Bogaert, 2017).

With her university students, Van Bogaert used this graphic to generate and organize points relevant to papers they were writing. For example, Figure 4.6 uses the force field analysis graphic organizer to generate ideas for a paper about why action related to climate change is so limited, with articulation of driving forces and restraining forces, which includes recognition of differing perspectives on whether climate change is occurring and what can be done about it. Figure 4.6 shows a sample of many ideas that can be generated.

Figure 4.6 Generating and Organizing Ideas for a Paper Using Force Field Analysis

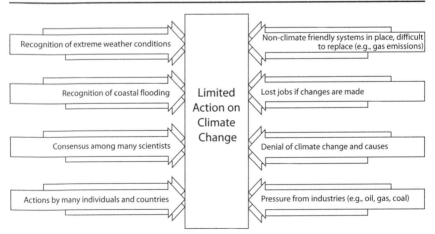

From Van Bogaert, 2017; used with permission.

■ Concluding Thoughts

Students engaged in academic writing need not only effective feedback on the writing they produce (as described in Chapter 6), but also the supports that place them in the context of a community of writers and help them to generate and organize their ideas before they begin writing. This chapter provides a number of ways that this can be done, through interactive writing and the use of graphic organizers. One way that we might continue to grow as a field is to document the ways that interactive writing and graphic organizers are used—in multiple contexts and with learners at many different levels—and then make these easily accessible to teachers working with adults learning English. We might do that through conference presentations, publications, and webpages, so that teachers have the information and resources they need. There is a great deal to be done in the field of adult ESL education to ensure that learners in these programs are learning to do what they need to do to be successful in further education and work. Educators are clearly interested in participating in needed changes, but they cannot do it alone. It is time for us to work together as a field in systematic ways to make the needed shifts.

———— Questions for Reflection and Application————

1. How much written interaction do the students in your classes engage in about the topics they are writing about? At what level do these interactions occur? How engaged are both parties in the interactions?

2. Are you able to engage with your students in written interaction/ dialogue journal writing?

3. What graphic organizers are you using now? What ones might be appropriate and helpful? At what levels? With what students? For what purposes?

References

Ashbury, J.E., Fletcher, B.M., & Birtwhistle, R.V. (1993). Personal journal writing in a communication skills course for first-year medical students. *Medical Education, 27*, 196–204.

Baez, T. (2005). Evidenced-based practice for anxiety disorders in college mental health. *Journal of College Student Psychotherapy, 20*(1), 33–48.

Baxter Magolda, M. (2001). *Making their own way: Narratives for transforming higher education to promote self-authorship.* Sterling, VA: Stylus.

Baxter Magolda, M. (2009). *Authoring your life: Developing an internal voice to navigate life's challenges.* Sterling, VA: Stylus.

Bohon, L. (2017, April 7). *Chinese undergraduate student self-authorship: Implications for faculty.* Presentation at the Conference on Language, Learning, and Culture, Virginia International University, Fairfax, Virginia.

Calderón, M.E., Carreón, A., Slakk, S., & Peyton, J.K. (2015). *Expediting comprehension for English language learners (ExC-ELL) foundations manual.* New Rochelle, NY: Benchmark Education.

Cazden, C. (1988). *Classroom discourse.* Portsmouth, NH: Heinemann.

Cheng, Y.-S. (2004). A measure of second language writing anxiety: Scale development and preliminary validation. *Journal of Second Language Writing, 13*(4), 313–335.

Common Core State Standards Initiative. (2007). *Common core state standards for English language arts (ELA) and literacy.* http://www.corestandards.org/ELA-Literacy

Cotterall, S., & Cohen, R. (2003). Scaffolding for second language writers: Producing an academic essay. *ELT Journal, 57*(2), 158–166.

Dialogue journal. Wikipedia. https://en.wikipedia.org/wiki/Dialogue_journal

Englert, C.S., Raphael, T.E., Anderson, L.M., Anthony, H.M., & Stevens, D.D. (1991). Making strategies and self-talk visible: Writing instruction in regular and special education classrooms. *American Educational Research Journal, 28*(2), 337–372.

Ferlazzo, J. (2017, April 22). Ways to teach ELLs to write academic essays: A discussion with Larry Ferlazzo. *Education Week.* http://blogs.edweek.org/teachers/classroom_qa_with_larry_ferlazzo/2017/04/response_teaching_ells_to_write_academic_essays.html

Fernández, R., Peyton, J. K., & Schaetzel, K. (2017, Summer). A survey of writing instruction in adult ESL programs: Are teaching practices meeting adult learner needs? *Journal of Research and Practice for Adult Literacy, Secondary, and Basic Education, 6*(2), 5–20.

Gee, J.P. (1989). Literacy, discourses, and linguistics: Essays by James Paul Gee. A Special Issue of the *Journal of Education, 171*(1), 5–17.

Heath, S.B. (1983). *Ways with words: Language, life, and work in communities and classrooms.* Cambridge, England: Cambridge University Press.

Hurt, F. (1998, May). Implementing great new ideas through the use of force-field analysis. *Direct Marketing, 61,* 1.

Jiang, X., & Grabe, W. (2007). Graphic organizers in reading instruction: Research findings and issues. *Reading in a Foreign Language, 19*(1), 34–55.

Kegan, R. (1982). *The evolving self: Problem and process in human development.* Cambridge, MA: Harvard University Press.

Kegan, R. (1994). *In over our heads: The mental demands of modern life.* Cambridge, MA: Harvard University Press.

Kim, J. (2005). A community within the classroom: Dialogue journal writing of adult ESL learners. *Adult Basic Education, 15*(1), 21–32.

Krashen, S.D. (1984). *Writing: Research, theory, and applications.* New York: Pergamon Institute of English.

Krashen, S.D., & Terrell, T. (1983). *The natural approach: Language acquisition in the classroom.* New York: Prentice-Hall. http://www.osea-cite.org/class/SELT_materials/SELT_Reading_Krashen_.pdf

Lee, O. (2017). Common Core State Standards for ELA/Literacy and Next Generation Science Standards: Convergences and discrepancies using argument as an example. *Educational Researcher, 46*(2), 90–102.

Lewin, K. (1951). *Field theory in social science.* New York: Harper & Row.

Lucas, C. (1990). Using dialogue journals in a graduate linguistics program. In J.R. Staton & R.C. Johnson (Eds.), *Conversations in writing: A guide for using dialogue journals with deaf post-secondary and secondary students.* Washington, DC: Gallaudet University.

Martinez, C. T., Kock, N., & Cass, J. (2011). Pain and pleasure in short essay writing: Factors predicting university students' writing anxiety and writing self-efficacy. *Journal of Adolescent & Adult Literacy, 54*(5) 351–360.

Matsuda, K. (2006). The myth of linguistic homogeneity in U.S. college composition. *College English, 68*(6), 637–651.

Minahan, J., & Schultz, J. J. (2015, January). Interventions can salve unseen anxiety barriers. *The Phi Delta Kappan, 96*(4), 46–50.

Peyton, J. K., & Schaetzel, K. (2016). Teaching writing to adult English language learners: Lessons from the field. *Journal of Literature and Art Studies, 6*(11), 1407–1423. http://www.davidpublisher.com/index.php/Home/Article/index?id=28304.html

Peyton, J.K., & Staton, J. (1993). *Dialogue journals in the multilingual classroom: Building language fluency and writing skills through written interaction.* Norwood, NJ: Ablex.

Prain, V., & Hand, B. (2016). Coming to know more through and from writing. *Educational Researcher, 45*(7), 430–434.

Rosenfeld, M., Courtney, R., & Fowles, M. (2004). *Identifying the writing tasks important for academic success at the undergraduate and graduate levels.* (GRE Board Research Report No. 00-04 R). Princeton, NJ: Educational Testing Service. Retrieved from https://www.ets.org/Media/Research/pdf/RR-04-42.pdf

Scheiber, H. J. (1987). Toward a text-based pedagogy in the freshman composition course—with two process-oriented writing tasks. *Freshman English News, 15*, 15–18.

Spack, R. (1988). Initiating ESL students into the academic discourse community: How far should we go? *TESOL Quarterly, 22*(1), 29–51.

Staton, J. (1988). An introduction to dialogue journal communication. In J. Staton, R. Shuy, J. K. Peyton, & L. Reed (Eds.), *Dialogue journal communication: Classroom, linguistic, social, and cognitive views* (pp. 1–32). Norwood, NJ: Ablex.

Staton, J., Shuy, R., Peyton, J.K., & Reed, L. (1988). *Dialogue journal communication: Classroom, linguistic, social, and cognitive views* (pp. 1–32). Norwood, NJ: Ablex.

Van Bogaert, D. (2017, April 8). *Force field analysis: A practical planning tool for professional development.* Presentation at the Conference on Language, Learning, and Culture, Virginia International University, Fairfax.

Vygotsky, L.S. (1962). *Thought and language.* Cambridge: MIT Press.

Vygotsky, L.S. (1968). *Mind in society: The development of higher psychological processes.* Cambridge, MA: Harvard University Press.

Walworth, M. (1985). Dialogue journals and the teaching of reading. *Teaching English to Deaf and Second-Language Students, 3*(1), 21–25.

Walworth, M. (1990). Interactive teaching of reading: A model. In J.K. Peyton (Ed.), *Students and teacher writing together: Perspectives on journal writing* (pp. 35–47). Alexandria, VA: Teachers of English to Speakers of Other Languages.

Wrigley, H., & Isserlis, J. (n.d.). *Into the box, out of the box—Grids, graphs, and ESL literacy.* http://www.centreforliteracy.qc.ca/sites/default/files/GridsSurveys. pdf.

ADDITIONAL RESOURCES

Supports for Developing Learners' Writing

- Center for Writing Studies, University of Illinois at Urbana-Champaign

This webpage (www.cws.illinois.edu/workshop/writers/tips/writersblock) has many writing resources that teachers can use in instruction and can teach students to use. A helpful section focuses on *Writing Tips: Strategies for Overcoming Writer's Block.* There is a brief discussion of one of the causes of writer's block, conflicted feelings: "We want the writing to be perfect, and we want the paper done as soon as possible. We know what we know, but we don't know what our readers know. We know how the memo should sound, but we don't have all the facts we need. We know everything about the software, but we don't know what an article should look like. We know what we have to say, but we are afraid that it won't measure up to our expectations or to our readers' expectations."

The page then describes weak strategies for overcoming writer's block (e.g., insisting on a perfect draft, waiting for inspiration) and effective strategies for overcoming it, including:

- taking notes: Jot down ideas and phrases as they occur to you.

- freewriting/brainstorming: Sit down for 10 minutes and write everything you can think of about the topic you are writing about (this could also be done orally with another person).

- WIRMI: When you're stuck and trying to find the perfect way to say something, think, What I Really Mean Is (WIRMI), and just say it the way you think it. When you know what you mean, it is easier to write it and then refine it.

ATLAS ABE Teaching & Learning Advancement System

- Writing Instruction Resource Library, Hamline University, Minnesota

This is a rich set of resources for teachers (http://atlasabe.org/resources/writing-instruction) that is focused on writing instruction and has these sections:

- *Research and professional development:* Published research reviews and national reports to guide the processes of learning to write and writing to learn.

- *Mechanics:* Describes, for the Roman alphabet, writing conventions that do not occur in oral language (letter formation, spelling, capitalization, and punctuation).

- *Grammar:* A discussion of how words are formed (morphology) and how phrases, clauses, and sentences are formed (syntax).

- *Sentence and paragraph writing:* Guidance and resources for teaching ways to write simple, compound, and complex sentences and cohesive paragraphs.

- *Essay writing:* Resources for teaching how to write narrative, informative, and argumentative essays.

- *Workplace writing:* Resources for teaching ways to write effectively the different types of pieces written in workplace contexts (e.g., cover letters, resumes, emails, memos).

- *Reading/writing connections:* A set of activities that can be used to make connections between reading and writing.

Interactive Writing in Dialogue Journals

- Dialogue Journal

This rich resource can be found at https://en.wikipedia.org/wiki/Dialogue_journal.

Graphic Organizers

Examples of different graphic organizers can be found on these sites:

- Wikipedia, *Graphic Organizer*

  https://en.wikipedia.org/wiki/Graphic_organizer

- *Into the Box, Out of the Box—Grids, Graphs, and ESL Literacy by* Janet Isserlis and Heide Spruck Wrigley.

  www.centreforliteracy.qc.ca/sites/default/files/GridsSurveys.pdf

- Venn Diagrams

  https://support.office.com/en-us/article/Create-a-Venn-diagram-D746A2CE-ED61-47A7-93FE-7C101940839D

- RAFT Writing Organizer

  www.readwritethink.org/professional-development/strategy-guides/using-raft-writing-strategy-30625.html

- RAFT Writing Template

  www.readwritethink.org/files/resources/printouts/RAFT Writing.pdf

Chapter 5

Leveraging Technology in Writing Instruction

Diana Satin, English for New Bostonians
Steve Quann, Consultant

Opening Questions ────────────────────

1. What are some effective language learning activities that you have used in class?

2. What technology have you used successfully, with your class or with learners outside of class?

3. What challenges do you encounter when using technology in your program and classes?

This chapter describes ways that teachers can leverage technology to support English language learners throughout the academic writing process. Because there are many approaches to integrating technology into instruction, our suggestions are based on more than 20 years in the field, creating and teaching lessons for adult learners at all levels, co-authoring books on the topic, and providing professional development nationally and internationally. We give special attention to instructional strategies for integrating these technologies into classes.

■ Theoretical and Research Background

Most researchers and teachers report that technology integration increases teaching and learning effectiveness (Mullamaa, 2010). Research indicates that, with technology, learners are more interested and involved in developing their writing skills, they produce more writing, and their writing is more advanced (Goldberg, Russell, & Cook, 2003; Sullivan & Pratt, 1996).

It is valuable to create opportunities for learners to interact with authentic audiences. Using technology is beneficial because it extends the possibilities beyond the classroom, which then provides students with a purpose for communicating and greater motivation to do their best writing (Sweeny, 2010; cited in Yunus, Nordin, Salehi, Redzuan, & Embi, n.d.). Using technology to collaborate on team assignments is common in academic and work settings, so providing authentic opportunities for learners to become comfortable with these types of experiences helps them develop necessary skills (Peyton, Moore, & Young, 2010).

Project- and problem-based learning (PBL) are approaches that successfully combine technology integration, writing for an audience, and collaboration. These approaches involve learners investigating authentic topics to find solutions to real-world problems. Teachers can also use these approaches to provide opportunities for learners to strengthen skills identified as necessary for success in today's college and career environments, often described as the 4 Cs: *critical thinking, communication, collaboration,* and *creativity* (Partnership for 21st Century Learning, 2017). Theories and approaches abound on how to use technology to address the 4 Cs.

- ☐ Teachers' knowledge of effective ways to combine technology, pedagogy, and content, or the TPACK Framework (Technological, Pedagogical, and Content Knowledge), is one.

- ☐ Another is the SAMR model, which guides teachers in moving students from lower levels of engagement (**S**ubstitution and **A**ugmentation) to higher levels (**M**odification and **R**edefinition), in correlation with Bloom's Taxonomy of Cognitive Processing (Bloom, Englehart, Furst, Hill, & Krathwohl, 1956).

- ▣ A similar model is Replacement, Amplification, Transformation (RAT), which moves the teacher from simply substituting technology and keeping the activity the same to creating a novel activity that requires the use of technology to carry it out.

- ▣ The Triple E Framework (Kolb, 2011) provides guidance for implementing these various approaches and brings together research findings on leveraging technology to engage, enhance, and extend learning, making learning goals the central focus instead of the use of the technology itself, asking students to leverage technology to investigate and build new understanding, and then asking them to use it to connect their learning to their lives outside the class.

In adult education, technology has been integrated into the College and Career Readiness Standards (U.S. Department of Education, Office of Vocational and Adult Education, 2013), which describe a set of writing anchors that call for learners to build skills in writing, citing evidence, and publishing. Those related to uses of technology are shown in Figure 5.1, where we describe a set of instructional activities that use technology to promote academic writing. As you read, think about ways that you could modify them in your classes but also keep in mind the standards that your program uses.

Figure 5.1   Writing Anchors Related to Technology in the College and Career Readiness Standards

Writing Anchor 6: Use technology, including the internet, to produce and publish writing and to interact and collaborate with others.
Writing Anchor 7: Conduct short, as well as more sustained, research projects based on focused questions, demonstrating understanding of the subject under investigation.
Writing Anchor 8: Gather relevant information from multiple print and digital sources, assess the credibility and accuracy of each source, and integrate the information while avoiding plagiarism.

■ Classroom Application: The Project

The writing anchors in Figure 5.1 correspond with what is often thought of as a six-step writing process: preparation, pre-writing, drafting, revising, editing, and publishing. Topic development with guiding questions, in Writing Anchor 7, is often part of the preparation process, followed by the sort of research described in Writing Anchor 8, which precedes or can occur during the process of drafting. Publishing relates to Writing Anchor 6.

This section describes how technology can be used to enhance each step of the process for both teachers and students. (The technologies mentioned here exist as of the timing of the publication of this book and are offered as illustrative examples only. As change and innovation are constant, these tools may become unavailable, switch from being free to requiring a fee, or be revised or replaced.)

1. Preparation

As an educator, you have, no doubt, experienced how planning ahead helps you use your time in class more efficiently. Planning is crucial when using technology, so we recommend considering these steps:

Plan the Activity

- **Use the POST method to inform lesson planning and technology selection.** We use the acronym POST to guide teachers with their selection of technology tools (Haydon, 2017). It helps them to first focus on the needs of the learners—*people* **(P)**, in this case, students—and the learning *objectives* **(O)**, before developing teaching *strategies* **(S)**. Then, only after considering these three, select the appropriate *technology* **(T)**. Be sure to address the learners' language and technology needs related to their academic or career goals, such as those listed in the College and Career Readiness Standards (U.S. Department of Education, 2013). As you select technology, think about whether one tool would support English language learners better than another. For example, you may decide to have students use a spreadsheet program rather than a word processing program if you plan to integrate math into your curriculum.

- **Analyze the activity to know the specific technology skills that learners will need to complete it.** To avoid the situation where learners feel overwhelmed, there needs to be a balance between their having enough skills before starting an activity and the new skills they will learn while carrying it out. It is important to break down the steps required to successfully complete an activity using the technology that you have selected before identifying the support and the practice that learners will need. Gaps in skills are fine, as long as there is value to the learners in going through the work to close those gaps, and the work is balanced with the time spent moving toward language goals. For example, if typing the address of a website into a browser would take undue time, you might want to place shortcuts to the website on learners' desktops or have the website open on their computer screens.

In these situations, asking learners to work in small groups or pairs is helpful because they can help each other. For example, some students might not be familiar with moving the cursor to the icon and double clicking. The students who know how can demonstrate and then their partners can repeat it several times for practice. This also makes more efficient use of the limited time in class because students do not have to wait for the teacher to help them.

- **Identify any technical terms or other challenging vocabulary that is new to learners and consider how you will pre-teach it.** Teachers who have been using technology for a long time may not realize that terms such as *cursor* and *search engine* are new to some learners and can leave them confused when trying to follow instructions. Demonstrate, for example, by pointing out the cursor on your screen and asking learners to locate the cursors on their devices. Write new terms on the board and repeat them a number of times while engaging in an activity to give learners enough exposure to develop mastery.

- **Consider grouping learners.** Most adult ESL classes are in some way multilevel, in terms of both language and technology skills. Varying student groupings in such cases can ensure that all learners feel both supported and challenged. Learners can be grouped either with others at the same level, so they can learn a skill together at the same pace (like-ability), or in mixed-ability levels, so that each learner has a strength to teach the others (cross-ability). Based on the lesson objectives, teachers may find value in grouping learners according to their technology skills or language levels. We find this especially useful when engaging in project-based learning. Doing this has the added benefit of providing opportunities for learners to connect with more people in the class, thereby building a sense of community.

- **Use the "I do, we do, you do" approach when teaching a new skill.** It can be a challenge helping a group of learners become familiar with a new skill and aiding the movement to mastery. An excellent method for scaffolding learning begins with "I do" (the teacher demonstrates the skill or activity), followed by "we do" (the teacher and learners do the skill or activity together), and finally, "you do" (learners do the skill or activity independently/ alone, in pairs, or in groups).

Prepare the Technology

Using technology requires additional steps to get ready. We recommend considering these questions for the best chance of a successful experience.

- **How do you use technology for writing instruction when resources are lacking?** Schools and learners have varying levels of access to technology and the resources to use it—devices such as tablets and laptops, projectors, the internet—and space, comfort, expertise, and time, to name a few. Lacking any of these can pose major barriers to teaching and learning. One way that teachers address limited technology resources is by making use of the mobile devices that learners own, since even low-income students today seem to own cell phones, smartphones, or tablets (Rideout & Katz, 2016). We strongly advocate for the use of a projector or other device that allows all learners to view the teacher's computer screen. It is indispensable for modeling how to do a task and for sharing exemplary learner work.

- **What do you need to reserve in advance of the class? Mobile devices or a computer lab? Wi-fi hotspot? A projector? A room with a Smartboard?** If you will be using your school's devices, check the availability ideally before class, particularly if you are using multimedia and especially if you share the computers with other classes. Click links and check audio to see if there have been changes to websites or device settings. If needed for learners with limited experience, be sure to open the programs on the devices that they will use in advance of the class. If you are fortunate to have an assistant, he/she can take on some of these responsibilities.

- **Which tools, apps, plug-ins, or setting adjustments are needed, if any?** Do you need to get a technology administrator's login to make those changes on the devices?

- **How will you send or share assignments with learners and, if applicable, among learners?** How will learners save the assignments? If using Google Drive, you may use a separate folder for each learner or group of learners and set sharing permissions accordingly. Beginners often struggle to key in web addresses, so share the addresses by using a class webpage with an easy-to-type web address, or email or text them. Another option is to use a web address shortener, such as goo.gl or tinyurl.com so you can easily write them on the board. Some teachers use QR codes (a type of barcode) when students have smartphones.

- **What do you do to prevent students from losing or forgetting passwords?** Because activities can often go awry if students are unable to access computers or websites because they have forgotten or lost their passwords, you should keep track of passwords or logins. Some sites (like Google Drive) and some course management systems (like Canvas) require them. Approaches that teachers have found effective include assigning learners passwords and keeping a list, or asking learners to use the same formula, such as their name with capital initial letters and no vowels, plus the name of the class.

As a final note, keep in mind that technology requires patience, flexibility, and a fairly high level of tolerance for glitches, more than is typical when using handouts or workbooks. This is also why it is useful for you to share with learners various ways of dealing with the challenges that can occur.

Design the Project

Most learners will need academic writing as well as presentation skills to meet their academic and career goals. Asking learners to solve a meaningful problem or answer a question using a project-based learning approach is an ideal way to integrate technology with writing. Next, we describe a specific project: Learners research job information online, create a presentation (e.g., PowerPoint, Google Slides, Keynote, or Prezi), and report their findings orally. We highlight instructional methods that transform the fairly standard use of presentations into a range of approaches to address learners' range of language and technology skills. The Learner Needs Matrix in Figure 5.2 gives some possible variations.

Figure 5.2   Learner Needs Matrix for Use in Developing a Project

Learner Needs Matrix		
Level	**Language Skill**	**Technology Skill**
Beginning	◘ Use an online bilingual or picture dictionary to find vocabulary and type three short sentences responding to the questions: ▪ What is the occupation? ▪ Where do people in this occupation work? ▪ What do they do?	◘ Use a template that is provided to create three slides. ◘ Add three images (photos or other images) plus text.
Intermediate	◘ Research mynextmove.org for information on the career each student wants. ◘ Summarize: ▪ What they do ▪ Education required ▪ One more section that learners select ◘ Include names of sites where resources were found.	◘ Copy a template or recreate a model and tweak the color, format, and font styles to personalize. ◘ Add images (photos or other images) plus text.
Advanced	◘ Research mynextmove.org for information on the career they want and summarize each section. ◘ Find another reliable website for information on one more subtopic of interest. ◘ Include full citations for information, video, and images.	◘ Search for slide layouts and select one. ◘ Add sized images (photos or other images) with borders. ◘ Search for or create a video to add. ◘ Select the desired alignment for text, images, and video.

As we provide broad strokes of the lessons, readers should understand that these are illustrative only and are not necessarily meant to be followed step-by-step. They will need to be adapted to your context.

2. Pre-Writing

Lesson 1: Activating Prior Knowledge

Objective: Learners are able to articulate and build on their previous experience with the topic.

Strategy: As with all adult learning, activating and sharing prior knowledge, or schema, on a topic creates a base that learners can tap into. They are able to activate schema and set the context that will inform their writing. An engaging way to do this is to ask learners to perform an online search for images or videos related to jobs they have become familiar with through friends, family, or other sources and review them as a class. Helping learners become comfortable using search engines is practical because they can use them for many other purposes as they advance in their writing studies in the future. Important goals for them are finding key resources on their own and knowing how to check the reliability of information.

Technology: View the image or video results of occupations using search engines such as Google or DuckDuckGo or on Wikimedia. For beginners, it might also be a good time to demonstrate how to capture images from the internet. Users intending to include images or videos in their projects need to be introduced to usage rights and ways to find free-to-use images.

Activity: Begin your classroom activity by projecting a website for the whole class and asking learners to enter an occupation or to spell it for you to enter. Review the vocabulary and pronunciation of words in the search results. Ask the class what they know about the occupation and to share experiences they have had with it. Learners can also work in small groups and share images on their device screens. Another option is for learners to share photos or videos they have taken at their places of work using their mobile phones. They can also print and post images on the classroom walls and have a gallery walk, where they walk around, look at the images posted, and possibly write comments on the pages with the images. For more advanced classes, consider having learners use a group photo-sharing app such as Cluster (https://cluster.co). Provide an overview of the project and share example slideshows from previous projects. If applicable, show choices for how the group will share their work and with whom. (See the Publishing section.)

Lesson 2: Generating Ideas

Objective: Learners will be able to list and organize their ideas prior to writing.

Strategy: Brainstorming is a typical classroom activity to generate and arrange ideas, normally carried out using a whiteboard or newsprint. One advantage of brainstorming, together using technology tools, is that it adds the energy that learners feel when they see their contributions immediately become visible to the whole group. Consider tools that allow learners or the teacher to prioritize ideas by reordering and highlighting them.

Technology: Private backchannel apps or websites, such as TodaysMeet, can be used by learners at almost all levels. Intermediate and advanced learners can generally handle generating ideas on shared online documents, such as Google docs. Technology-savvy classes can use mind mapping tools like Popplet (https://popplet.com/).

Activity: Ask learners to use a dictionary (see description in Figure 5.3) or spell checker to make sure they know the correct spelling of the jobs they are considering looking into and type the jobs on the backchannel app or shared document for others to see. Ask them to review one another's contributions and to note commonalities or clusters; for example, they might note that many jobs involve helping people or that only a few are in the technology sector. Then, pairs should ask one another questions to find out more about the jobs they chose and why they are interested in them. Ask them to report out to the whole class and note which learners share interest in the same career cluster. Group them accordingly for the next step, researching information.

Figure 5.3 Online Dictionaries

An online dictionary or app is indispensable. For the benefit of learners who do not know of one, other learners can be invited to demonstrate how to access a favorite of theirs. Ones that use common words in their definitions, like the *Longman Dictionary of Contemporary English Online* (http://www.ldoceonline.com/), make switching to an English-English dictionary easier. All levels of learners can benefit from using tools that include an audio feature, such as Google Translate, as well as picture dictionaries like Learning Chocolate (http://www.learningchocolate.com/).

Lesson 3: Researching Information

Objective: Learners are able to locate and select information that is appropriate for their project.

Strategy: Locating and understanding information on the internet is a necessary skill in the academic world, and including this activity in the project helps learners become comfortable doing it.

Technology: Use a projector to show the class the dictionary or job information webpage.

Activity: Ask learners to discuss who writes the information that is posted on websites and how to know the type of organization behind the website, such as the .com address suffix for businesses and .edu for educational institutions. Tapping the group's collective knowledge, guide learners in understanding how to locate information and navigate the website. Ask the class questions such as, "What is the name of the website?" and on the dictionary webpage, "Where do I type the word we want to find a definition for?" Distribute and review handouts that list the information that learners need to gather, including space to take notes if they prefer doing so by hand. With advanced language learners, help them to find the additional reliable web sources they need to locate and experiment with search terms that they generate so that they can figure out which ones are most useful; for example, "health educator job" may produce better results than "health." Brainstorm how to know whether a website is reliable and what the reader will learn and gain by using it. Pairs should collaborate on going through this process for the jobs they choose.

Plagiarism is an issue that is especially worthwhile covering with intermediate and advanced learners. They may be unaware that simply copying the language that others have used can be viewed as idea theft. With the whole class, practice rephrasing pieces of information from websites that several learners are using for their research. Depending on learners' language levels, show them how to give credit for sources by citing the title and author (and the date if it is stated), or by including a full-fledged citation. Websites such as Citation Machine™ (www.citationmachine.net) compose these in various formats, while the Google Explore tool allows learners to both research and cite sources from within their Google Doc.

Lesson 4: Organizing Ideas

Objective: Learners will be able organize and rearrange information in ways that clearly communicate their ideas.

Strategy: There are many ways to help learners organize their ideas, whether through semantic mapping or a basic outline, and technology might not be the best solution. (Pencil and paper is probably best for those who prefer to complete the organizing and editing process before keying it in.) Using the slide sorter or SmartArt graphics in PowerPoint to organize topics and subtopics allows more advanced learners to try out various ways to organize the information they have gathered. Unless learners struggle with editing on a computer screen, it is efficient as well, since they eventually will need to type the information in.

Technology: Several types of presentation software might be used: Google Slides, Keynote, PowerPoint, Prezi (https://prezi.com), or TesTeach (www.tes.com/lessons).

Activity: Ask learners to begin to prepare the slides for their presentation. Whichever presentation software they use, facing a blank screen can be intimidating, especially when they are writing in English. Using a prepared template will help beginning technology users to enter the job title on the title slide for their presentation and the questions you asked them to investigate in the title areas of the remaining three slides.

Advanced learners can choose a blank template and type in the sections they researched on the job website as the slide titles. They will be relieved to discover that writing their first draft will be easier for them since they already thought about, researched, and did some basic organization on their topic during this pre-writing step. To help them feel more relaxed about working with the slideshow software, show them how to use the Undo and Redo buttons. Seeing the neat and clear appearance of their writing gives learners confidence. After they have created their slides, demonstrate how they can drag slides into a new order using the Outline View and Slide Sorter features. Pairs should then ask one another for input and suggestions regarding the appearance of the slides.

3. Drafting

Objective: Learners are able to write an organized draft for their project.

Strategy: Learners review the ideas from the pre-writing process and embark on composing complete sentences and paragraphs, building on the language that they have found on the websites they are using for their project. English language learners might know how to turn an eloquent phrase in their own language, but they soon realize that direct translation has its pitfalls. They need additional support to craft a phrase in a way that is used by native English speakers. Whether you think English language learners need to pay attention to grammar or to check spelling as they type or after they formulate their ideas, there are tools that can improve productivity.

Technology: Numerous technology tools and resources are available to help English language learners get just-in-time grammar and writing-related lessons, expand their vocabulary and strengthen their use of new words and phrases, and use text-to-speech and audio input to help with pronunciation. Intermediate and advanced learners may want to try using a voice typing tool, such as the one that can be enabled in

Google Slides for speaker notes, along with a spell checker and a dictionary to resolve questions on pronunciation and the meanings of similar-sounding words that they mispronounce.

Language corpora (sets of words and phrases, used in different settings and for different purposes) can be useful for learners to get exposure to the context and usage of words that are new to them. (For the largest freely available corpus of English, see the Corpus of Contemporary American English (COCA) (https://corpus.byu.edu/coca/). For learners at lower levels of proficiency, checking with corpora is helpful in the drafting stage, but for learners at higher levels, it is best to write when drafting and improve word choice when revising or editing. Beginning- and intermediate-level learners would benefit from having a list of sample words and phrases from the teacher. Programs such as the Ginger Software Sentence Rephraser (www.gingersoftware.com/) can help push learners to add to their vocabulary and sentence formation. This will enable them to communicate their ideas in a more accurate and interesting manner, which will be expected of them when writing in academic contexts.

A checklist or rubric can guide students regarding what features of their writing to focus on and can focus on features that have been covered in class, such as clarity, grammar, and word choice. For example, a checklist for beginners could include ensuring that all sentences have a subject, verb, and object and that initial words are capitalized; one for advanced students might require varied sentence structure and, perhaps, five words from an academic word list. Sites such as Rubistar (http://rubistar.4teachers.org/) have customizable rubrics, and Google Forms can be used to create students' own checklists. Teachers may also choose to develop rubrics and checklists with the class to build learners' ability to create such tools for themselves in the future.

Activity: Provide learners with websites that help them develop ways to express their ideas effectively, such as multimedia lessons on spelling, grammar, vocabulary, and style, on

JenniferESL (www.youtube.com/user/JenniferESL). Invite learners to demonstrate other websites that they find useful. Teaching them to search for resources themselves is a skill that is invaluable for their lifelong learning, so we suggest reviewing the earlier lesson on search terms, asking a few learners for lessons they would like to locate, and then using the class computer with a projector to search for them together. Use the "I do, we do, you do" approach to model how to implement the checklist or rubric to create a strong first draft, explaining that this saves time on revision and editing later.

4. Revising

Objective: Learners are able to interpret and apply feedback from others on clarity and organization of ideas to improve their writing.

Strategy: Learners receive feedback from and work with the teacher and other learners to make sure that they are communicating their ideas clearly to their audience(s).

Technology: English language learners find personalized comments on their writing using the Comment feature in their software to be a helpful way to receive and save feedback. Most computer programs provide text-only commenting but do not overlook the option of voice commenting if that is available within the computer program or as an add on (e.g., at this time, Word and Google Docs have the option but PowerPoint and Google Slides do not). Although writing comments in a text can be labor intensive, we have found through our experience that English language learners benefit from this type of individualized feedback.

At this stage, advanced learners can use corpora such as an online thesaurus, words from the Academic Word List, and the Corpus of Contemporary American English (https://corpus.byu.edu/coca/) themselves to investigate words and phrases that more precisely express ideas that other learners and the teacher noted as being unclear.

Taking feedback to another level, an excellent way to model and provide mini-lessons for just-in-time support is by keeping a repository of existing teacher videos found on sites such as TeacherTube (www.teachertube.com/) and YouTube and creating your own brief three- to five-minute screencasts as needed, focusing on text features such as capitalizing proper names or employing advanced sentence structures. This is especially useful when teachers do not have the time to meet with learners individually and when learners find reading a text-based lesson too daunting. English language learners particularly appreciate learning from multimedia. It allows them to replay the videos as needed. And, of course, online tutorials are especially appropriate in a distance or blended learning context.

Activity: Ask learners to share their writing with one another and to exchange feedback. Show the class a sample project to help learners understand what the end-product ought to look like. Teachers sometimes provide the class with a rubric so that learners know how the project will be graded and the steps needed to successfully complete it. However, we find a checklist to be the easiest way to communicate expectations and guide students as they provide constructive feedback to one another. Employ the "I do, we do, you do" approach to demonstrate how learners will use the checklist or rubric, so they can get a clear idea on how best to direct their attention to skills already covered in class. Then ask pairs to check one another's work and provide feedback in a constructive way. Explain that, aside from communicating orally, exchanging thoughts and teaching one another strengthens their ability to independently edit their own work, a skill crucial to their success in higher education.

Using the slideshow commenting tool, concentrate on one or two major areas for clarification that interfere most with clear communication of the ideas in the written piece. Minimize the length of the comments to maintain learner focus. Use the comments as jumping off points for mini-lessons: In the comment, paste a link to a study resource and

Figure 5.4 The ARRR Approach to Using Computer Functions While Editing

---

Add—*Word Count:* Add text in sufficient detail, and use this for writing assignments that have word requirements or limits.

Rearrange—*Edit Menu:* To improve the flow, familiarize learners with cut, copy, and paste as well as how to highlight and drag text to reorganize their draft.

Remove—*Highlight and Delete:* Using backspace and delete keys are great, but highlighting the text and then deleting it can be more efficient.

Replace—*Find and Replace*: If a word or phrase needs to be changed throughout the text, this feature can be a big time-saver.

---

exercise, ideally one that provides answers. This way, learners can easily return from the resource to their writing and apply what they have learned.

During the revising stage, writers find the Add, Rearrange, Remove, and Replace (ARRR) approach, shown in Figure 5.4, to be helpful. These are basic word processing functions that teachers can introduce to more advanced writers and technology users. We suggest that these be used judiciously.

5. Editing

Objectives: Learners are able to modify and refine their drafts for correct grammar, mechanics, and word choice.

Strategy: Learners clean up the spelling, grammar, punctuation, and other technical elements of a text they have written.

Technology: The grammar and spell-check tools included in many computer programs can be useful, but learners need to have enough knowledge of phonics to spell words closely enough to the correct way for spell checkers to offer relevant options. They also need a large enough vocabulary to make a selection from the list of suggestions. For this reason, we recommend considering these factors when making a decision about using such tools. They may be most helpful to learners at high-intermediate and advanced levels.

Activity: Add a second round of comments about the text, with edits, along with follow-ups on previously suggested revisions. As before, it is most effective to focus on one or two specific errors that impede clear communication (Ferris & Hedgcock, 2014) and to have learners support one another as they make corrections. After they have implemented the corrections, check their work.

6. Publishing

Objective: Learners share their projects and written texts with an audience.

Strategy: Technology is especially useful at this step because it allows learners to interact around their writing with people in their class and beyond.

Technology: If learners are sharing only within the class and you are already using a learning management system (LMS) such as Canvas (https://canvas.instructure.com/login/canvas), Edmodo (www.edmodo.com/), or Schoology (www.schoology.com/), they can post their slideshows and exchange comments there. In lieu of an LMS, a private texting app such as WhatsApp (www.whatsapp.com/) can be used. Platforms such as SlideShare (www.slideshare.net/), blogs, and websites also have settings that are either private (available only to those with a password or the direct link to that page) or open to anyone, so that learners can invite other classes or the general public to comment and participate in conversations about their slideshows.

   Another exciting way to exchange work with an audience is to arrange to do so with a class somewhere else in the country or the world by web meeting, using a program such as Skype in the Classroom's Skype Collaborations (https://education.microsoft.com/skype-in-the-classroom/skype-collaborations).

Activity: Pair learners by like- or cross-ability levels to collaborate on the process of posting their presentations online. Use a checklist or rubric that describes how to successfully give a presentation of their slideshow, including level-appropriate criteria that are expected in presentations in academic settings, such as clear speech and eye contact. If available, have the group analyze videos of exemplary presentations from previous classes. Put learners in groups of three or four and ask each to rehearse their presentation, taking turns videotaping one another on their cell phones to review, and giving feedback according to the rubric or checklist. If individuals are presenting and there are many members in the class, scheduling the presentations during several class periods may be the best way to maintain the class' attention. With permission, learners' presentations can be shared with friends and family and used as documentation of progress in their oral language skills. A learner can record presentations via cell phone and then transfer them to a computer.

■ Concluding Thoughts

It is easy to feel overwhelmed by the array of technological possibilities available for the classroom. The choices multiply exponentially as people find applications to learning that are increasingly inventive and easier to use. We suggest resisting any sense of self-imposed pressure to keep on top of every development. Instead, focus on learners' language and technology skill needs and the class' goals and then choose one or several tools. Stick with them unless there is sufficient reason to change. Some of the best tools have been around for many years. That said, some learners will come with technological experience that has the potential to improve your teaching and the added benefit that learners are already adept at using them. For example, once almost exclusively used by youth, educators are now using Snapchat (www.snapchat.com/) with classes.

As teaching and learning strategies are honed to address learners' needs and paces of learning, personalized learning is beginning to be implemented in the field of adult education. Along with this, we are likely to see more and more classrooms with learners grouped at "digital access stations," areas in the classroom that are set up with digital devices and specific tasks for students to engage in, either related to an activity that the rest of the class is working on and using other materials, or activities that help students who need to build specific skills like writing to catch up with the rest of the class.

One emerging technology to consider to augment the writing process with advanced English language learners is SAS Writing Navigator (www.writingnavigator.com/), available as a free Google add-on. It is a suite of online tools that aid in planning, drafting, editing, and revising. In the future, Automated Writing Evaluation (AWE) might be a tool that some teachers will choose to use. AWE allows learners to receive accurate automatic feedback tailored to the writing they produce, avoiding the lag time needed for the teacher to check each piece of work individually.

To keep abreast of new technologies, such as AWE, professional development can be accessed in a number of ways. The U.S. Department of Education's Literacy Communication and Information System (LINCS) (https://lincs.ed.gov) provides a number of free resources, including discussion forums on topics such as integrating technology and reading and writing, where educators can share ideas and best practices. These resources, along with local professional development centers, provide materials around which professional learning communities and mentoring can form. Because changes in technology and research findings on pedagogy are a constant, connecting with professional development opportunities is a way for educators to support their students in ways that will help them reach their goals.

———— Questions for Reflection and Application ————

1. What is a project that you might undertake with learners that would combine use of different technologies?

2. What is one technology tool or technology-based idea that you will consider using with your classes? What do you need to learn more about it so that you feel comfortable using it? How will you need to modify it to match your learners' needs and goals?

3. What additional information, if any, is necessary for you to learn about learners' interests and needs before planning a technology-based project or lesson?

4. Are there trainings for technology integration or technology resources that you would like to advocate for in your program? Who would have information on ways to acquire them?

References

Bloom, B., Englehart, M., Furst, E., Hill, W., & Krathwohl, D. (1956). *Taxonomy of educational objectives. Handbook 1: The cognitive domain.* New York: Longmans, Green.

Ferris, D., & Hedgcock, J. (2014). *Teaching L2 composition: Purpose, process, & practice* (3rd ed.). New York: Routledge.

Goldberg, A., Russell, M., & Cook, A. (2003). The effect of computers on student writing: A meta-analysis of studies from 1992 to 2002. *The Journal of Technology, Learning, and Assessment, 2*(1). https://ejournals.bc.edu/ojs/index.php/jtla/article/view/1661

Haydon, J. (2017). *Here's the secret to successful social media campaigns (Hint: P.O.S.T.).* https://www.postplanner.com/secret-to-successful-social-media-campaigns-post-method

Kolb, L. (2011). *Triple E Framework.* http://www.tripleeframework.com/

Mullamaa, K. (2010). ICT in language learning—Benefits and methodological implications. *International Education Studies, 3*(1). http://www.ccsenet.org/journal/index.php/ies/article/view/4965

Partnership for 21st Century Learning. (2017). *The 4Cs research series.* Washington, DC: CONVERGENCE. Center for Policy Resolution. https://education-reimagined.org/resources/partnership-for-21st-century-learning

Peyton, J. K., Moore, S., & Young, S. (2010). *Evidence-based, student-centered instructional practices.* CAELA Network Brief. Washington, DC: Center for Applied Linguistics. http://www.cal.org/caelanetwork/resources/student-centered.html

Rideout, V., & Katz, V. S. (2016). *Opportunity for all? Technology and learning in lower-income families* (Winter Ed., Rep.). New York: Families and Media Project.

Sullivan, N., & Pratt, E. (1996). A comparative study of two ESL writing environments: A computer-assisted classroom and a traditional oral classroom. *System, 24*(4), 491–501. http://www.sciencedirect.com/science/article/pii/S0346251X96000449

Sweeny, S. (2010). Writing for the instant messaging and text messaging generation: Using new literacies to support writing instruction. *Journal of Adolescent and Adult Literacy, 54*(2), 121–130.

U. S. Department of Education. Office of Vocational and Adult Education. (2013). *College and career readiness standards for adult education.* Washington, DC: Author. http://lincs.ed.gov/publications/pdf/CCR StandardsAdultEd.pdf

Yunus, M. M., Nordin, N., Salehi, H., Radzuan, N., & Embi, M. A. (n.d.). *A review of advantages and disadvantages of using ICT tools in teaching ESL reading and writing.* http://www.academia.edu/28260734/A_Review_of_Advantages_and_Disadvantages_of_Using_ICT_Tools_in_Teaching_ESL_Reading_and_Writing

ADDITIONAL RESOURCES

- Buck Institute for Education. (n.d.) *Why project-based learning (PBL)?* https://www.bie.org/

- Jenkins, R. (2016). *Integrating digital literacy into English language instruction: Companion learning resource.* Washington, DC: Literacy Information and Communication System.

- National Research Council. (2012). *Improving adult literacy instruction: Supporting learning and motivation.* Washington, DC: The National Academies Press. https://doi.org/10.17226/13469

- Quann, S. (2015, June). *Integrating digital literacy and problem solving into instruction.* Washington, DC: U.S. Department of Education.

- Weisspol, A. (2016, June 9). *Teaching effectively with technology: TPACK, SAMR, RAT.* https://micool.org/updates/blog/2016/06/09/teaching-effectively-with-technology-tpack-samr-rat/

Chapter 6

Providing Feedback on Students' Writing

Dana Ferris, University of California, Davis

Opening Questions ─────────────────────

1. How would you describe the purposes of the teacher providing feedback on students' writing?

2. If you have typically provided feedback on students' writing, what issues have you struggled with or wondered about?

3. In your own experience or observations, have you found— either as a student writer yourself or as a teacher—that teacher feedback tends to be *helpful and facilitative* to students or *harmful and discouraging* to them? How do your views about this question influence your attitudes toward responding to your own students' writing?

All writers need feedback on how successfully they have communicated their ideas, and students who are building confidence and competence in writing in a second language (L2) especially need thoughtful, supportive feedback from expert mentors (i.e., their teachers). Though few teachers or student writers would disagree that feedback is important, instructors may struggle at times with providing effective commentary on student writing and with efficiently using the time they spend providing feedback to their students. Teachers of students learning to write in a second or additional language (L2 writers) must also consider whether their feedback will empower and encourage their students, rather than demoralize them. This concern is especially salient for teachers who work with adult L2 learners, who may come from a range of educational backgrounds and may not be especially confident about their writing abilities in any language.

Responding to student writing in ways that are effective, efficient, and empowering is an art, not a science, and there is a learning curve for new teachers and an opportunity for experienced teachers to consider and improve their responding strategies. This chapter discusses best practices in providing feedback to L2 writers about their texts, focusing especially on three practical points: (1) providing selective, prioritized feedback; (2) providing clear, specific feedback; and (3) providing encouraging, empowering feedback. It closes with suggestions for ways for new L2 writing teachers to develop their feedback skills and for already practicing teachers to reflect on and sharpen their approaches. These suggestions will not only help student writers but will also help L2 writing instructors feel less harried and frustrated and more satisfied with their efforts.

◼ Background: Theory and Research on Response to Student Writing

Response to student writing has been an area of scholarly inquiry in first language (L1) composition since the 1970s and in L2 writing since the 1980s. Early writings on teacher feedback typically cast the endeavor in quite a negative light. For example, in an influential piece, Knoblauch and Brannon, citing Marzano and Arthur (1977), described teacher commentary as "an exercise in futility" (Knoblauch & Brannon, 1981, p. 1). A year later, in a pair of related articles in *College Composition and Communication*, Brannon and Knoblauch (1982) criticized teachers who use feedback as a way to shape student writing into the teacher's "Ideal Text," and Sommers (1982) characterized teacher commentary as overbearing: "The teacher appropriates the text from the student by confusing the student's purpose in writing the text with her own purpose in commenting" (p. 149). Sommers further criticized teacher commentary, as observed in the study she conducted with Brannon and Knoblauch, as reflecting poor priorities (for example, commenting prematurely on grammar and mechanics when a paper was still in its early stages of development) and being generic ("Good job!") rather than text-specific. These early indictments of teacher feedback, especially Sommers's notion of teacher "appropriation" of student texts, were very influential in composition research and practice, leading to strong suggestions that teachers avoid written commentary in favor of in-person writing conferences and that they privilege peer feedback over teacher response (see, e.g., Anson, 1989; Hairston, 1986; Moxley, 1989).

An early study of L2 writers by Zamel (1985), building on the findings of Brannon and Knoblauch and Sommers, reported similar conclusions: "ESL composition teachers…are even more concerned with language-specific errors and problems. The marks and comments are often confusing, arbitrary, and inaccessible" (p. 79). Two late-1980s studies of student views about teacher response noted that, in students' perceptions, teacher feedback was mainly focused on grammar rather than on their ideas or organization (Cohen, 1987; Radecki & Swales, 1988).

In the 1990s, however, the research and discussion on teacher feedback took a more productive and less negative turn, possibly reflecting changes in writing pedagogy in L1 and L2 composition that privileged the writing process (i.e., students writing multiple drafts of papers and receiving formative, intermediate-draft feedback that helped them revise, rather than simply corrections and a grade). For example, Reid (1994), taking on "the myths of appropriation," argued that expert feedback from teachers on student writing should be considered a form of positive intervention, not a mean-spirited attempt to undermine and "take over" students' work. Studies of student reactions to teacher feedback generally found that L2 writers appreciated their teachers' efforts and found them helpful; some of these studies, unlike those completed in the 1980s, reported that teachers commented on a range of writing issues beyond grammar or error (Cohen & Cavalcanti, 1990; Ferris, 1995; Hedgcock & Lefkowitz, 1994; Leki, 1991).

Another line of research on response to writing in the 1990s focused on descriptions of teacher commentary and its effects on student revision (Conrad & Goldstein, 1999; Fathman & Whalley, 1990; Ferris, 1997; Ferris, Pezone, Tade, & Tinti, 1997; Straub & Lunsford, 1995). These studies, taken together, generally found that teachers have a broad range of commenting purposes and strategies (see also a more recent study by Ferris, 2014) and that teacher feedback did help students to make successful revisions to their texts, though some types of feedback were more helpful than others (discussed more specifically in the next section). In short, contrary to early assertions that teacher feedback may do more harm than good by appropriating students' work and confusing and demoralizing student writers, later work suggested that thoughtful, principled teacher commentary could benefit students and indeed was greatly valued by novice writers.

Beyond the more general trends in research on teacher commentary already outlined, it is important to mention the major role that more specialized studies of teacher/expert error correction, more recently known as written corrective feedback (CF), have played in L2 writing pedagogy and scholarship (see, e.g., Bitchener & Ferris, 2012; Bitchener & Storch, 2016; see also the 2012 special issue of the *Journal of Second Language Writing* on this topic). Until the mid-1990s, there was relatively little research on the effects of error correction or CF in L2 writing. However, in response to a provocative paper by Truscott (1996; see also Ferris, 1999; Truscott, 1999), who argued strongly that "grammar correction" in L2 writing should be "abandoned" because it was ineffective, counterproductive, and impractical, the past years since 1996 have seen an enormous amount of empirical work on the efficacy of written CF in facilitating both second language acquisition and L2 writers' development. Space does not permit a full review of this work here, but best-practice suggestions derived from the recent studies are summarized in the next section, and additional sources are mentioned at the end of the chapter.

To summarize this section, while early theoretical and empirical work on teacher commentary in general and written corrective feedback in particular suggested that such interventions were, at best, ineffective and, at worst, harmful to students, subsequent research has provided, if not always a ringing endorsement of teacher feedback, at least a more nuanced view that it can, under the right conditions, be helpful, encouraging, and motivating for student writers. It is to these "right conditions" that we turn in the next section.

■ Classroom Applications

The various lines of research since the mid-1980s, taken together, lead to some clear directions as to what have been described as best practices in response to student writing. These are summarized in Figure 6.1.

Figure 6.1 Best Practices Suggestions from Response Research

1. Teacher feedback (whether written or oral) should focus on a range of issues, including content, organization, language, mechanics, and style, and the focus of response should depend on individual students' needs at that point in time.
2. Feedback should be provided on multiple drafts of student papers, not only final graded drafts.
3. Students should receive feedback from multiple sources (e.g., teacher and peers) so that they can benefit from reactions from different readers.
4. One-to-one writing conferences may be more effective than written teacher commentary.
5. Teachers should give clear and text-specific feedback that includes both encouragement and constructive criticism and that avoids appropriation (taking over) the student's text. Where possible, questions are preferable to imperatives, as they are less directive and promote student autonomy.
6. Teachers should focus primarily on issues of content and organization early in the writing process, saving grammar and mechanics issues for the end of the writing process.
7. Selective error feedback on several patterns of error is more beneficial than comprehensive error correction, as the latter is exhausting and overwhelming to teachers and students.
8. If feedback on errors is provided, indirect error feedback (in which the error is indicated but not corrected) is more beneficial to long-term student development than direct correction (in which the teacher or peer provides the correct form to the writer).
9. For peer response activities to be successful, the teacher should (a) model the process for students before beginning (i.e., provide training); (b) structure peer response tasks carefully; (c) form peer review groups thoughtfully; and (d) include accountability/reflection mechanisms so that students take the process seriously.
10. To alleviate problems that some students might have with teacher-student writing conferences, teachers should (a) discuss the goals and format of conferences with students ahead of time; (b) suggest that the student take notes or record the conference for later review; (c) consider holding conferences with students in pairs or small groups to minimize any discomfort that students might feel with one-to-one meetings with the instructor and to maximize instructor time (particularly with small groups of students struggling with similar writing issues).

Source: Ferris, 2014, p. 8.

The list in Figure 6.1 makes it clear that written teacher commentary is not (or need not be) the only source of feedback to student writers as they go through the writing process for a particular assignment or through a writing course (or course that includes significant amounts of writing). Other sources of feedback might include tutors in a writing or learning center, peers, or the writers themselves while rereading and reflecting on their own texts (see Andrade & Evans, 2013; Ferris, 2015). Further, teachers may find that in-person writing conferences with students (Points 4 and 10 in Figure 6.1)—whether conducted in office hours, in class, or even virtually over a course management system such as Canvas or an online application such as Google Hangouts—may be more effective in some instances than written commentary. Some instructors have also experimented with audio commentary inserted into students' electronic texts, an option available in the Canvas Speed Grader and in other applications such as iAnnotate®, an app for iOS devices such as iPhone or iPad.

Nonetheless, for a variety of practical reasons, teachers' written commentary still tends to be the most common way in which students receive feedback on their writing (see Ferris, 2014), and thus, the discussion turns to specific considerations for written response provided by teachers to their students, where three important principles for written teacher commentary are discussed: being selective, being clear, and being encouraging. Readers interested in learning more about peer response for L2 writers, the role of writing centers in L2 writing instruction, or guided self-evaluation as a form of response will find suggestions along those lines in the Additional Resources section.

Written Teacher Commentary Should Be Priority-Driven

While the initial musings on teacher feedback by Brannon, Knoblauch, Sommers, and Zamel may have been unnecessarily pessimistic and even cynical about the potential value of teacher response to student writing, they were right about a very important point: Teachers should have a principled approach and be clear in their own minds as to why and how they respond to student papers. Specifically, teachers should not believe that they must address every single problem they see on each student paper to which they respond. Experts agree that feedback is most beneficial to students when it is *selective* and focused on the most major issues, problems, or patterns observed in the text at that particular point in its development. There are two reasons for this assertion. One is that too many comments, corrections, and symbols at one time can be overwhelming to students. It can discourage them ("The teacher hates my writing"; "I'm a terrible writer"), and it can confuse them, providing more information than they can apply to that paper or generalize and learn from for future writing tasks. The danger of visual and cognitive overload seems equally possible, whether the teacher handwrites comments and corrections on a hard copy with a (red) pen or whether she uses Track Changes (from Microsoft Word) on a computer.

Beyond the potential to demoralize and overburden students, leading to diminishing returns as to learning from the feedback, it makes sense to prioritize content, idea development, and organization on student texts before providing feedback on grammar, vocabulary, or mechanics (see Points 2 and 6 in Figure 6.1). As Sommers (1982) noted, premature attention to form and surface issues might mislead student writers into believing that all they need to do is tidy up a few mechanical errors rather than substantively revise their content by adding, deleting, or rearranging their ideas. It also may be a wasted effort on the part of the teacher if extensive line editing is applied to a section of text that might disappear during the process of content revisions.

In adult L2 writing contexts, students may not initially be writing long, source-driven papers as they will in later classes—they may instead be writing paragraph-length texts based on personal experience or opinion or limited outside information. Even so, teachers can and should prioritize idea development in their feedback in earlier stages of the writing process by: asking questions that elicit more information, details, evidence, or analysis; suggesting ways in which the text could be structured or organized more effectively (e.g., adding a transition or topic sentence, adding a summary sentence, rearranging details, or moving extraneous details out of a paragraph to maintain better paragraph focus); guiding students back to the assignment or writing prompt to make sure they have understood and fulfilled task specifications (an important academic skill in all courses); and asking students to consider the knowledge and expectations of a target audience or hypothetical reader. Figure 6.2 shows a response rubric for a "report paragraph," in which students were asked to present well-focused, useful information about an assigned topic (in this instance, their chosen or potential field; the focus could similarly be what a student's chosen or potential career goal is). The rubric provides ideas about how an instructor (or peer reviewers) could respond to a first draft, focusing first on ideas and arrangement.

Figure 6.2   Sample First-Draft Feedback Rubric ("Report Paragraph")

Structure	Yes	Maybe	No
▫ Is there a topic sentence that states what the writer's career goal is?			
▫ Does the paragraph report enough details about the career goal?			
▫ Are the details arranged in a logical order?			
▫ Is there a concluding sentence that recommends, based only on the reported information, what the writer expects this career will do for him/her in the future?			
Content			
▫ Does the paragraph describe the reason(s) he/she chose this career?			
▫ Does the paragraph describe the types of steps he/she will have to take to pursue this goal?			
▫ Does the paragraph discuss other details such as internships and/or employment opportunities?			
Write an endnote: Remember to compliment what the writer did well (marked YES). Then, discuss what was confusing or missing (MAYBE/NO). Finally, give some advice about how he/she might improve this paragraph.			

Note: I am grateful to my colleagues, Catherine Hatzakos and Kelly Crosby, for sharing these materials.

In this assignment, students were also, in this assignment, asked to include at least three reporting verbs (e.g., *argue, suggest, discuss*) from a list provided and to stay consistent with verb tenses. These issues could be addressed as part of the first-draft feedback, but they could also be part of later feedback on a penultimate draft that focuses specifically on language issues.

Written Teacher Commentary Should Be Clear and Specific

It is surprising how often teacher commentary can be cryptic, vague, overly abstract, jargon-filled, and sometimes even illegible (see Ferris, 1995). These problems were a large part of why earlier researchers such as Sommers (1982) and Zamel (1985) were so critical of teacher commentary. Zamel, for example, cited a teacher comment in the margins (p. 90)—"INC SEN"—that was completely unsuccessful in guiding the student writer toward revision of the offending sentence fragment. In one publication (Ferris, 2003), I similarly cited a case study of a student writer named "Antonio," whose teacher exhorted in the margins "Change it to weaker!" when he wrote that being an immigrant to a new country had made him a "stronger" person—a request/order that was simultaneously confusing and overbearing.

It should be self-evident that teacher commentary should not be a reading comprehension exercise for the student and that feedback that students do not understand cannot help them. With this principle in mind, some practical suggestions for making teacher written commentary clear and accessible are discussed briefly here. A sample student text with teacher marginal and end comments is also provided as an illustration in Appendix 6A (adapted from Ferris & Hedgcock, 2014).

1. **Reduce visual clutter.** As already noted, student texts that are covered with teacher markings—whether they be in pen or using Track Changes or other digital means—can be visually overwhelming to students. Adhering to the previous principle—be selective and prioritize in written commentary—will help curb this unfortunate teacher tendency, but other practical advice along these lines includes: Use a computer for providing feedback

where possible (e.g., use typed comment boxes rather than handwritten notes in the margins); keep sentences relatively short and straightforward; consider breaking up longer comments (e.g., in an endnote) into bullet points or numbered lists to make the most important suggestions easily identifiable; and consider using non-verbal cues, such as color-coding, for specific error patterns (e.g., blue for verb tense errors, yellow for missing noun plurals, etc.).

2. **Avoid jargon.** Teachers should assume nothing about terms, rules, and labels that students might or might not already know. In other words, avoid marking papers with codes such as "tense" or "VT" (verb tense) or "transition" unless (a) that structure or concept has already been explicitly taught in class or (b) it has been determined, via a pre-test or questionnaire, that all of the students have previously learned this concept. This principle refers to rhetorical jargon, such as "introduction," "counterargument," or "audience," as much as it does to grammatical or mechanical labels.

3. **Privilege clear statements over abstract questions.** Teachers are often trained to ask questions of students rather than spitting out directives in the margins, again following Sommers's (1982) warnings about not appropriating students' texts. Questioning is also considered a student-friendly "reader-response" strategy, in which the teacher assumes the role of an interested reader, having a dialogue with the writer, rather than an evaluator or judge. However, in my own previous research (e.g., Ferris, 1997, 2001), I found that some types of questions may be more accessible to L2 writers than others:

Type 1: Request for information known to the writer: *What is her major?*

Type 2: Indirect request phrased as a yes-no question: *Can you give an example here?*

Type 3: Higher-order question to challenge the writer's thinking, logic, or argument: *Isn't it true that…? Have you considered…?*

Most students in this study were much more able to deal
in their revisions with questions that asked them for more
information (known to the writer but not the reader; Types
1 or 2) than with abstract questions that challenged their
logic or argumentation (Type 3). Only the strongest writers
in the sample were able to revise effectively in response to
Type 3 questions; often, the student would just delete that
portion of the text in the next draft! One way for teachers
to address this problem is to pair a Type 3 question with a
straightforward revision suggestion, such as "Maybe you
could add a sentence or two here that explains...."

4. **Give students a plan or specific steps to take.** It can
be difficult for novice writers to turn reader (teacher or peer)
suggestions into a concrete revision plan or to apply advice
given to future writing tasks. Thus, it can be very helpful
for teachers to summarize their suggestions in an endnote
under "suggestions for revision" (if the text is a preliminary
draft) or "advice for future papers" (if it is a final draft that
will not be further revised). Otherwise, it can be difficult for
students to take a wide-ranging list of suggestions, questions,
and corrections and know what to do next. Teachers can
facilitate this ability to generalize and apply feedback both
through their own summary comments and by walking
students through a guided revision activity, in class or for
homework, to apply feedback received. (See Ferris, 2015, for
several examples of such activities.)

5. **Finally, teachers should *require* that students read,
think about, and apply feedback they have received,**
not simply *hope* that they will do so. This can be accomplished
through asking students to write a reflective memo or letter
to the teacher about the feedback, through revising or
rewriting a text after receiving feedback, or through analyzing
(e.g., through an error patterns chart) the feedback they
have received. (See a sample error codes chart in Appendix
6B.) Teachers are often frustrated when they put time and
energy into written feedback, only to suspect or discover that
students have never even read it, let alone benefited from it
(see Ferris, 2014, 2015; Ferris, Liu, & Rabie, 2011). However,
this does not have to be left to chance or student whim, if
teachers are intentional about requiring follow-up steps.

Written Teacher Feedback Should Be Encouraging

Writing for academic or professional purposes is hard work. Doing so in a second language is a daunting challenge. It is not surprising that student writers in general, and L2 writers in particular, tend to dislike writing and lack confidence in their abilities as writers. Teachers, caught up in their own time constraints and frustrations, can sometimes forget that there is a vulnerable (and usually young) human being who wrote the text. Thus, as previously discussed, early critics of teacher feedback characterized it as being careless, insensitive, arbitrary, and sometimes even mean-spirited.

There is no excuse for teacher feedback being snappish and mean—*ever.* If a teacher truly thinks that students are not putting forth a good-faith effort, there are more professional and constructive ways to convey and enforce expectations than to snarl at them in the margins of their texts. Beyond avoiding meanness or rudeness, though, teachers can take positive steps to encourage L2 writers and build their confidence. First, **treat students as individuals.** While a rubric, such as the one shown in Figure 6.2, can be useful for both focusing teacher feedback and communicating assignment criteria clearly and consistently, a filled-out checklist should not be the only feedback that students receive from their teachers. Teachers should use students' names, refer to their ongoing work (e.g., "You've really improved your verb tense consistency since your last paper!" "You did a great job of adding support since your last draft!"), and treat each student and text equally (don't be overly negative with weaker students; don't shortchange the stronger students with just an A grade and a "Great job" comment) and individually (write text-specific comments that focus on the strengths and weaknesses of that particular paper, not a generic comment that you might give to the whole class).

Second, **praise students for what they have done well.** Teachers tend to be so focused on looking for problems and errors that they may forget to notice what *is* working in student papers. If the student writes an engaging introduction, let him or her know that right away in the margin. If a quotation from a source is well chosen and effectively integrated, teachers can note that, too, and they can begin an endnote with a summary of the strengths of the text before jumping into criticisms or suggestions. Sometimes finding positive things to say can be difficult if a paper is very weak and full of problems. This is why a feedback rubric structured like the one in Figure 6.2 can be helpful—any column with a Yes checkmark can provide ideas for what the teacher can praise. However, there are a couple of caveats to keep in mind. It is probably not necessary to strive for a 50-50 split in positive vs. critical comments. Students generally understand that the purpose of teacher feedback is to help them improve and will not expect too much praise (see Ferris, 1995), but it is also important for teachers to clearly explain their purposes and approaches in feedback to student writers. Also, if the feedback is on a preliminary draft that will be revised, teachers should bear in mind that students generally are reluctant to change sections of a paper that a teacher has praised (see Ferris, 1997). If there is a section of a paper that needs work or rethinking, it might be counterproductive to write a cheerful comment of praise in the margins next to it (or, a positive comment can be carefully hedged in an endnote: "You did a good job with _____, but _____, so maybe you could _____").

Finally, **help students reflect on their progress to build their confidence.** Teacher feedback, combined with students' own guided self-evaluations, can help students feel less overwhelmed. Students can be asked, at the end of each assignment or between drafts, to note in a chart or a short reflective writing activity (even just a couple of sentences) what the teacher commented on, if that issue (grammar, organization, support, cohesion, etc.) showed improvement, and what they still need to work on. They can then be guided to review those reflections regularly and at the end of the course. While it can be challenging to take the time for this and to make specific feedback points concrete and measurable, if students can observe that they're not simply writing papers, getting grades and criticisms, and then repeating the process—but that they are actually learning and improving from practice and feedback—then writing assignments can be seen as productive and as moving toward important goals (better writing for future school and workplace tasks) rather than disheartening teacher-induced drudgery.

■ Concluding Thoughts

As already noted, providing feedback to L2 writers can be time-consuming, challenging, and frustrating—but it is also very important. As one teacher noted a few years ago:

> Responding to student writing IS the job of teaching writing. If they don't write and we don't respond, then how else are they going to learn to write? I can't learn to ride a bicycle by talking about it or watching PowerPoint presentations about it or even thinking about it. (Ferris, Liu, & Rabie, 2011, p. 40)

Though early L1 and L2 composition scholars disparaged teacher commentary on student writing as being at best futile and at worst harmful, later researchers have found that feedback can help student writers revise their texts more effectively and that students themselves (mostly) value and appreciate their instructors' efforts in responding. With this research in mind, we have looked at three major principles for teacher response—**prioritization, clarity,** and **encouragement**—offering specific suggestions as to how those principles could be applied in real-world writing instruction.

For new L2 writing instructors, there can be a learning curve in responding to student writing, as pre-service teachers ask questions such as, "On what should my comments focus?" "How can I provide feedback that my students can understand and apply?" "How can I avoid demoralizing my students with too much criticism?" or "How can I avoid exhausting myself from spending too much time on the responding task?" New teachers seeking to develop their feedback skills are encouraged to consider their approach to response (purposes and goals), to develop specific strategies for response (e.g., using a rubric, color-coding, being selective), and to be intentional about designing follow-up activities for students to reflect on and apply feedback they have received (see Ferris, 2007, 2015; Ferris & Hedgcock, 2014). Experienced teachers who want to sharpen their existing strategies may benefit from an objective analysis of their own commentary (see Ferris, 2007, for suggestions), reflecting on questions about how much their feedback seems to help their students make progress, or asking the students themselves, in a questionnaire or letter-writing task, what aspects of teacher feedback they find helpful—or not. A hands-on workshop in which teachers in a program or department share and discuss their feedback approaches can also be an excellent topic for an in-service professional development activity.

Responding to student writing can be the aspect of the job that teachers dread and resent most—but it doesn't have to be. With some thoughtfulness and advance planning, giving feedback can be a satisfying, intellectually stimulating, and meaningful task for L2 writing teachers (yes, really!). Perhaps more important, if teachers take time to develop and improve their feedback approaches according to the principles discussed, it will be a great gift to their present and future students.

Questions for Reflection and Application

1. The last point of the Classroom Applications section focuses on being encouraging and positive in responding to student writing. Is this something you would naturally do, or do you agree that many or most teachers immediately start looking for problems when reading student papers? Do you agree that encouragement is an important facet of teacher feedback? Why or why not?

2. The first principle discussed in the Classroom Applications section is to be selective in giving feedback rather than trying to comment on every single aspect or problem seen in a student text. What is your response to this idea? Does it make sense to you, confuse you, or raise concerns?

3. What is one area in which you would like to improve your approach to giving feedback on students' writing?

References

Andrade, M. S., & Evans, N. W. (2013). *Principles and practices for response in second language writing.* New York: Routledge.

Anson, C. M. (Ed.) (1989). *Writing and response: Theory, practice, and research.* Urbana, IL: National Council of Teachers of English.

Bitchener, J., & Ferris, D. R. (2012). *Written corrective feedback in second language acquisition and writing.* New York: Routledge.

Bitchener, J., & Storch, N. (2016). *Written corrective feedback for L2 development.* Bristol, England: Multilingual Matters.

Brannon, L., & Knoblauch, C. H. (1982). On students' rights to their own texts: A model of teacher response. *College Composition and Communication, 33,* 157–166.

Cohen, A. (1987). Student processing of feedback on their compositions. In A. L. Wenden & J. Rubin (Eds.), *Learner strategies in language learning* (pp. 57–69). Englewood Cliffs, NJ: Prentice-Hall.

Cohen, A., & Cavalcanti, M. (1990). Feedback on written compositions: Teacher and student verbal reports. In B. Kroll (Ed.), *Second language writing: Research insights for the classroom* (pp. 155–177). Cambridge, England: Cambridge University Press.

Conrad, S. M., & Goldstein, L. M. (1999). ESL student revision after teacher-written comments: Text, contexts, and individuals. *Journal of Second Language Writing, 8,* 147–180.

Fathman, A., & Whalley, E. (1990). Teacher response to student writing: Focus on form versus content. In B. Kroll (Ed.), *Second language writing: Research insights for the classroom* (pp. 178–190). Cambridge, England: Cambridge University Press.

Ferris, D. R. (1995). Student reactions to teacher response in multiple-draft composition classrooms. *TESOL Quarterly, 29,* 33–53.

Ferris, D. R. (1997). The influence of teacher commentary on student revision. *TESOL Quarterly, 31,* 315–339.

Ferris, D. R. (1999). The case for grammar correction in L2 writing classes: A response to Truscott (1996). *Journal of Second Language Writing, 8,* 1–10.

Ferris, D.R. (2001). Teaching writing for academic purposes. In J. Flowerdew & M. Peacock (Eds.), *The EAP curriculum* (pp. 298–314). Cambridge, England: Cambridge University Press.

Ferris, D. R. (2003). *Response to student writing: Implications for second language students.* Mahwah, NJ: Lawrence Erlbaum.

Ferris, D. R. (2007). Preparing teachers to respond to student writing. *Journal of Second Language Writing, 16*(3), 165–193.

Ferris, D. R. (2014). Responding to student writing: Teachers' philosophies and practices. *Assessing Writing, 19*, 6–23.

Ferris, D. R. (2015). Inclusivity through community: Designing response systems for "mixed" academic writing courses. In M. Roberge, K. M. Losey, & M. Wald (Eds.), *Teaching U.S-educated multilingual writers: Practices from and for the classroom* (pp. 11–46). Ann Arbor: University of Michigan Press.

Ferris, D. R., & Hedgcock, J. (2014). *Teaching L2 composition: Purpose, process, & practice* (3rd ed.). New York: Routledge.

Ferris, D. R., Liu, H., & Rabie, B. (2011). "The job of teaching writing": Teacher views on responding to student writing. *Writing and Pedagogy, 3*(1), 39–77.

Ferris, D. R., Pezone, S., Tade, C. R., & Tinti, S. (1997). Teacher commentary on student writing: Descriptions and implications. *Journal of Second Language Writing, 6*, 155–182.

Hairston, M. (1986). On not being a composition slave. In C. W. Bridge (Ed.), *Training the new teacher of college composition* (pp. 117–124). Urbana, IL: NCTE.

Hedgcock, J., & Lefkowitz, N. (1994). Feedback on feedback: Assessing learner-receptivity in second language writing. *Journal of Second Language Writing, 3*, 141–163.

Journal of Second Language Writing (2012, December), *21*(4). Special issue: Exploring L2 writing–SLA interfaces.

Knoblauch, C. H., & Brannon, L. (1981). Teacher commentary on student writing: The state of the art. *Freshman English News, 10*(2), 1–4.

Leki, I. (1991). The preferences of ESL students for error correction in college-level writing classes. *Foreign Language Annals, 24*, 203–218.

Marzano, R. J., & Arthur, S. (1977). Teacher comments on student essays: It doesn't matter what to say. *ERIC ED* 147864.

Moxley, J. (1989). Responding to student writing: Goals, methods, alternatives. *Freshman English News, 17*(2), 3–11.

Radecki, P., & Swales, J. (1988). ESL student reaction to written comments on their written work. *System, 16,* 355–365.

Reid, J. (1994). Responding to ESL students' texts: The myths of appropriation. *TESOL Quarterly, 28*(2), 273–292.

Sommers, N. (1982). Responding to student writing. *College Composition and Communication, 33,* 148–156.

Straub, R., & Lunsford, R. F. (1995). *Twelve readers reading: Responding to college student writing.* Creskill, NJ: Hampton Press.

Truscott, J. (1996). The case against grammar correction in L2 writing classes. *Language Learning, 46,* 327–369.

Truscott, J. (1999). The case for "the case against grammar correction in L2 writing classes": A response to Ferris. *Journal of Second Language Writing, 8,* 111–122.

Zamel, V. (1985). Responding to student writing. *TESOL Quarterly, 19,* 79–102.

ADDITIONAL RESOURCES

- Ferris, D.R. (2011). *Treatment of error in second language student writing* (2nd ed.). Ann Arbor: University of Michigan Press.

- Goldstein, L.M. (2005). *Teacher written commentary in second language writing classrooms.* Ann Arbor: University of Michigan Press.

- Hyland, K., & Hyland, F. (eds.) (2006). *Feedback in second language writing: Contexts and issues.* New York: Cambridge University Press.

- Liu, J., & Hansen, J.G. (2018). *Peer response in second language writing classrooms* (2nd ed.). Ann Arbor: University of Michigan Press.

- Rafoth, B. (2015). *Multilingual writers and writing centers.* Boulder, CO: Utah State University Press.

Appendix 6A: Sample Student Paper with Margin and End Comments (adapted from Ferris & Hedgcock, 2014)

Lying is not always wrong, if it is used for good intentions. Lying can be very manipulative, yet that particular quality, Goodrich mentioned, "is also exciting". Instead of using it for evil, lying can be a vital source for good, whether it from sparing a child feelings or doing it just to get something out of it. There are numerous explanations why people would create white lies. One reason why people lie is to surprise or distract a love one. Another reason why people do it is to create a diversion, in order to escape the difficulties that may take place by telling the truth.

> **Comment [DF1]:** Good clear response to the essay question
>
> **Comment [DF2]:** Who is Goodrich? You need to explain that she is the author of the article and give the title.

There is no greater rush than getting away with a good, harmless lie. For example, on one occasion, I have used lies for good intention. My close friend birthday was coming up. My friends and I were planning a surprise birthday. We did not want the birthday girl to know of this, so we manipulated her into thinking that we did not remember her birthday. Making up stories that we were busy on that day, to convince her so. Seeing the hurt in her eyes further greaten our smile. Like Goodrich said, "even though people lie for good reason, lying can be harmful". My friends and I knew that by lying to her, the surprise party would be a total success. Yes, our way of springing the party on her was wrong, but when the surprise was successful, seeing the joy on her face gave everyone involve a great rush, and that is exciting.

> **Comment [DF3]:** Is getting a "great rush" good if it hurts someone's feelings?
>
> **Comment [DF4]:** Would you do anything differently next time? You seem to be saying that you did a good thing but also that it was "wrong." This is a bit confusing.

When Goodrich said that, "everyone lie" it could very well be the truth. People lie constantly to avoid difficult situation by telling the truth. For instant, I was at my friends' house for dinner. His mother was cooking her best dish that took hours to make.

During the course of the meal she asked me how was it. The truth is that I didn't like it, maybe is because I hate shrimp, but to avoid being an unwanted guess, I bit my lips and told her that the meal was excellent. Besides my stomach hurting from the shrimp, no feelings got hurt.

> **Comment [DF5]:** Good example of lying to spare someone from hurt feelings!

To conclude, small, harmless lies can be exciting and fun. Not knowing if you will get caught in a lie, or knowing that you just got away with a lie is a great thrill. The truth is, some lies can be damaging when it is discovered, but if done properly, lies can be very benificial. No one really likes to lie, but not everyone is aware that they are lying. Lying is not always wrong.

> **Comment [DF6]:** When might lies be "damaging"?

> **Comment [DF7]:** Lies are "exciting, and fun—but "no one really likes to lie"? This seems to be saying two opposite things.

Lucy,

You did a nice job of taking a clear stand on the essay question by saying that "lying is not always wrong." Your two examples—the surprise party and the shrimp dish—were both effective in illustrating times when a lie may be harmless and even beneficial.

There are a couple of issues you need to think about as you write your next draft:

(1) You should also discuss times when lying is harmful. You hint at this a couple of times in your introduction and conclusion by saying that lying can be "manipulative" and "damaging," but the rest of your essay presents a very positive view of lying. I'd suggest adding a paragraph or two that defines the types of lies that are harmful and provides an example or two and perhaps ideas from Goodrich's article.

(2) The story about your friend's birthday is a bit confusing. You are honest about the fact that your lying caused her pain, and you even describe it as "wrong," yet you present it as an example of when lying can be beneficial. See if you can make this clearer by explaining either (a) what you might have done differently or better; or (b) why you think the positive aspects of the surprise "erased" the hurt she felt when she thought you had forgotten her birthday.

(3) You need to use Goodrich's article more in your essay. Be sure to introduce it clearly at the beginning—author's full name, article title, and a brief summary of the main idea(s)—and see if you can use facts, examples, or specific quotations to support your own arguments and examples throughout the paper.

You are off to a great start with clear organization and nice examples. I will look forward to reading your next draft! Be sure to e-mail me, talk to me in class, or come by my office if you need any help as you revise!

Good luck!

—Teacher

Appendix 6B: Sample Error Codes and Student Error Log

Error Codes

Your paragraphs will be marked using the error codes found in the Error Codes chart. Global errors are errors that interfere with meaning. Local errors and other errors do not interfere with meaning but can still be distracting, especially if they occur frequently. Therefore, you should treat all errors seriously.

Error Log

You will keep a log of the number and types of errors that you make on each paragraph. You must keep this log with you at all times and keep it up to date. You will need it for in-class workshops and a reflection assignment at the end of the quarter.

Major Error Category	Brief Description
Punctuation	Missing/unnecessary/incorrectly used commas, semicolons, apostrophes, quotation marks
Mechanics	Spelling/typing errors, capitalization
Nouns/Noun Phrases	Missing/unnecessary/incorrect plural markers, possessive markers, articles/determiners
Subject-Verb Agreement	Error in the noun/verb phrase leading to disagreement between subject and verb
Verbs/Verb Phrases	Incorrect tense/form, modal auxiliary incorrect
Sentence Structure	Run-ons, comma splices, fragments, word order, missing/unnecessary words
Word Form	Wrong word form for context
Incorrect Word Choice	Any word choice error; including preposition errors

Error Category	TWP #*	TWP #	TWP #	TWP #	TWP #	TWP #	TWP #
Noun Phrases (N)							
Verbs/Verb Phrases (V)							
Word Choice (WC)							
Sentence Structure (SS)							
Subject-Verb Agreement (SV)							
Word Form (WF)							
Punctuation (P)							
Mechanics (M)							
TOTAL							

*TWP = times within paper.

PART 3

Working with Beginning Writers

Chapter 7

Getting Started with Writing from the Beginning

Betsy Lindeman Wong,
Northern Virginia Community College

Opening Questions ————————————————————

1. Describe the ESL literacy learners that you work with. What types of skills do they need to develop literacy in English?

2. What instructional strategies have you used with learners with low or no literacy in their native language?

3. What instructional practices have helped the adult learners you work with acquire the ability to write in English?

Imagine that it is your first night teaching an ESL class for adult English learners at low-beginning levels in a community-based adult education program. As you had anticipated, the class has adults of varying ages from many different countries who have limited proficiency in English but intense motivation to learn. What you had not predicted, however, is that several students have never attended school, for a variety of political, economic, or cultural reasons, or they had to quit school at a young age. Through no fault of their own, these learners have limited literacy skills in both their native language and in English. How can you help them learn to read and write in another language when they cannot do so in their own language and when many of them are just beginning to understand the English words and phrases that they hear?

This chapter summarizes the characteristics of adult ESL literacy learners, highlights the types of literacy skills they need as a precursor to academic and professional writing, and presents instructional strategies that have proven effective. It explores how to align classroom instruction for ESL literacy learners with the English Language Proficiency Standards for Adult Education (U.S. Department of Education, 2016). It concludes with a thematic, standards-based lesson that promotes writing from the beginning.

■ Literacy of Immigrant Adults

Literacy development is a need addressed by educators around the world. According to UNESCO (2017a), literacy is the ability "to read and write with understanding a simple statement related to one's daily life." There are currently 750 million adults aged 15 and older across the world who are not literate, and the majority are female (UNESCO, 2017b).

This phenomenon is also evident in the United States. Approximately 40 percent of U.S. immigrant adults—about 11.5 million—have low levels of English literacy skills, according to an international adult competency test administered in 2012 by the Organization for Economic Cooperation and Development (OECD, 2013). Results from the test, the Program for the International Assessment of Adult Competencies (PIAAC), show that U.S. immigrants with low English literacy and numeracy skills suffer a "severe wage penalty" (Batalova & Fix, 2015): Their monthly salary is roughly half that of adult native and non-native English speakers who are literate and have numeracy skills.

Analysis of the PIAAC data (Batalova & Fix, 2015) also reveals an uneven ethnic distribution of English literacy levels. Among U.S. immigrant adults, approximately 62 percent of Hispanics were classified at or below Level 1 of five literacy levels, compared with 21 percent of Asians, 40 percent of African Americans, and 11 percent of whites. Level 1 or below denoted minimal or no English literacy, whereas Levels 3–5 corresponded to varying degrees of the English literacy skills needed to effectively function in modern society. Although the test did not measure native-language literacy skills, the results may indicate that a number of learners classified as Level 1 or below had limited access to formal education in their native countries. These results seem to correlate with the U.S. Census Bureau (2010) American Community Survey, which found that about 53 percent of immigrants from Latin America had completed high school, and about 40 percent of immigrants born in Mexico and 50 percent from Central America were high school graduates. This trend suggests that roughly half of Latino immigrants arriving in the United States may not have had the chance to fully develop writing skills in their own language, making it exponentially more challenging to learn to write in English. One may infer that these learners will need substantial classroom support to acquire not only basic writing skills but also the academic skills inherent in writing tasks at school and work.

The same support may be needed for refugees in the U.S., as many of its members possess low levels of literacy and English language skills, according to a 2015 Migration Policy Institute report (Capps et al., 2015). Among refugees arriving in the U.S. from Burma, Bhutan, Liberia, and Somalia between 2004 and 2013, 50 percent or fewer had literacy skills in their native language (Capps et al., 2015). Likewise, data from PIAAC (as cited by Richwine, 2017) show that approximately 72 percent of immigrants in the U.S. who self-identified as refugees have literacy skills that are below a basic level upon their arrival. This is still true for 58 percent of the U.S. refugee population (Richwine, 2017).

Yet despite this need, a recent survey indicates that many teachers are ambivalent about teaching academic writing to low-level English learners (Fernández, Peyton, & Schaetzel, 2017). The survey of more than 400 teachers of adult English learners showed that more than half spent less than an hour a week teaching writing, and that those who tended to devote the least amount of time to writing instruction (30 minutes a week or less) were teachers of learners at lower proficiency levels. This finding calls for greater amounts of writing instruction tailored to the real-world needs of adult learners, including development of the basic literacy skills that are the foundation of writing.

■ Literacy Learners in the Adult ESL Classroom: A Profile

Literacy learners come to the ESL classroom with reading and writing skills ranging from "little or no comprehension of how print corresponds to spoken language, to the ability to read most sight words and familiar phrases and simple sentences, with limited understanding of connected prose" (Burt, Peyton, & Schaetzel, 2008). While some adult programs have separate classes for language learners with limited literacy, others place these students in low- or high-beginning classes. To illustrate this point, here are some examples of the types of learners who may be placed in a low-beginning ESL class (for a similar discussion, see Florez & Terrill, 2003).

- **Amina** has never been to school in her native Somalia. She does not speak any English, nor does she read or write in any language.

- **Gustavo** went to school for three years in El Salvador. He speaks almost no English and has minimal literacy skills in Spanish and English.

- **Maria** went to school for three years in El Salvador, but she converses easily in English and has a wide vocabulary. She can sight-read some high-frequency words in English and Spanish but cannot sound out words in either language that she does not know.

- **Laxmi** is a professional from Nepal who speaks and writes Bengali. She does not know the Roman alphabet and speaks very little English.

- **Negusa** is a senior citizen from Ethiopia. He was educated in his country and reads and writes English but has great difficulty understanding spoken English.

- **Rena** was a language teacher in her native Tunisia. She has strong written and oral English language skills but wanted a slower-paced beginner course that would allow her to feel "at the top" of the class.

According to Florez and Terrill (2003), adult ESL literacy learners in the United States have usually had six or fewer years of formal education in their home country. They come from many different countries and have spent varying lengths of time in this country. They are of all ages and have different goals. Some may have experienced trauma in their home countries or when resettling to other countries as refugees.

Of course, many ESL students come from countries with a strong oral, rather than print, tradition (Vinogradov, 2008). This contributes to what Marshall and DeCapua (2013) refer to as *cultural dissonance*, "a sense of confusion and dislocation that students coming from different cultural backgrounds and ways of learning experience when confronted with the expectations and demands of Western-style formal education" (Cole & Elson, 2015, p. 203). Moreover, some ESL students have not had access to education "due to distance, poverty, civil unrest, or a host of other reasons" (Vinogradov, 2008). They are encountering the "double challenge" of acquiring English proficiency and learning to read and write in any language. Some of these learners may have much stronger speaking skills, to the point where they can communicate orally with relative ease but struggle with even basic reading and writing tasks.

Indeed, writing is often the weakest of the four language skills that adult English learners bring to the classroom. The "mismatch" between literacy and speaking skills can cause learners to place into higher-level ESL classes, writes Vinogradov (2008), where they are unable to keep up with the reading and writing demands of the class. This creates additional problems: If learners cannot access level-appropriate instruction in writing, they may not develop this essential support for reading- and oral-skill development. They will also face an obstacle to learning about other subjects, given that writing about texts in different content areas increases knowledge of them (Graham & Hebert, 2010).

■ Instructional Needs of Adult ESL Literacy Learners

If we think about the backgrounds of literacy-level learners in adult ESL classes, we realize that there is a significant gap between what they know and what they need to know to acquire academic writing skills. Some of the different types of knowledge and competencies that ESL literacy learners need are evident in the interdependence of writing and reading. Comprehending this interdependence starts with an understanding of the concept of print, including the ideas that texts "have a beginning, a middle, and an end; that English is read from left to right and from up to down; and that written words can represent a story, just as pictures do" (Florez & Terrill, 2003). In addition to understanding the concept of print, some ESL learners must also gain comfort and ease with basic classroom skills and expectations, such as sitting at a desk, using a pen or pencil, listening to the teacher, and interacting with fellow classmates (Burt, Peyton, & Schaetzel, 2008).

In order to develop literacy skills, learners need to develop four components of reading, which Burt, Peyton, and Schaetzel (2008) summarize as follows:

1. **Alphabetics,** or connecting the sounds of the spoken language with the written alphabet

2. **Fluency,** as seen in the ability to decode words with speed and ease and apply correct rhythm, intonation, and stress

3. **Vocabulary,** or the knowledge and understanding of distinct words

4. **Reading comprehension,** which calls for processing syntax, understanding grammar and mechanics, and being familiar with the organization and structure of English texts to understand overall meaning.

Learners must master these pre-reading and literacy skills to develop Roman alphabet literacy. Working on these skills simultaneously helps learners to gradually develop an awareness of "the big picture" of how a text is organized and what it represents. These five types of literacy activities (developed by Wong, 2011) help with the development of these skills, ranging from tracing letters to developing the fine motor skills needed to hold and use a pencil, to recognizing words by sight and understanding how to place them together to make sentences, which form the basis of a text.

Types of Literacy Activities for Use with Adult Beginning Writers

1. "Pencil Work"

tracing letters and numbers
"connect the dots"
copying letters

2. Letter Recognition

matching letters
circling a letter as a partner says it
matching uppercase and lowercase letters
finding a letter in a series
reading alphabet flashcards
sequencing letter cards

3. Sight Recognition of High-Frequency Words

copying words
matching words
crossing out the different word(s) in a series
identifying a word within a sentence or series
seeing and saying words

4. Sound-Symbol Correspondence

identifying sounds with letters

"sound grids" (charts with a letter or sound in each square, similar to a "Bingo" card)

initial consonant dictations

grouping or circling words with the same initial consonant

word strips (put initial consonant card with correct word)

discriminating between similar sounds (e.g., /b/ /v/, minimal pairs)

5. Sentence and Paragraph Structure

copying sentences

sentence completion

sentence strips

Language Experience Approach stories

cloze exercises

Instructional Strategies for Promoting Writing Development

Although there has not been a great deal of research on instructional strategies that have proven effective with ESL literacy learners (Burt, Peyton, & Schaetzel, 2008; Florez & Terrill, 2003), a few studies and anecdotal evidence from the field have suggested some ways to help adult ESL learners develop literacy skills as they build oral English proficiency. Perhaps most notably, the *What Works Study for Adult ESL Literacy Students* (Condelli & Wrigley, 2008) found three instructional strategies that fostered growth in English literacy and oral communication skills: (1) varied language-skill practice and student-to-student interaction; (2) use of the native language to clarify instructions and facilitate small-group discussion of relevant problems and scenarios; and (3) connection of classroom materials and activities to the outside world. On this last point, the researchers found that connecting what ESL literacy learners already knew to what they needed to learn in English motivated learners and helped them to build literacy skills (Condelli & Wrigley, 2008).

Similarly, research from community-based adult education programs serving English learners with limited literacy (Cole & Elson, 2015; Frydland, 2017) suggests that implementing a framework known as the Mutually Adaptive Learning Paradigm (MALP) (Marshall & DeCapua, 2013) increases learner engagement in the classroom and fosters the development of basic academic skills, including literacy. The paradigm has three essential tenets (Marshall & DeCapua, 2013): (1) incorporating themes and creating instructional materials that are relevant to learners' lives and allow them to share personal experiences and prior knowledge; (2) using speaking and listening as a mode of instruction before moving to print-based activities; and (3) engaging learners at all ability levels with collective projects related to real-life contexts or tasks—and using content from these projects as a bridge to more academically oriented activities.

In another study, the National Literacy Panel on Language-Minority Children and Youth (August & Shanahan, 2006) found that cooperative learning involving group problem-solving scenarios or tasks had a positive impact on student learning when combined with direct instructional approaches and a focus on form. This research suggests that adult ESL learners who are at the beginning literacy level benefit when letter-sound association exercises are incorporated into lessons on specific knowledge and skills, such as those needed for a job.

A study of literacy learners in multilevel class settings (Wrigley & Guth, 1992) recommended instructional strategies. Among them were assigning cooperative projects; organizing the class into groups (at times heterogeneous, at times homogeneous); conducting ongoing, informal assessments to get a feel for learners' needs, abilities, and challenges; and peer teaching, pairing or grouping students with different types of expertise (both linguistic and non-linguistic) to share knowledge and complete cooperative tasks.

Florez and Terrill (2003) summarize effective practices in the adult ESL literacy classroom as: (1) draw on the principles of adult learning (including the idea that adult learners bring a wealth of life experiences and cognitive skills to the classroom and can direct their own learning); (2) integrate all four language skills; (3) involve learners in choosing what topics to study; and (4) connect instruction to learners' lives.

Vinogradov (2008) draws on research and ESL practitioners' experiences to offer five guiding principles to help ESL literacy learners succeed in the classroom: (1) contextualize lessons, (2) integrate bottom-up and top-down approaches to reading, (3) teach to varied learning styles, (4) build on learners' strengths and life experiences, and (5) foster learners' self-confidence. She argues that literacy instruction must be meaningful, so that learners can grasp *why* they are learning to read and write. She recommends moving from top-down to bottom-up reading instruction in order to help students connect their background knowledge and real-life experiences to a text (top-down instruction) and then using the text to teach decoding skills (bottom-up instruction).

To develop literacy skills, learners need varied ways to learn new concepts and processes (Vinogradov, 2008)—including hands-on activities that involve pictures, flashcards, and story strips—and different grouping strategies, such as tasks for the whole class, small groups, pairs, and individuals. Using these groupings, learners can do many different activities with the same text, such as sorting word cards by sound, spelling words with letter tiles, or searching for words with the same initial consonant. Since learners benefit much from significant repetition, Vinogradov recommends allotting only one-third to one-half of class time to the use and learning of new material.

Teaching literacy skills paves the way for not only higher-level writing but also academic reading and content knowledge. As learners write, they create their own texts, which leads to increased understanding of other texts (Graham & Hebert, 2010). Three instructional practices related to writing that promote enhanced reading skills and understanding of content areas, according to a study by Graham and Hebert (2010), are:

1. writing about content-area texts to analyze, interpret, and react to the information in them
2. teaching about the writing process itself, including the structure of different kinds of texts, paragraphs, and sentences; ways to create or combine sentences; and spelling skills
3. asking learners to write more frequently.

These practices are reflected in the research-based strategies for ESL instruction suggested by Burt, Peyton, and Schaetzel (2008), which address the four components of reading (alphabetics, vocabulary, fluency, reading comprehension) described by the National Literacy Panel (August & Shanahan, 2006). The research-based instructional strategies, along with the approaches that promote writing presented in this chapter, are summarized here.

- ☑ Capitalize on learner motivation by explicitly connecting classroom instruction and materials to learners' needs outside of the classroom.
- ☑ Conduct ongoing, informal assessments to determine learners' needs and goals.
- ☑ Draw on the principles of adult learning: Build on learners' knowledge, experiences, and cognitive skills; allow learners to choose what topics to study.
- ☑ Select activities that cater to different learning styles and integrate different language skills.
- ☑ Use the native language to clarify instructions and facilitate small-group problem-solving tasks.
- ☑ Provide a real-world context for literacy activities in class.
- ☑ Teach specific strategies for approaching and understanding a passage.
- ☑ Teach word recognition skills and alphabetic literacy.
- ☑ Integrate top-down and bottom-up strategies for reading instruction.
- ☑ Build vocabulary knowledge.
- ☑ Allow for repetition, with multiple ways to practice skills with the same text.
- ☑ Create opportunities for peer-to-peer teaching and interaction, including communication about written texts.
- ☑ Use varied grouping strategies so that learners work with peers of similar or different ability levels.

- ☐ Consider providing direct feedback when appropriate, rather than teacher recasts (the teacher simply restating the student's utterance with proper grammar), to help learners acquire correct grammatical forms.
- ☐ Involve learners' family members in literacy activities (Burt, Peyton, & Schaetzel, 2008).

■ The Role of the English Language Proficiency Standards

As discussed in other chapters in this volume, the English Language Proficiency Standards (ELPs) outline competencies in the four language skills at five levels of English proficiency. The writing standards reflect the College and Career Readiness Standards' emphasis on incorporating evidence from texts to make and support claims in writing. The texts used to support writing tasks are informative or literary in nature and contain the types of academic language that learners are likely to encounter in future careers or post-secondary education.

At first glance, aligning standards that emphasize academic language and evidence-based writing with instruction for learners with limited formal academic experiences and English language proficiency may seem a daunting task. However, many of the tried-and-true ESL activities that teachers regularly use with this population can be aligned with the ELPs, as described earlier in this chapter. To that end, the activities presented for a low-beginner ESL class with the learners described (Literacy Learners in the Adult ESL Classroom: A Profile) show how to align the ELPs with research-based instructional ESL literacy practices.

■ Classroom Applications: Aligning Writing Instruction with the English Language Proficiency Standards

The lesson presented is designed for a two-hour, low-beginning adult ESL class that meets twice a week in the evenings. Students in the class are exploring jobs, a topic chosen based on a needs assessment that the teacher conducted. The lesson shows how the six literacy activities align with the ELPs.

Lesson Set-Up: Introduction to Occupations and Work Schedules

As learners enter the class, they complete the nightly routine of copying sentences about the evening's lesson topic. (Having a class routine lessens anxiety because learners know what to expect, and it helps them acclimate to classroom practices, such as noting information from the board.) On the board at the front of the room are large, simple pictures of a cook and a painter, each taped above three sentences, shown in Figure 7.1. Students begin copying the sentences, and one learner who is just beginning to write traces the sentences on a handout.

Figure 7.1 Sentences on the Board

Van is a cook.
He cooks food.
He works on weekends.

Sofie is a painter.
She paints houses.
She works on weekdays.

After all students have copied these sentences, the teacher brings the class together by asking learners what they see in the pictures on the board. She reads the sentences aloud, pointing to each word as she says it, and then asks learners to read as she motions to each word. She points out two consonant sounds, asks learners which words start with them, and elicits other words they know that start with them. After some word-recognition activities (see Figure 7.2), the teacher leads students in a brief discussion of the meaning of the sentences.

Using the sentences as a springboard, learners then complete a series of integrated-skill activities aligned with the ELPs.

ELP-Aligned Classroom Activities

As students finish copying the sentences on the board that introduce the topic they are working on, they complete different activities based on their literacy and language levels and needs. Some activities involve multilevel grouping configurations:

- ☐ A student with slightly higher literacy skills sequences pre-made word flashcards to form the sentences on the board (see Figure 7.3). She then works with two classmates by reading the word cards aloud for one of the sentences. The classmates then repeat the sentences aloud to practice pronunciation.
- ☐ The first student then jumbles the word cards for the sentence. The two classmates work together to re-sequence the word cards, reading them aloud as they do so.
- ☐ The group repeats this sequence for several sentences.

Figure 7.2 Sequence Word Cards to Make Sentences (ELP Standard 10)

> **ELP Standard 10:** An ELL can ... demonstrate command of the conventions of standard English to communicate in level-appropriate speech and writing.
>   **Level 1:** By the end of the English language proficiency level 1, an ELL can ... with support,
> - **Recognize and use a small number of frequently occurring nouns, noun phrases, verbs, conjunctions, and prepositions.**

Figure 7.3 Match Flashcards to Words in a Text (ELP Standards 1, 7)

ELP Standard 1: An ELL can ... construct meaning from oral presentations and literary and informational text through level-appropriate listening, reading, and viewing.

> **Level 1:** By the end of the English language proficiency level 1, an ELL can ... use a very limited set of strategies to:
> - **Identify a few key words and phrases in oral communications and simple spoken and written texts.**

ELP Standard 7: An ELL can ... adapt language choices to purpose, task, and audience when speaking and writing.

> **Level 1:** By the end of the English language proficiency level 1, an ELL can ...
> - **Recognize the meaning of some words learned through conversations, reading, and being read to.**

This sequence of activities introduces sentence structure and helps students recognize and say common words that they see in the sentences. It reinforces subject-verb word order, which may be different from the word order in students' native languages. The precursor to this activity sequence, tracing or copying sentences on the board, may seem rote in nature, but it is important "pencil work" that helps develop the fine motor skills needed to hold a pencil and write. It also reflects the National Research Council (2012) recommendation to explicitly teach basic writing skills—including spelling and handwriting—so that they become automatic processes for learners.

Activity 1

After listening and reading aloud the sentences on the board about the painter and cook, students identify words in the sentences with the initial consonants of *c*, *p*, and *w*. They then:

- ☐ match word cards (*cook, cooks, works, painter, paints, weekends, weekdays*) to words in the story on the board, holding each card over the corresponding word as the rest of the class says it together.
- ☐ find and say words with the same base (*cook/cooks; painter/paints; weekends/weekdays*).
- ☐ say what each word card means, pantomiming actions such as *cooks* and *paints* to demonstrate understanding.

Students are reading sentences related to a lesson theme that was identified in a learner needs assessment. They practice sight recognition of high-frequency words, an important literacy activity, as well as letter recognition and sound-symbol correspondence.

After students have discussed the pictures on the board, read the sentences aloud several times, and worked on letter and word recognition, the teacher "unpacks" the content of the sentences by stating the topic and helping students make a personal connection to it (see Figure 7.4).

- The teacher asks:

  What does the story talk about?

  What is Van's job?

  What does he do at work?

  Do any of you work as a cook?

  Do you have any friends or family who work as a cook?

  Would you like to have this job? Why or why not?

- The teacher repeats the questions, asking about Sofie's job.

- The teacher asks about the characters' work schedules:

  When does Van work? What days are weekend days?

  When does Sofie work? What days are weekdays?

  Which job would you prefer to have, Van's job or Sofie's job? Why?

- After students discuss reasons why they would prefer to have one person's job rather than the other person's job, the teacher has students vote on which job they would like to have.

Focusing on the global meaning of the sentences and helping students connect them to their own lives helps them see a purpose for reading: They are learning about people like themselves and putting ideas together from the text. Indeed, connecting content to learners' lives is a key component of Marshall and DeCapua's MALP (2013). Learners also identify the topic of the text and cite specific details about the characters from the text. Citing information from

Figure 7.4 State the Topic and Give a Personal Opinion
(ELP Standards 4, 6)

> **ELP Standard 4:** An ELL can ... construct level-appropriate oral and written claims and support them with reasoning and evidence.
> **Level 1:** By the end of the English language proficiency level 1, an ELL can ...
> - **Express an opinion about a familiar topic, experience, or event.**
>
> **ELP Standard 6:** An ELL can ... analyze and critique the arguments of others orally and in writing.
> **Level 1:** By the end of the English language proficiency level 1, an ELL can ... with support,
> - **Identify a point an author or a speaker makes.**

a text is an essential precursor to academic writing. Even if students answer the comprehension questions based on what they remember from the oral reading (as opposed to what they see in print), they are gaining the useful pre-academic skill of analyzing and synthesizing information. Moreover, briefly discussing which work schedule or job students prefer is a first step to formulating an opinion and giving reasons to support the opinion.

Activity 2

After students have worked with the sentences on the board, they learn about six other jobs: cashier, babysitter, waiter, landscaper, driver, and janitor. The teacher writes the words on the board and asks them what people do in each job, using pantomime to reinforce meaning as necessary.

- ☐ Students identify the initial consonant of the words, match word flashcards to the words written on the board, and read the words aloud several times (see Figure 7.5).

- ☐ Groups of three receive a zip-lock bag with picture cards of the jobs and six blank flashcards and markers. Students take turns writing the job names on the flashcards, copying the words from the board. They also copy the names in their notebooks.

- ▣ Working together, students match the picture and word cards. They scramble the cards and repeat the activity several times.

- ▣ As students finish, they take turns holding up picture cards and having group members find and read aloud the corresponding word cards.

- ▣ For more practice with the words, groups receive a small bag of dried beans and a grid for each student with six large, blank squares. Students copy the name of each job onto their grid.

- ▣ One student in each group says a word in the grid, and classmates place a bean on the word on their grid; they do so until their grid is filled with beans. They repeat this, taking turns saying the words.

- ▣ In the full group, the teacher repeats the activity but gives prompts related to letters and sounds (e.g., *Put a bean on the word that starts with the letter B. Put a bean on the word that starts with a "w" sound)*. Students then briefly practice with each other.

Although students may appear to be simply writing words on flashcards or in a grid, they are completing activities that call for labeling pictures or a graphic organizer (grid), which align with ELP Standard 5 (see Figure 7.5). They practice the literacy skills of letter recognition, sound-symbol correspondence, and sight recognition of high-frequency words. Thus, writing supports and helps extend overall language and literacy. The teacher saves the sets of cards and grids to use as pair or group review activities in the initial phase of the next lesson.

Figure 7.5   Match Words-Pictures and Label Grids (ELP Standard 5)

ELP Standard 5: An ELL can ... conduct research and evaluate and communicate findings to answer questions or solve problems.
  Level 1: By the end of the English language proficiency level 1, an ELL can ... with support,
  - **Label collected information, experiences, or events.**

Activity 3

After they have learned about different occupations and practiced reading and writing the words for them, students participate in this dialogue (see Figure 7.6):

> *What do you do?*
>
> *I'm a __.*
>
> *When do you work?*
>
> *I work on __.*

- ☐ Half of the students (the "As") have two flashcards: One has an occupation, and the other has a work time (*weekdays, weekends,* or *weekdays and weekends*).
- ☐ They line up, with their backs to the wall and some space between each other.
- ☐ The other half of the students (the "Bs") form a line facing the students with flashcards. A and B students across from each other form a pair.
- ☐ Student A holds up his or her occupation flashcard and asks Student B a question (*What do you do?*).
- ☐ Student B looks at the card and uses the word on it to say a response (*I'm a painter.*).
- ☐ Pairs repeat this question-and-answer sequence with the work time cards (*When do you work? I work on weekdays.*).
- ☐ Students in the B line then move down one space to face the next classmate in the A line. New pairs repeat the activity but use the information on different flashcards. The pair rotations continue until students in the B line have rotated all the way through.
- ☐ If Student B cannot say the word on a card or makes a mistake, Student A helps.

Figure 7.6 Perform a Line Dialogue (ELP Standards 2, 8)

ELP Standard 2: An ELL can ... participate in level-appropriate oral and written exchanges of information, ideas, and analyses, in various social and academic contexts, responding to peer, audience, or reader comments and questions.

Level 1: By the end of the English language proficiency level 1, an ELL can ...

- **Participate in short conversations and written exchanges about familiar topics and in familiar contexts.**

ELP Standard 8: An ELL can ... determine the meaning of words and phrases in oral presentations and literary and informational text.

Level 1: By the end of the English language proficiency level 1, an ELL can, relying heavily on context, questioning, and knowledge of morphology in their native language(s),

- **Recognize the meaning of a few frequently occurring words, simple phrases, and formulaic expressions in spoken and written texts about familiar topics, experiences, or events.**

☐ The teacher shadows a student who is not yet reading or writing. She moves through the rotation with the student, offering cues to decode the word cards (*What letter does the word start with? What sound does it start with? What job begins with that sound?*).

☐ To accommodate students with high oral proficiency, the teacher encourages adding information to answers. She models this: *I'm a painter. I paint houses and office buildings. I work weekdays, Monday through Thursday, from 6 AM to 3 PM*).

Although students are participating in a short oral exchange about a work-related topic, they need to use written information—the words on flashcards—to complete the oral exchange and make meaning. This makes reading purposeful, as it allows students to ask and answer very basic questions about occupations and work schedules, thus "connecting to the outside."

Activity 4

To reinforce in print the language structures used in the line dialogue, and to give students a chance to personalize the topic with their own information (see Figure 7.7), the teacher gives students a handout, shown in Figure 7.8. It has the questions from the line dialogue, with answers to fill in, space to copy all of the questions and answers, and space to record answers from a friend or family member.

Figure 7.7 Write Information about a Text and Yourself (ELP Standards 3, 9)

ELP Standard 3: An ELL can ... speak and write about level-appropriate complex literary and informational texts and topics.

    Level 1: By the end of the English language proficiency level 1, an ELL can ... with support,

- **Communicate information and feelings about familiar texts, topics, and experiences.**

ELP Standard 9: An ELL can ... create clear and coherent level-appropriate speech and text.

    Level 1: By the end of the English language proficiency level 1, an ELL can ... with support,

- **Communicate basic information about an event or topic.**
- **Use a narrow range of vocabulary and syntactically simple sentences.**

Figure 7.8 Writing and Talking about "My Story"

My Story	_My Story_
What do you do?	_What _____?_
_I'm a _____._	_____._
When do you work?	_____?_
_I work on _____._	_____._

My Friend's Story
_What is your name? _____
What do you do?
_I'm a _____._
When do you work?
_I work on _____._

- ☐ The teacher reads aloud the sentences, eliciting occupations from students and writing them on the board. She includes *family caregiver* and *student* for those who aren't working.
- ☐ Students fill in the missing information about themselves in the left column on the handout. The teacher sits with two students and helps them write.
- ☐ Students who finish first read their stories to each other.
- ☐ Students then walk around the room and ask and answer the questions with classmates.
- ☐ For homework, students copy the questions and answers in the right column of the handout. They also ask a friend or family member about their job and write it on the sheet (under "My Friend's Story"). They then share this information in the next class.

Students are writing about a level-appropriate, familiar topic—themselves and their jobs. They ask and answer a frequent question: *What do you do?* By writing about their own job and asking someone else what his or her job is, students are "connecting to the outside" and linking what they read and write to what they experience in their daily life.

This lesson began with students working with two sets of three sentences and built in complexity from there. As students become more proficient, the text can be a story or a narrative. The form the students are practicing mimics expository academic writing in that students make a generalization and support it with information from the text; in this case, the sentences about the two workers. This type of writing builds literacy skills and provides the basis for higher levels of writing that involve synthesizing, interpreting, and stating ideas and supporting them with details from informative texts.

■ Concluding Thoughts

As the lesson shows, English literacy is a skill that is best developed in a meaningful context that allows students to see connections between writing and meaning and between their tasks in the classroom and their lives outside of it. Most important, it represents a tool for learners to use in reaching their goals. Given that many students have goals related to the workplace or post-secondary education, they need to develop not only English but *academic* English. Aligning English literacy classroom activities with the ELPs can help teachers to ensure that students are acquiring a foundation of academic language from the very beginning.

─────── **Questions for Reflection and Application** ───────

1. How can the classroom strategies and activities described promote the development of adult learners' English literacy skills?

2. How can ESL practitioners ensure that learners of differing ability levels are both supported and challenged as they develop writing skills?

3. How can you align your existing instructional practices with the English Language Proficiency Standards?

References

August, D., & Shanahan, T. (Eds.). (2006). *Executive summary. Developing literacy in second-language learners: Report of the National Literacy Panel on language-minority children and youth.* Washington, DC: Center for Applied Linguistics. http://www.cal.org/projects/archive/nlpreports/executive_summary.pdf

Batalova, J., & Fix, J. (2015). *Through an immigrant lens: PIAAC assessment of the competencies of adults in the United States.* Washington, DC: Migration Policy Institute. http://www.migrationpolicy.org/research/through-immigrant-lens-piaac-assessment-competencies-adults-united-states

Burt, M., Peyton, J. K., & Adams, R. (2003). *Reading and adult English language learners: A review of the research.* Washington, DC: Center for Applied Linguistics. http://www.cal.org/caela/research/RAELL.pdf

Burt, M., Peyton, J. K., & Schaetzel, K. (2008). *Working with adult English language learners with limited literacy: Research, practice, and professional development.* Washington, DC: Center for Applied Linguistics. http://www.cal.org/caelanetwork/resources/limitedliteracy.html

Capps, R., & Newland, K., with Fratzke, S., Groves, S., Fix, M., McHugh, M., & Auclair, G. (2015). *The integration outcomes of U.S. refugees: Successes and challenges.* Washington, DC: The Migration Policy Institute. https://www.migration policy.org/research/integration-outcomes-us-refugees-successes-and-challenges

Cole, S. M., & Elson, A. B. (2015). Implementing the Mutually Adaptive Learning Paradigm in the LESLLA classroom. In I. van de Craats, J. Kurvers, & M. Young-Scholten (Eds.), *Adult literacy, second language, and cognition: Proceedings from the 2014 Low-Educated Adult Second Language and Literacy Acquisition (LESLLA) symposium* (pp. 199–216). Nijmegen, The Netherlands: Centre for Language Studies.

Condelli, L., & Wrigley, H. (2008). The what works study: Instruction, literacy and language learning for adult ESL literacy students. In S. Reder & J. Bynner (Eds.), *Tracking adult literacy and numeracy skills: Findings from longitudinal research.* London: Routledge.

Fernández, R., Peyton, J. K., & Schaetzel, K. (2017). A survey of writing instruction in adult ESL programs: Are teaching practices meeting adult learner needs? *Journal of Research and Practice for Adult Literacy, Secondary, and Basic Education, 6*(2), 5–20.

Florez, M. C., & Terrill, L. (2003). *Working with literacy-level adult English language learners.* Washington, DC: Center for Applied Linguistics. http://www.cal.org/caela/esl_resources/digests/litQA.html

Frydland, N. (2017, Spring). Implementing the Mutually Adaptive Learning Paradigm: Applications for literacy-level through academic ESL. *College ESL Quarterly.* http://www.languageartspress.com/ceq/Implementing%20the%20Mutually%20Adaptive%20Learning%20Paradigm%20-%20CEQ%20-%20Spring%202017.pdf

Graham, S., & Hebert, M. (2010). *Writing to read: Evidence for how writing can improve reading.* A Carnegie Corporation Time to Act Report. Washington, DC: Alliance for Excellent Education. https://www.carnegie.org/media/filer_public/9d/e2/9de20604-a055-42da-bc00-77da949b29d7/ccny_report_2010_writing.pdf

Marshall, H. W., & DeCapua, A. (2013). *Making the transition to classroom success: Culturally responsive teaching for struggling language learners.* Ann Arbor: University of Michigan Press.

National Research Council. (2012). *Improving adult literacy instruction: Developing reading and writing.* Washington, DC: The National Academies Press. https://www.nap.edu/catalog/13468/improving-adult-literacy-instruction-developing-reading-and-writing

OECD (Organization for Economic Cooperation and Development). (2013). *Technical report of the Survey of Adult Skills (PIAAC).* Washington, DC: OECD. http://www.oecd.org/skills/piaac/_Technical%20Report_17OCT13.pdf.

Richwine, J. (2017, September 25). *Rough estimates of refugee literacy.* Washington, DC: Center for Immigration Studies. https://cis.org/Richwine/Rough-Estimates-Refugee-Literacy

UNESCO. (United Nations Educational, Scientific, and Cultural Organization). Institute of Statistics. (2017a). http://uis.unesco.org/en/glossary-term/literacy

UNESCO. (United Nations Educational, Scientific, and Cultural Organization). Institute of Statistics. (2017b). *UNESCO eAtlas of literacy* [data file]. http://tellmaps.com/uis/literacy/#!/tellmap/-601865091

U.S. Census Bureau. (2010). The foreign-born population in the United States: 2010. *American Community Survey Reports.* Washington, DC: U.S. Census Bureau. https://www.census.gov/prod/2012pubs/acs-19.pdf

U.S. Department of Education. Office of Vocational and Adult Education. (2013). *College and career readiness standards for adult education.* Washington, DC: Author. http://lincs.ed.gov/publications/pdf/CCRStandardsAdultEd.pdf

U.S. Department of Education. Office of Career, Technical and Adult Education. (2016). *English language proficiency standards for adult education.* Washington, DC: Author. https://lincs.ed.gov/publications/pdf/elp-standards-adult-ed.pdf

Vinogradov, P. (2008). "Maestra! The letters speak": Adult ESL students learning to read for the first time. *MinneWITESOL Journal, 25.*

Wong, B. L. (2007). Online discussion on *Practical strategies for working with literacy-level adult English language learners.* Electronic discussion list. Washington, DC: National Institute for Literacy. https://lincs.ed.gov/lincs/discussions/englishlanguage/07strategies_summary.html

Wong, B. L. (2011). *Reaching your adult ESL literacy learners* [Workshop Facilitator's Guide]. Richmond: The Virginia Adult Learning Resource Center.

Wrigley, H. S., & Guth, G. J. A. (1992). *Bringing literacy to life: Issues and options in adult ESL literacy.* (ERIC ED 348896) https://eric.ed.gov/?id=ED348896

ADDITIONAL RESOURCES

Activities to Promote Reading Development

- *Practitioner Toolkit: Working with Adult English Language Learners.* Washington, DC: Center for Applied Linguistics.

  This document (www.cal.org/caela/tools/program_development/elltoolkit/Part2-57ActivitiestoPromoteReadingDevelopment.pdf) gives helpful background information and activity ideas for ESL literacy learners.

- Adult ESL Video Training Project. New American Horizons Foundation.

  The online video series *Teaching ESL to Adults: Classroom Approaches in Action* (www.newamericanhorizons.org/training-videos) shows literacy and mixed-beginner classes, followed by expert commentary.

Articles, Books, and Resource Collections

- Brod, S. (1999). Focus on teaching: Seven easy pieces. *Focus on Basics, 3*(D).

  This practical article (www.ncsall.net/index.php@id=335.html) offers a range of writing activities for beginning ESOL learners.

- *MinneWITESOL Journal.* (2008). Volume 25.

  Section 1 of the 25th anniversary edition of the *MinneWITESOL Journal* is devoted to the instruction of adult ESL learners with low literacy.

- Nishio, Y. W. (2013). *Longman ESL Literacy.* New York: Pearson Education.

  This resource (http://www.longmanusa.com/longman_esl_literacy), which includes a student book and a teacher resource book, is organized thematically, with life-skill lessons that promote literacy development. The teacher resource book has flashcards, an audio CD, and extra stories to use with the text.

- *Working with Literacy-Level Adult English Language Learners.* Washington, DC: Center for Applied Linguistics.

  This collection (http://www.cal.org/caela/esl_resources/collections/literacy.html) includes many different resources (including reports, articles, organizations, databases, and materials) for ESL practitioners working with literacy-level ESL learners.

Chapter 8

Oral Language as a Bridge to Academic Writing

Patsy Egan, Hamline University

Betsy Parrish, Hamline University

Opening Questions ─────────────────────────

1. What have you noticed about learners' oral language skills compared to their writing skills? What factors may influence those differences?

2. What are some ways that you draw on learners' oral language in preparation for writing?

3. What supports do you think adult ESL learners may need to engage in academic conversations?

Academic writing is often neglected in adult ESL curricula, where the focus tends to be on basic instrumental writing tasks (e.g., filling in forms or applications) and where more extensive writing is often limited to the narrative genre (Fernández, Peyton, & Schaetzel, 2017; Johnson & Parrish, 2010). Adult learners who are preparing for workplaces, career training, and post-secondary education need preparation in the complex writing demands they will encounter, such as making claims and writing an argument supported by evidence, writing clear procedures, making comparisons, or reporting information. These academic writing demands can be challenging for many adult English learners, but they are particularly difficult for those who have interrupted or limited prior formal schooling or limited experience with academic literacy (Bigelow & Vinogradov, 2011). These same learners may bring strong oral skills to the classroom, gained through their experiences as active community members or workers in an English-speaking environment, but this language may represent what Gee (1990) refers to as their primary discourse, and they may lack the secondary discourses of school or specialized professions. How can we leverage students' oral language as the basis for academic writing, and what would be the benefits of doing so? This chapter explores these questions by first articulating the rationale for building bridges between oral and written language and then by giving four examples of these principles in practice at a range of adult ESL proficiency levels. The chapter closes with additional resources for adult ESL educators to further explore the connections among purposeful classroom conversations and stronger academic writing.

■ Building a Bridge from Oral to Written Discourse

Moving beyond basic writing tasks involves deeper levels of thinking, where learners organize ideas, provide evidence to support claims, identify points of view and challenge assumptions, and analyze and evaluate ideas. The three instructional shifts (also referred to as the key advances) reflected in the English Language Arts standards of the College and Career Readiness Standards (CCRS) for Adult Education also speak to this move away from using basic tasks: engaging with complex texts, extracting and employing evidence, and building content knowledge (U.S. Department of Education, 2013). A critical way to engage learners in this level of thinking and knowledge building is through classroom dialogue and structured academic conversations (Gibbons, 2009; Zwiers & Crawford, 2011). The power of classroom talk has been explored extensively (see, Mercer, 2000) and, as Zwiers and Crawford (2011) remind us, "Oral language is the cornerstone on which we build our literacy and learning throughout life" (p. 7).

In the context of adult education, students with interrupted or limited prior schooling (sometimes referred to as **SLIFE** or **SIFE**) may be working to develop academic literacies (oral, print, graphic, digital) for the first time. Even so, all students can engage in what Gibbons (2009) refers to as "intellectual quality" in the classroom, which she suggests should "include students' construction of knowledge and their participation in deep inquiry, higher-order thinking, deep knowledge and understanding, and substantive conversations" (p. 19). These cognitively challenging classrooms are more engaging for adults (Vinogradov, 2016), and our job as educators is to provide the language supports needed, both oral and written, to engage in those academic conversations, and from there, apply the ideas and knowledge generated to writing academic texts.

■ Applying the Practice

In this section, we present four sample lessons representing a variety of adult ESL contexts, from beginning to advanced proficiency, with a focus on general and more career-specific purposes, to demonstrate how to build academic language orally in preparation for writing in a variety of genres. Each sample lesson includes:

- ▣ an **interactive oral task** that allows learners to generate ideas and content for their writing and to build academic language through structured dialogues and conversations.
- ▣ a focus on the **academic language** connected to the genre of the text to be written.
- ▣ a **writing task** that uses the ideas generated through dialogue and conversations and that uses the academic language that was practiced orally.

Sample 1

Level: high-beginning ESL

Text genre: informational/explanatory, specifically report writing

Final writing objective: a short written report about the strategies that people in class use to practice their English

Summary of lesson: This sample lesson, which focuses on community engagement, allows learners to explore a topic of relevance to them while practicing important academic skills such as collecting and tabulating data, analyzing and discussing the data, graphing and reporting on data, and finally, writing a short report about the research they conducted in class. The lesson starts with a one-question interview.

Step 1: Use an oral task for generating ideas and content: One-question interview.

Learners are given one of the questions in Figure 8.1 and asked to talk to everyone in class, tallying their responses. Two to four students are given the same question, so that later in the lesson they can work together on the same topic.

Figure 8.1 Sample Question Strips

| 1. How often do you talk to your neighbors in English? |
| Every day   Once a week   Once a month   Never   Other_____ |

| 2. How often do you read news online in English? |
| Every day   Once a week   Once a month   Never   Other_____ |

| 3. How often do you listen to news in English? |
| Every day   Once a week   Once a month   Never   Other_____ |

| 4. How often do you ask a co-worker for help with new words in English? |
| Every day   Once a week   Once a month   Never   Other_____ |

| 5. How often do you attend neighborhood meetings? |
| Every day   Once a week   Once a month   Never   Other_____ |

| 6. How often do you attend events in your community (concerts, plays)? |
| Every day   Once a week   Once a month   Never   Other_____ |

Step 2: Analyze data: Language with language frames.

Once learners have interviewed everyone in class, they collaborate with others who were assigned the same question and analyze their results. To begin building the academic language they will need for their writing, the teacher provides learners with the language frames needed for describing trends based on data. Language frames like those in Figure 8.2 may be provided on a poster, on small cards, or projected for the class.

Step 3: Create a graph and report to others.

Those learners with the same question now create a graph like the one in Figure 8.3, which depicts the results of Question 6: How often do you attend events in your community (concerts, plays)?

Figure 8.2   Useful Language to Talk about Data

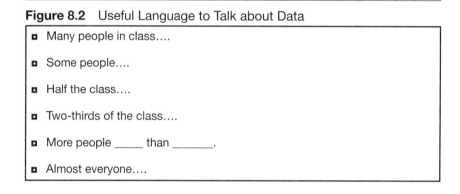

- Many people in class....

- Some people....

- Half the class....

- Two-thirds of the class....

- More people _____ than _____.

- Almost everyone....

Figure 8.3   Sample Bar Graph of Class Data for One Question

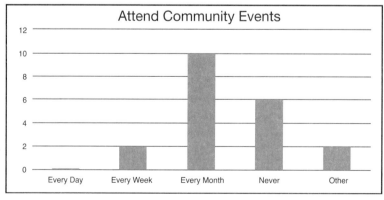

Next, learners work in small groups made up of members representing different questions and present the results for their question to other group members using only their graph. Group members are asked to take notes about what they see and hear. In their presentations, students use the academic language function of presenting results, which they can use in their writing as well. Phrases such as these can now be presented to students:

- ☐ We found that _____.
- ☐ The data show that _____.

Step 4: Write a report about class results.

Using the information that they learned from one another in the presentations, learners can now synthesize information in a short report using a paragraph frame, as shown in Figure 8.4. This can be expanded, or less language can be provided, depending on the level of the learners.

As a culminating task, learners are asked to write a report without the paragraph frame. This sequence of tasks can be used for virtually any topic, and the one-question interview can be used to generate ideas to write other text genres—for example, compare and contrast (comparing class results). Students could conduct a one-question interview on the sequence of steps in a procedure and then use the responses to fill in a simple graphic organizer displaying the steps, along with the academic language frames needed to describe a sequence. Finally, they can write the procedure.

Figure 8.4 Reporting Results using a Paragraph Frame

Our class uses many techniques for practicing English. We _____ that

_____ read the news online in English _____. _____

people _____. The data show that more

_____ than _____. This shows

that _____.

Sample 2

In the current landscape of adult ESL education, where we are moving away from basic life skills to rigorous instruction that prepares learners for the demands of work and school (U.S. Department of Education, 2013), adults benefit from working on academic topics (e.g., psychology, environmental studies, history) (Parrish, 2015). Within a typical adult ESL unit theme such as family, we can bring in an informational text (oral or written) on the topic of personality and birth order theory, for example, thus upping the level of rigor and engagement. For this sample lesson, a teacher can choose a written or oral text on the topic of personality and birth order theory (a simplified article, a video, a web search of reliable sites). (If the teacher finds that personality and birth order theory might be difficult for students because of past experiences with losing siblings, etc., other topics might be language learning theories, child-raising principles/practices, or ways to make a community stronger.) The steps provided can then be used with the level-appropriate text(s) chosen.

Level: intermediate to high-intermediate ESL

Text genre: argumentation

Final writing objective: Write a three-paragraph essay presenting an argument supported by evidence from multiple sources.

Summary of task: This sample helps learners construct and write an argument, a task they will encounter if they pursue postsecondary studies or if they prepare to complete a high school equivalency diploma. The lesson begins by building prior knowledge that students have about a topic and provides information about the topic (print or oral) and the academic language needed to develop and present an argument supported by evidence.

Step 1: Explore the topic: Explore the benefits and drawbacks of each birth order.

Learners create groups with others with the same birth order (including an "only child" option), or they select the birth order group they would like to participate in. (The teacher may need to help some learners select a group to participate in, based on a birth order they choose, if they were adopted, separated from their parents at an early age, simply want to talk about a specific birth order, etc.) Each group brainstorms the benefits and drawbacks of the birth order that is the focus of their group, using one T-chart, like the one shown in Figure 8.5, to record their ideas.

Step 2: Learn about academic research.

The teacher explains to learners that they will read about (or listen to a video about) personality and birth order theory. As they read or listen, they complete one portion of a chart like the one in Figure 8.6, focusing on the birth order that they discussed in their group.

Notice that graphic organizers can help learners recognize the structure of a text, in this case, the categorization of birth order and characteristics of each. (See Additional Resources for links to ready-made graphic organizers and also Chapter 4.)

Figure 8.5 T-Chart to Record Ideas

Benefits | **Drawbacks**

(Steps 1 and 3 are adapted from Parrish & Johnson, 2010.)

Figure 8.6   Chart for Use with a Reading or Listening Activity on Personality and Birth Order Theory

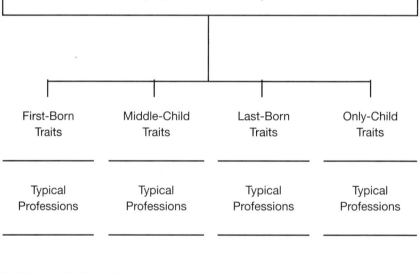

Personality and Birth-Order Theory

What are some traits of the birth order that you are discussing? Read your assigned section of the article and fill in at least four traits given in the article and two sample professions under your birth order.

| First-Born Traits | Middle-Child Traits | Last-Born Traits | Only-Child Traits |

| Typical Professions | Typical Professions | Typical Professions | Typical Professions |

Step 3: Talk about the research using academic language frames.

First, the birth order groups discuss among themselves how the research they read about or listened to on a video compares to their own experience or the experiences of others. They then mingle to complete the rest of their chart graphic organizer using language frames for the academic language function of reporting on research:

- ☐ *It was found that* _____.
- ☐ *The study showed that* _____.
- ☐ *The researchers found that* _____.
- ☐ *According to one study* _____.
- ☐ *The text said that* _____.

Step 4: Conduct their own studies and develop an argument.

Learners create a short survey based on what they have learned. If the source text suggests that first-born individuals tend to be in leadership roles, they may ask, "What kind of jobs do you (if you are first-born) or first-born individuals whom you know or have heard or read about have?" Learners could also review different readings and research on mitigating factors that are addressed in other research (e.g., the effects of temperament, age, gender).

Now learners are ready to write an argument supported by evidence. Here they draw on information gathered from multiple sources: the course text(s), their own experiences in their families and communities, the results of their own survey, and further reading and research. A learner may say, for example: My argument: *Cultural beliefs and differing family roles affect personality more than birth order.*

Learners can use the same language frames provided in Step 3 above, possibly starting with paragraph frames or a template to develop their academic writing. Graff and Birkenstein (2014) suggest that we need to make academic discourse explicit to learners and argue that providing templates for academic writing allows learners to shape their ideas more effectively.

Sample 3

Level: high-intermediate ESL, Career Pathways class focused on healthcare professions

Text genre: narrative, specifically retelling a sequence of events

Final writing objective: Write brief narratives of three patient care interactions clearly, accurately, and concisely, using professional language and tone.

Summary of lesson: This series of tasks helps students develop the narrative writing required in a healthcare position such as personal care or nursing, specifically documenting patient care and interactions. Such writing must be clear, concise, and articulate in a short amount of space. In the end, narrative writing in this context (although certainly these skills transfer to other professions as well) should be of high enough quality that if the chart were used in court, the information would not be challenged due to inaccuracies or confusion. In this activity, students work together first to improve poorly written patient care narratives and then to write their own. After they have used their background knowledge and oral language through vocabulary work and guided conversations, students are able to achieve clarity and coherence before composing three strong patient care narratives.

Step 1: Talk about this genre of narrative writing.

Students are asked to tell a partner briefly why narrative documentation is important in patient care, a topic they studied in a previous lesson. The teacher elicits a few responses, such as ensuring high-quality care and continuity of service with many caregivers. Shifting to the nature of these narratives, a mind map, depicted in Figure 8.7, is provided with five key elements of good medical documentation (Kalitzkus & Matthiessen, 2009). Students are asked to write two words they associate with that element, guided by the question: "What does it mean to 'Be factual [precise/complete, etc.]?'" Then they circulate around the room, talking to others, finding two more words, and filling out their thinking on each concept.

Figure 8.7   Mind Map for Organizing Features of a Clear Narrative

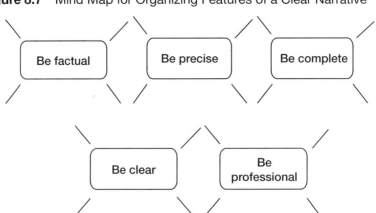

Step 2: Identify weaknesses and strengths in a patient care narrative.

Students are shown this poorly written example of a patient care narrative on the board: *The patient was mean to me today.* With a partner, they talk about the five elements discussed in Step 1 in relation to this example—*Is it factual? Is it precise? Is it complete? Is it clear? Is it professional?* (The teacher will ensure ahead of time that students know the meanings of these words.)

The teacher now offers a more appropriate narrative, such as: *The patient appeared restless, getting up from his bed and pacing back and forth across the room. His fists were clenched, and he yelled at me and other staff members, 'I hate this hospital!'* Again, students discuss the five elements from Step 1 in relation to this new example.

Step 3: Talk through a patient care narrative.

Each student is given a piece of paper with one poorly written patient care narrative statement and three empty boxes (see Figure 8.8). Students are directed to make a quick attempt at an improved patient care narrative in the first box. Next, they talk with two different people, sharing first the original prompt and then their attempt(s) at improving it. Their conversation partner gives his/her feedback and suggestions for making it stronger and clearer (Zwiers & Crawford, 2011), and the student records a new attempt in the next box. Details of the patient interactions are left to the writers' imaginations!

Figure 8.8 Writing Patient Care Narratives

Patient looks like her leg hurts.	Patient is holding her leg funny.	Patient is holding her leg and making a face.	Patient clutches leg, grimaces, and complains of lower leg pain.

Patient couldn't answer my questions.			

Step 4: Write three well-written patient care narratives.

In this final step, care is taken to simulate a more realistic timeframe and task. Students are shown a video with three patient care interactions. They are given limited time and space to write a patient care narrative for each one that is factual, precise, complete, and professional. This writing serves as a summative assessment of the lesson for the teacher. As an extend-your-thinking question to conclude the lesson, students are asked what other jobs might require similar narrative writing (child care provider, maintenance record keeper, security guard, etc.).

Sample 4

Level: advanced ESL, College Bridge reading and writing class

Text genre: argumentation

Final writing objective: Argumentative essay based on textual evidence from sources presented in diverse formats, integrating multiple perspectives

Summary of lesson: This sample of a lesson leading to an argumentative writing assignment is designed for students at a very advanced level of adult basic education, preparing for college entrance. Even at this level of language and literacy, academic conversations enhance students' thinking and provide needed support for clearer, more coherent writing. This sample is a culminating writing activity, situated at the end of a line of inquiry that spanned several lessons: *Is the United States progressing toward racial equality?* It requires students to understand and synthesize excerpts from multiple textual sources and think critically about these texts and how they represent current and past events around racial inequality. Students are asked to present their own case in answer to the essential question and support their claim with evidence. The sources for the readings/viewings are all speeches that can be both viewed and read. The steps described here come at the end of several lessons, when students have completed close readings of the various speeches and are now ready for further synthesis and to begin their own argumentative essay writing. This lesson's content, while challenging, exemplifies a tenet of the CCRS, which emphasizes using texts worth reading and responding to questions worth answering.

Step 1: Recognize multiple perspectives and identify the author/speaker's audience and purpose.

As a warm-up, interactive task, students are presented one of two quotes to re-enter the topic at hand (progress toward racial equality) and to recognize multiple perspectives. Half of the group is given this quote:

> The death of Michael Brown is a grave tragedy the community of Ferguson, Missouri, should not have to bear...What kind of a police department is it that would refer to the people it should be trying to protect as animals? It is unbelievable that these ideas could run rampant in 2014. This is not 1940 or 1950 in America, but today it is hard to see the difference. (Congressman John Lewis, August 2014, press release upon the events in Ferguson, MO)

The other half is given this quote:

> That is the story of this country, the story that has brought me to this stage tonight, the story of generations of people who felt the lash of bondage, the shame of servitude, the sting of segregation, but who kept on striving and hoping and doing what needed to be done so that today I wake up every morning in a house that was built by slaves. And I watch my daughters, two beautiful, intelligent, black young women playing with their dogs on the White House lawn. (First Lady Michelle Obama, July 2016, Democratic National Convention)

Students are given a few moments to read and reflect on the quote they have been given and confer with others who have the same quote to confirm their understanding. They are asked to generate with their

Figure 8.9 Responding to Quotes about Racial Equality: Venn Diagram

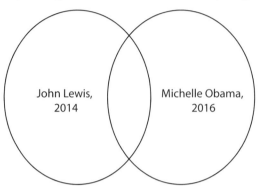

same-quote group/partner: (1) what they know about the speaker and the context where the quote appeared and (2) what the excerpt is saying about the United States's progress toward racial equality. A Venn diagram, shown in Figure 8.9, is provided to capture notes.

Step 2: Compare differing perspectives: Warm-up quote comparison.

Next, students are paired with someone with the other quote and are asked to talk about these questions, adding to the ideas already in the half-completed Venn diagram.

1. What do you know about the speaker in each case, and what else is going on in the world at that time that frames his/her statement?
2. Does the speaker believe that the United States is making progress toward racial equality? Why do you say that?

Step 3: Synthesize multiple text analysis into a graphic organizer and work collaboratively to articulate one's text analysis.

In previous lessons in this unit, students have studied the civil rights movement as well as some of the more recent racially charged events nationwide. They have, in lessons leading up to this one, already completed close readings of three texts/speeches, viewed each speech on video, and also read and analyzed the written text in class. By viewing the speeches, they engaged their listening comprehension skills and built understanding of the context, tone, and substance of each speech. Close readings were completed using the written transcripts from the speeches. Now, in small groups of three or four, students are asked to recall those close readings and together fill out one graphic organizer about the three texts (see Figure 8.10), paying particular attention to evidence from the texts that illustrates how the speaker views the United States' progress toward racial equality.

Figure 8.10 Notes on Racial Equality Texts

Speaker/Author	Recall and make notes about the speaker and the context for this speech.	Does the speaker believe that America is progressing toward racial equality?	What evidence in the text leads you to say that?
Robert F. Kennedy's speech on the death of Martin Luther King (April 4, 1968)			
President Obama's speech on the 50th Anniversary of Bloody Sunday in Selma, Alabama (March 7, 2015)			
Common and John Legend's Oscar Acceptance Speech for Best Song, "Glory" (February 22, 2015)			

The teacher provides language for sustaining a discussion and seeking the ideas of others to assist with this group work:

- *Can you clarify what you mean by _____?*
- *What's your perspective?*
- *I'd like to build on that idea.*
- *The speaker is likely biased, because _____.*
- *What in the text leads you to say that?*

Step 4: Write an argumentative essay.

Now, given all the previous work to explore the essential question in this unit, students are prepared for the final culminating writing activity. They have synthesized excerpts from multiple textual sources (from diverse media formats) and considered various perspectives presented in these texts. The structured academic conversations they participated in during this sample lesson worked to clarify their text analyses and helped to build their own arguments. Now students are asked to present their own response to the question of the United States' progress in racial equality in the form of an essay, supporting their claim with evidence from the readings/viewings in this unit. They may integrate information from other sources they find relevant as well in this first draft, with peer feedback and revisions to follow in subsequent lessons and outside of class, as needed.

■ Concluding Thoughts

Writing is, ultimately, a quiet, individual activity. However, the path to becoming a strong writer need not be quiet or individual! The four sample lessons in this chapter demonstrate highly engaging, interactive steps that capitalize on students' oral language and lead toward a high-quality written product. Showcased tasks range across English proficiency levels and across contexts for adult education. Activities include one-question interviews to collect data, jigsaw reading and speaking tasks, graphic organizers to collect and organize information, structured conversations, and more. Such speaking, listening, reading, and writing tasks move students toward career and college readiness.

The language, often oral, that students already possess is the raw material for great literacy development. Zwiers and Crawford (2011) remind us that "the language that happens in each person's head is the main set of tools for constructing meaning from texts and for writing" (p. 13). By harnessing and building on students' oral language, we can build bridges to the strong academic writing they need for full participation in their communities as family members, citizens, and workers.

—————— **Questions for Reflection and Application** ——————

1. Of the four sample lessons provided, which is closest to your context? What can you glean from the example to inform your instruction?

2. In each of the sample lessons, a graphic organizer is used to extend thinking, make connections, and give structure to a conversation task. Which graphic organizers might you try with the learners you work with?

3. Students often have a "mismatch" between their oral language and written language proficiency. Is this true for the learners you work with? How can you bridge the gap?

References

Bigelow, M., & Vinogradov, P. (2011). Teaching adult second language learners who are emergent readers. *Annual Review of Applied Linguistics, 31*, 120–136.

Fernández, R., Peyton, J. K., & Schaetzel, K. (2017). A survey of writing instruction in adult ESL programs: Are teaching practices meeting adult learner needs? *Journal of Research and Practice for Adult Literacy, Secondary, and Basic Education, 6*(2), 5–20.

Gee, J. P. (1990). *Social linguistics and literacies: Ideologies in discourses.* New York: Falmer Press.

Gibbons, P. (2009). *English learners' academic literacy and thinking.* Portsmouth, NH: Heinemann.

Graff, G., & Birkenstein, C. (2014) *They say, I say: The moves that matter in academic writing* (3rd ed.). New York: W.W. Norton and Company.

Johnson, K., & Parrish, B. (2010). Aligning instructional practices to meet the academic needs of adult ESL students. *TESOL Quarterly, 44*(3), 618–628.

Kalitzkus, V., & Matthiessen, P. F. (2009). Narrative-based medicine: Potential, pitfalls, and practice. *The Permanente Journal, 13*(1), 80–86.

Mercer, N. (2000). *Words and minds: How we use language to think together.* London: Routledge.

Parrish, B. (2015). *Meeting the language needs of today's English language learner.* Issue Brief, Online Module. Washington, DC: American Institutes for Research and OCTAE. LINCS ESL Pro. https://lincs.ed.gov/programs/eslpro/meeting-the-language-needs-of-todays-english-language-learner

Parrish, B., & Johnson, K. (2010, April). *Promoting learner transitions to postsecondary education and work: Developing academic readiness from the beginning.* CAELA Network Brief. Washington, DC: Center for Applied Linguistics. http://www.cal.org/caelanetwork/resources/transitions.html

U.S. Department of Education. Office of Vocational and Adult Education. (2013). *College and career readiness standards for adult education.* Washington, DC: Author. http://lincs.ed.gov/publications/pdf/CCRStandardsAdultEd.pdf

Vinogradov, P. E. (2016). *Meeting the language needs of today's adult English language learner: Companion learning resource.* Washington, DC: Dept. of Education, Office of Career, Technical and Adult Education. https://lincs.ed.gov/programs/eslpro

Zwiers, J., & Crawford, M. (2011). *Academic conversations: Classroom talk that fosters critical thinking and content understandings.* Portland, ME: Stenhouse.

- *TEAL Just Write! Guide.*

  This resource guide (https://lincs.ed.gov/state-resources/federal-initiatives/teal/guide/toc) for adult educators works to increase familiarity with evidence-based writing instruction and to disseminate research findings through practical teaching suggestions to enhance the quality of instruction.

- ATLAS Writing Resources.

  ATLAS, ABE Teaching & Learning Advancement System (http://atlasabe.org/resources/writing-instruction), is a professional development provider in Minnesota funded by the Minnesota Department of Education. This section of the ATLAS website (Writing Resources) is for all ABE/ESL writing teachers, from those teaching basic writing skills to those teaching GED, adult diploma, and transition to the workplace or post-secondary. Organized around seven categories, educators can find links to practical classroom resources and relevant research.

- Jeff Zwiers Website.

  This site (http://jeffzwiers.org) provides tasks and tools for developing academic language for English language learners. While focused on K–12 contexts, much is immediately applicable to adult education.

Graphic Organizers

These sites provide links to ready-made graphic organizers that can help learners structure writing projects:

- Graphic Organizers—Education Place. Houghton Mifflin Harcourt Publishing Company. www.eduplace.com/graphicorganizer
- TeacherVision Graphic Organizers. www.teachervision.com/lesson-planning/graphic-organizer

PART 4

Aligning Writing with Accountability Systems

Chapter 9

Using Writing Test Prompts to Develop Academic Writing

Kirsten Schaetzel, Emory University School of Law

Opening Questions ─────────────────────────

1. What do you think are the purposes of the writing section on high-stakes exams? Do you think high-stakes exams fulfill these purposes?
2. What are ways that students can practice for these exams?
3. How much practice do you think students need before taking a high-stakes exam that includes writing? Why?

Writing exams are a fact of life in academic classrooms. They come in many shapes and sizes, some with gate-keeping properties and some without. We find writing exams given in college and university classes to measure student learning, for placement into classes, for moving into higher-level classes, for obtaining a GED or a professional degree, and for other purposes in academic and professional programs of study. Whether the writing exam prompts students to display knowledge, as in an exam for a psychology course, or to display that they can use exam reading materials as support in their answer, doing well on a writing exam means that a student can exemplify the skills of good academic writing. This chapter focuses on one high-stakes writing exam, the writing section of a high school equivalency exam. The chapter examines the purposes behind high school equivalency writing exams and the writing skills and habits of mind they test, all of which are applicable to any high-stakes writing exam. It then argues that writing exam preparation can occur at all levels of English language proficiency and walks through an example of a high school equivalency read-to-write test. It examines each stage that students move through when crafting an answer and emphasizes the thinking processes that they use at each stage. Helping students learn the thought processes for each stage of writing results in their being better prepared not only for high-stakes writing exams, but also for the academic and professional writing they need to do. Ultimately, the chapter aims to "forge stronger links between teaching and assessment [which] is essential if educators hope to optimize classroom learning" (Stoynoff & Chapelle, 2005, p. 4).

In this chapter, the writing sections of exams are called *writing exams*, not *written exams*, for two reasons. First, the act of writing is emphasized because that is what students are asked to do on these exams; they are "writing" during the exam. While writing, they need to bring the requisite thinking processes, strategies, and skills to bear. Most writing exams are timed, so writing quickly and confidently is important. Second, the phrase *written exams* brings to mind the finished, written product. The focus of this chapter is not on the result but on the thinking processes, strategies, and skills that students need to develop to write an effective response.

■ Purpose of High-Stakes Writing Exams

Students have been writing exams for hundreds of years. Although educational testing began through oral exams, students began being tested through writing in post-Reformation Europe (the late 1600s) because more of the populace had become literate. As Faught (2006) writes, "Since then, exams have had a long and colourful history, their alleged tyranny being routinely decried by some, but their effectiveness in determining academic ability has remained pretty much unassailable" (p. 53).

All three high school equivalency programs, the General Educational Development (GED), the High School Equivalency Test (HiSET), and the Test Assessing Secondary Completion (TASC), culminate in a high-stakes exam. Part of each of these exams involves producing a written essay using source materials provided. Students passing the exam earn a high school equivalency certificate. The GED is the oldest of the three programs, beginning as part of the GI Bill of Rights after WWII to help returning soldiers get a high school diploma if they were too old to return to high school. Since 1947, non-veteran civilians have been allowed to take the GED, and in the 1970s, the minimum age requirement for the GED was lowered so that students who have dropped out of high school are eligible to take it.

In 2014, the GED became aligned with the Common Core State Standards and so now focuses more on critical thinking and only uses a computer-based test. (It does not offer a paper format.) That same year, two other high school equivalency programs came on the market: the HiSET and the TASC. Both are as rigorous and as focused on critical thinking as the GED, but they offer paper-based tests as well as computer-based tests (Adams, 2015). According to a July 2015 report issued by the Education Commission of the States amid concerns about testing center infrastructure and staff capacity to offer only the GED, a computer-based test, states now offer one, two, or all three high school equivalency tests (Zinth, 2015).

All three high school equivalency tests include a timed written response (30–60 minutes). For many years, the GED's timed written response was a writing prompt that students were asked to respond to. These essays were often patterned on the famous (or infamous) five-paragraph essay, and topics resulted in one of the main essay forms, such as comparison-contrast, definition, and cause and effect. These essays were graded and accorded a pass or a fail. Because they were subjectively graded, they were criticized for lack of consistency in rater markings, for not having authentic writing tasks for students to do, and for whether the essays actually tested the ability to produce academic writing (Cumming, 1997; Lumley, 2005; Plakans, 2008; Weigle, 2004).

Because of these criticisms, when the GED was revised and the HiSET and TASC were developed, these tests no longer used only a writing prompt; instead, they all created read-to-write tasks. A read-to-write task is a task in which the student reads two or more source materials, which are provided in the test, and then responds to a prompt by writing an essay that uses information from the source materials as support (Hirvela, 2016). These read-to-write tasks are thought to more closely mirror university writing assignments and, thus, to be a more authentic measure of students' academic writing ability (Braine, 1989; Carson, 2001; Horowitz, 1986). This new approach to assessing students' academic writing skills tests not only their writing abilities but also their reading abilities. Students need to be able to read the materials provided and understand them, read the writing prompt and determine what they are being asked to produce, and then use the materials provided to write an essay that conforms to the guidelines of the prompt and demonstrates their academic writing skills.

This type of writing task is a difficult one for many adult learners, and a lack of preparation to successfully complete it may be one reason why community college and university students are not completing their degree programs. As reported by Coon and Jacobsen (2014), many adult English learners are not completing their degree programs because they do not finish required and remediation courses, and they do not have the requisite skills to do well in classes that require academic reading and writing skills. One reason adult learners are struggling with academic reading and writing may be that the writing taught in adult education classes does not align with the types of writing they are required to do. In one recent survey, adult education teachers said that they assign narrative, descriptive, and expository writing tasks more often than they assign argumentative tasks (Fernández, Peyton, & Schaetzel, 2017), but in fact, argumentative writing tasks are the most common type of writing done in community college and university courses and are exemplified on the new high school equivalency tests. If we can prepare students to formulate and develop an argument using selected readings, for a high school equivalency test, then we are also preparing them for the academic writing they need in higher education.

■ Habits of Mind

To help students develop the skills needed to write successfully in community college and university classes and to carry out all the steps in reading, planning, and writing a read-to-write task, the National Council of Teachers of English (NCTE) has analyzed the skills necessary and listed them as "Habits of Mind" (Council of Writing Program Administrators, National Council of Teachers of English, & National Writing Project, 2011; Johnson, 2013). These Habits of Mind describe "the rhetorical and twenty-first-century skills as well as habits of mind and experiences that are critical for college success" (Ericsson, 2005, p.105). These Habits of Mind can inform teaching and provide focus for lessons as we strive to prepare students for writing exams. We can teach—and students can learn—Habits of Mind at any level of English language proficiency: "Teachers can do much to develop activities and assignments that foster the kind of thinking that lies behind these habits and prepare students for the learning they will experience in college and beyond" (Council of Writing Program Administrators, National Council of Teachers of English, & National Writing Project, 2011, p. 4). By designing lessons focused on developing one or more Habits of Mind, teachers can give students consistent practice in thinking processes.

Figure 9.1 lists the Habits of Mind and activities that teachers can design to help students acquire each Habit of Mind throughout the writing process. For example, we take one Habit of Mind, Engagement, and the related activity of stating and supporting an opinion to see how teachers can incorporate this framework into any lesson at any level of English language proficiency. In the U.S. educational

Figure 9.1 Habits of Mind Teaching Activities

Habit of Mind	Activity
Curiosity: the desire to know more about the world	Looking for and reporting information: asking questions; surveying students and others; asking students to interview one or more people; helping students work with written texts: find, summarize, synthesize, and present material
Openness: the willingness to consider new ways of being and thinking in the world	Discovering more than one way: asking students to find different solutions to a problem; leading students to discover different ways of interpreting a text or oral response; asking follow-up questions to gain clarification; helping students to analyze a situation to determine the best answer/solution/course of action and to weigh alternatives; guiding students to see and examine "gray" areas
Engagement: a sense of investment and involvement in learning	Forming and supporting an opinion: giving choices in assignments; asking students their opinions; asking students to state their opinions and support them with specific data; stating rationales for class assignments; asking students to state rationales for choices
Creativity: the ability to use novel approaches for generating, investigating, and representing ideas	Performing new and different tasks: including a variety of tasks in lessons; incorporating multiple modalities for displaying skills; having students brainstorm alone or with others; asking students to share their approaches to a task and ideas for the task; commending students when they take a risk and try something different
Persistence: the ability to sustain interest in and attention to short- and long-term projects	Assigning a variety of tasks: assigning short- and long-term projects; breaking down projects into steps; scaffolding longer projects; assigning individual, pair, and group work
Responsibility: the ability to take ownership of one's actions and understand the consequences of those actions for oneself and others	Scaffolding to develop independent learners: scaffolding group and individual work; lessening scaffolding over a term/class; giving time-on-task guidelines; supervising groups and pairs as students divide up work; providing feedback opportunities to members of a group; designing group assignments to ensure equal participation of all group members; varying group members during a term/class
Flexibility: the ability to adapt to situations, expectations, or demands	Making changes: assigning work in steps (not as a whole); using a draft or final product in another way; shifting point-of-view/audience in writing or telling; helping students develop their ideas by asking clarification questions; exposing students to new and different audiences
Metacognition: the ability to reflect on one's own thinking as well as on the individual and cultural processes and systems used to structure knowledge	Reflecting: giving students questions to reflect on their own or others' work; asking students to analyze pros and cons, strengths and weaknesses, differences and similarities; asking students to give one another feedback; helping students respond to feedback they receive to improve a product

system, teachers emphasize stating and supporting an opinion starting in preschool with Show and Tell, an activity that young learners engage in almost every day. Students are asked to show something, such as a favorite toy, color, food, or activity, and tell the rest of the class why it is their favorite. In doing this, they state their personal opinion about what they like. They follow up this statement with their reasons for liking it. For example, *I like my teddy bear because it is soft and I can hold it every night* or *I like apples because they are crunchy and sweet.* Through Show and Tell, students learn that their personal opinions have value, and they learn to state and support their opinions for an audience. In essence, they are speaking an expository paragraph: opinion + support.

This "opinion + support" formula can be incorporated into any class at any age or English proficiency level. Teachers can frequently ask students to state their opinions and then ask them why they like or dislike something or why they hold that opinion (or those opinions). For example, students can talk about whether it is best to wash a car by hand or take it to a car wash, or whether we become who we are because of our genetics or because of the environment in which we are raised. Students state an opinion and give reasons for their opinion: *I think genetics determine who we are, because I have my mother's brown eyes, long legs, and flat feet, and I am as stubborn as my grandfather was about changing my mind*: generalization + details (physical features) + an example (my grandfather's stubbornness). The teacher or student can later write out this talk so that students become accustomed to writing and supporting their opinions. These are very simple examples, but they demonstrate a way of teaching that facilitates student engagement in ideas and how, over time, students can acquire the Habits of Mind that they need to write well academically.

Likewise, a teacher can develop students' engagement through asking what the rationale for an assignment is. By asking, *Why are we doing* _____? a teacher can help students think about the assignment not only as a way of practicing a grammar item, vocabulary, or sentence structure, but also as a way of expanding their ability to communicate to a particular audience or learn alternative ways of saying or writing (thinking processes). Through this, teachers can help students realize that different assignments serve different and multiple purposes, thereby developing students' Engagement and Metacognition (reflective thinking).

◼ Habits of Mind and High School Equivalency Test Read-to-Write Tasks

Now that we have examined the Habits of Mind needed for academic writing, we examine how they are tested in a read-to-write high school equivalency test question. The writing tasks on all three high school equivalency tests are read-to-write tasks, using two passages that state two different opinions on a topic. Both passages use source materials as the basis for supporting a point of view. However, the writing prompts ask slightly different questions. The GED test asks students to analyze each reading passage and determine which side of the argument has better support. (The prompt warns them that the better argument may or may not match their own thinking about the topic). After students have decided which is better, they write an essay in which they use information from both passages to support the better-supported argument, even though this may not match their own thinking about the topic. As shown in Figure 9.1, engagement in such an assignment requires that they first examine the support in each passage and decide which passage has stronger, more convincing support.

The TASC and the HiSET read-to-write tasks ask students to form their own opinions on a topic and use information from both passages to support it. They can examine both passages and evaluate the evidence provided. The strong information can support their arguments, and the weak information can help them refute counterarguments, or opinions opposite to theirs. In some writing tasks, they are asked to use information to argue for their opinion. In others, they are asked to give someone advice using information from the passages.

In all three tests, students need to use these Habits of Mind to read and understand the passages and then formulate a response:

- ▣ Curiosity: finding information in the passage that is relevant to the test prompt; summarizing and synthesizing information
- ▣ Openness: seeing different positions in an argument; choosing the best position

- ☐ Engagement: giving an opinion regarding the best alternative; determining why it is the best alternative
- ☐ Creativity: taking a risk to list their arguments or the best arguments
- ☐ Persistence: determining what steps they need to take to write a well-supported answer and then following those steps
- ☐ Responsibility: putting forth and taking ownership of their own opinions/arguments
- ☐ Flexibility: using arguments from both sides (information from both passages) to examine both sides and find one to be better
- ☐ Metacognition: analyzing pros and cons and determining that one side is better; weighing strengths and weaknesses of arguments.

All of these Habits of Mind can be used in many different contexts, modalities (oral and written), and English language proficiency levels. Students with good grounding in them will be able to apply these Habits of Mind to their read-to-write tasks.

An Example of a Read-to-Write Task Followed by Class Activities to Prepare for It

To plan lessons that develop Habits of Mind in students and familiarize them with a high school equivalency test, this section analyzes a sample read-to-write question. After analyzing the test question and determining the Habits of Mind and skills it tests, we walk through the thinking processes, strategies, and skills that students need to write a good answer. We break down the process of answering the test question into three stages: (1) analyzing the prompt, (2) reading the passages, and (3) writing the answer. Although these stages overlap, we examine each stage separately. In addition to developing these thought processes and skills, students gain by seeing sample test readings and writing prompts as a regular part of class. These materials familiarize students with the test and lessen test anxiety.

A Sample Read-to-Write Test Question

This test question is one of the sample GED Extended Response Passages and Prompts for Classroom Practice (https://ged.com/wp-content/uploads/extended_response_classroom_practice.pdf). The instructions ask students to answer the prompt by writing four to seven paragraphs of three to seven sentences each.

Source Material #1

Game-Based Learning Is Merely a Fad
Solomon Robles, Ed.D., Professor of Education, Winborne College
Workplace Training Journal

Electronic learning, or "eLearning," was sold to many CEOs as the wave of the corporate future. There's no need to hire human beings to train staff, managers were told. All the information you require can be accessed online—at a reduced cost for the company, and more flexible scheduling for employees. It sounded too good to be true—and it was. As one writer noted, "Most eLearning is nothing more than online lectures or course notes." To teach skills beyond basic facts, the person-to-person method is still more effective than any form of electronic learning.

And yet, along comes the next eLearning fad: "gamification," which means using video games to teach. Video-game-based learning is already widely used in schools and has spread to corporations as a tool for training workers and motivating customers. This approach is even used in the military. But does it work?

Most research on game-based learning has looked at schools. Results have been inconsistent but not especially encouraging. One 2013 study found that "students who completed the gamified experience got better scores in practical assignments and in overall score, but … performed poorly on written assignments and participated less during class activities." This makes sense: If you're playing video games, you are not developing the so-called "soft skills"—also known as "people skills"—that are necessary for success in any job. In a traditional classroom, on the other hand, students can ask questions and engage with the teacher and with other learners.

In the workplace, game-based learning is yet another wedge driven between younger employees, who might applaud gamification, and older workers, who may now feel obsolete. What's more, the prestigious magazine *The Economist* points out that "many of the aspects of gamification that do work are merely old ideas in trendy new clothes." For example, the points and other rewards that are selling features of video games are just online versions of sales contests or "employee of the month" perks. Like other trends, game-based learning is likely to fade away as the next new teaching fad appears on the horizon.

Source Material #2

Game-Based Learning: An Effective Training Strategy
Janette Morgan, PhD, Professor of Business,
Saratoga State University
Innovative Trends in the Workplace

Already a multi-billion-dollar business, game-based learning in the corporate world continues to grow at a steady pace, and is here to stay. Executives are smart—they are not going to waste resources on training methods that don't work. Let's look at some of the advantages of "gamifying" workplace training.

First, many people are "gamers" in their non-work lives, so playing video games is something they are already comfortable with and enjoy. This makes game-based learning in the workplace more attractive and motivating than traditional instruction. And according to the Entertainment Software Association, despite the image of video-game players as teenaged boys, "the average gamer is now 37 years old." Further challenging the stereotype, nearly half of gamers are girls or women. Even 29 percent of those over age 50 are getting into the video-game habit. Teenagers and young men, in fact, make up only 15 percent of the over 190 million video-game users in the United States.

Evidence supporting the effectiveness of game-based learning is starting to emerge. Researchers point out that video games have "compelling storylines, attainable challenges, rewards, recognition and control," all of which stimulate learners. A 2012 report on game-based learning notes that "there is research evidence demonstrating positive impact on higher order skills such as decision making and problem solving." The report adds that using video games can also reduce training time, an advantage for both managers and employees.

Finally, unlike one-time training in a classroom, game-based learning is infinitely repeatable. If employees miss something or need more practice, they can always start the game again, using the feedback provided by the game to gauge their progress. This leads to a sense of accomplishment and creates a supportive learning environment, which is what we all want in an education strategy.

Extended Response Prompt:

Analyze the arguments presented in the two journal articles. In your response, develop an argument in which you explain how one position is better supported than the other. Incorporate relevant and specific evidence from both sources to support your argument.

Remember, the better-argued position is not necessarily the position with which you agree. This task should take approximately 45 minutes to complete.

From: https://ged.com/wp-content/uploads/extended_response_classroom_practice.pdf

Activity 1. Analyze the test prompt as the basis for writing an answer.

To help students write a passing essay for this question, students first analyze the prompt to know what it is asking them to do, as shown in Figure 9.2. Teachers identify the Habits of Mind that students need to perform and focus on them in leading students through developing their response. In analyzing the prompt and developing a response, students should begin with actions suggested in Column 1. Next, teachers can teach the sub-skills in Column 2 to help students do these actions and use the class activities in Column 3 to develop the listed thinking processes and skills. These activities can be adapted

Figure 9.2 Class Activities to Develop Habits of Mind Needed to Answer a Test Prompt

1. Student Actions to Analyze and Answer the Prompt (Directions in the Prompt)	2. Sub-Skills and Habits of Mind Inherent in the Action	3. Class Activities That Build These Habits of Mind
Read the prompt and identify the actions (verbs) to see what the prompt is asking you to do. To help students focus: 1. The articles support different positions about game-based training. I need to decide which article has stronger support. 2. After I decide which article has stronger support, I write an essay arguing for that position and material from both articles to support what I say.	□ Determine what you are being asked to do (Openness and Engagement) □ Plan the steps you will take to do this (Creativity and Responsibility)	□ Give different directions and different tasks so that students become accustomed to reading and responding to directions accurately. □ Show students the steps they need to do embedded in the prompt.

to all levels of English language proficiency by using combinations of oral and written language and by using vocabulary appropriate for students' proficiency levels.

Activity 2. Read the passages.

After analyzing the prompt, students read the passages. After reading each passage, students review it to determine its claim (opinion) and what arguments it uses for support. In the example, the first passage does not support game-based training, whereas the second passage does. If we examine the actions that learners take to analyze these passages, we can practice these actions with students at lower levels of language proficiency.

Several actions, based on Habits of Mind, help students understand and analyze a reading passage. (Much more can be said about reading strategies. See Grabe & Stoller, 2013; Koda, 2005.) These actions, with reference to the first passage of the test, "Game-Based Learning Is Merely a Fad," are:

- ▣ Identify arguments and support.

- ▣ Examine each paragraph and sentence for "what it says" (the words the writer uses) and "what it does" (the function the sentence or paragraph performs, such as introducing an idea, stating an opinion or argument, giving support, rejecting an argument, stating why an argument is strong or weak) (Bean, 2011; Bean, Chappell, & Gillam, 2011; Bruffee, 1993; Ramage, Bean, & Johnson, 2009).

- ▣ Weigh the arguments the author is making through the "believing game" and the "doubting game" (Elbow, 1973, 1986). When reading a passage and believing what the author says, the student "puts herself in the author's shoes" and tries to accept everything the author is saying. When reading a passage and doubting what it says, the student "plays the devil's advocate" and questions what the author is saying. Through these ways of reading, students can begin to figure out which arguments are strong and which are weak.

Figure 9.3 lists these actions, usually completed by more advanced students, in the first column, and lists several activities that teachers can do at advanced, intermediate, and beginning levels to build these skills and thought processes. Teachers can use course-reading materials but should also use test materials so students become familiar with reading test passages. If students can build solid academic reading habits at lower levels of proficiency, then they can develop the skills further at higher levels of proficiency (Grabe & Stoller, 2013). These practices will consistently engage them with academic texts.

For example, when students read "Game-Based Learning Is Merely a Fad," they determine that it does not support game-based learning. The title gives the clue that game-based learning is "merely a fad." This training technique will not become permanent. At the end of the introductory paragraph, the last two sentences, "As one writer noted, 'most eLearning . . . .' . . . " and "the person-to-person method is still more effective than any form of electronic learning," state the writer's opinion, that eLearning is not a good training method. The writer then moves from eLearning to game-based training, categorizing game-based training as one kind of eLearning.

The writer uses support from three sources. He includes a quotation in the first paragraph, the results of a 2013 study in the third paragraph, and a quotation from an article in *The Economist* in the final paragraph.

If students look at the second reading and compare it to the first, they see which passage contains stronger arguments, and they think about how to write a response to the prompt. A graphic organizer, like the one shown in Figure 9.4, helps students compare the passages.

Once students identify each of the arguments and their support, teachers help them evaluate their merits. There are many methods for evaluating arguments. One common, easy method is called STAR: Is the evidence **S**pecific, **T**ypical, **A**ccurate, and **R**elevant? (Ramage, Bean, & Johnson, 2011). If working on a GED test prompt, like the example presented, the student must decide which passage contains the best evidence, using the arguments and support in the passage. If working on a HiSET or TASC prompt, students decide which side of the argument they agree with and use the best arguments and support given in their answers.

In addition to stating which arguments are the best and why, students also might argue that some support is weak. If a piece of

Figure 9.3 Activities to Build Text Analysis Skills

Advanced-Level Actions to Analyze Readings	Advanced/Intermediate-Level Activities to Build Reading Analysis Skills	Beginning-Level Activities to Build Reading Analysis Skills
1. Identifying arguments and their support	◘ Annotating reading passages: labeling main ideas and support ◘ Labeling different kinds of support ◘ Keeping a reading log of ideas and reactions to these ideas ◘ Keeping a double-entry reading log: a summary on one side and reaction on the other side ◘ Asking students to put passages or parts of passages into their own words	◘ Asking students to state their opinions or the main idea and support them (show and tell) ◘ Labeling sentences as general and specific ◘ Labeling sentences as fact and opinion
2. Examining paragraphs and sentences for "what they say" and "what they do"	◘ Labeling functions in a text (for example, introducing, explaining, giving an example, contrasting one idea with another) ◘ Underlining the words that carry out these functions	◘ Giving students instructions with language functions (for example, *introduce us to . . ., give us an example of . . ., contrast these two ideas—what are their differences?*) ◘ Writing words on the board or a chart that carry out these functions
3. Weighing the arguments the author is making	◘ Teaching students to distinguish academic and popular kinds of support (for example, a quotation from a book or journal vs. what a friend thinks) ◘ Labeling strong and weak support in readings ◘ Using a graphic organizer to list and compare the support in two readings	◘ Introducing students to which kinds of support are more highly valued in academics—as in scientific support (research) vs. the advice of a community member

Figure 9.4 Graphic Organizer to Compare Arguments in Two Passages

<u>Robles's claim</u>: Game-based learning is not a good training tool.	<u>Morgan's claim</u>: Game-based learning is a good training tool.

<u>Arguments and support</u>:
1. Argument: eLearning is only lectures and course notes, not people interacting, which is a better training method.
<u>Support</u>: quotation
2. Argument: Research on game-based learning in school is not "encouraging"
<u>Support</u>:
  a. One study shows mixed results of effects on students (some skills better and some skills worse)
  b. Students are not learning interpersonal skills
3. <u>Argument</u>: Game-based learning at work separates older and younger people
<u>Support</u>: A quotation from an article in *The Economist* showing that game-based learning does not offer anything new
	<u>Arguments and support</u>:
	1. <u>Argument</u>: People already game, so game-based training uses a learning method they are already familiar with.
	<u>Support</u>: Statistics about the characteristics of gamers from the Entertainment Software Association
	2. Argument: Research showing that game-based learning is effective
	<u>Support</u>:
	  a. A quotation from researchers
	  b. A 2012 report: builds the abilities to make decisions and solve problems. It also takes less time for training.
	3. <u>Argument</u>: The game can be repeated
	<u>Support</u>:
	  a. Good if an employee missed the training
	  b. Good if an employee has trouble understanding a concept the first time

support is weak, it does not conform to STAR, or other criteria: It is not specific; it is not typical, or representative of the group; it is not accurate; or it is not relevant to the argument made. Students may cite weak arguments and state why they are weak. Figure 9.5 shows a simple chart that can be used to teach students how to evaluate support.

Teachers can do these types of exercises with students at all levels of English language proficiency, although with those at lower levels, they would do them orally first. After introducing "argument and support," teachers ask students what is the strongest support for an

Figure 9.5 How to Analyze the Strength of Arguments

Argument and Support	Specific?	Typical?	Accurate?	Relevant?

argument and then discuss that as a whole class or in small groups using a chart, such as Figure 9.5. There are many ways that teachers can introduce evaluation early in a course sequence and build on it at higher levels of proficiency. Thinking and evaluating builds students' Habits of Mind and fosters their engagement with learning, helping them to make connections between their own and others' ideas. Evaluation also builds students' confidence in reflecting on ideas and strengthens their metacognitive capabilities.

Activity 3. Write a response.

Finally, after reading and analyzing the prompt and the passages, students are ready to plan and write their response. Responses are usually four to seven paragraphs long, with each paragraph being three or more sentences.

At all levels of proficiency, students need to believe that they are active agents in the writing process: They are *doing*. Writing prompts set goals for what students need to accomplish: Write an argument and adequately support it. Thus, students plan their responses based on what they will do as a writer: Introduce the topic, state a claim, support the claim with several arguments, use information from the passages as support for each argument, and conclude. These writing actions achieve goals (Chandrasegaran & Schaetzel, 2004; Flower & Hayes, 1981) so that when students are writing, "instead of concentrating on 'What to say' in an essay, the student writing with a rhetorical approach plans 'What to do'" (Chandrasegaran & Schaetzel, 2004, p. 33). If students identify what they are doing when they write each part of their responses, they think about writing as doing, rather than as filling pages with words.

230 Preparing Adult English Learners

If a student has answered the prompt and analyzed the reading passages, their arguments, and support, the written response will follow the structure of a typical argument:

1. my claim/the author with the strongest claim
2. strong argument(s) and its/their support (from the reading passages)
3. weak argument(s) and explanation(s) of why it is that they are weak (from the reading passages)
4. conclusion

This is not to say that students must address both strong and weak arguments in their responses. They choose the arguments and their support from the passages that best substantiate the claim they are making.

Moreover, we are not suggesting that teachers neglect sentence-level writing issues that often interfere with English learners' ability to develop persuasive arguments. By focusing on teaching and developing the underlying thinking processes for academic and professional writing, we give purpose to writing and motivate students to apply what we teach them about the mechanics of writing, paragraph organization, sentence structure, grammar, and vocabulary. Thus, we need to teach thinking processes and writing skills simultaneously.

■ Concluding Thoughts

If students acquire the Habits of Mind to answer a read-to-write prompt, to analyze the prompt and readings, and to organize a written response, they will pass their high school equivalency read-to-write test and be well prepared for other academic tasks. By beginning to teach students academic Habits of Mind early in their classes and at all levels of English language proficiency, teachers give them the ability and confidence to pass their high school equivalency test and be successful learners in higher education.

———— **Questions for Reflection and Application** ————

1. When you write for academic purposes, which Habits of Mind do you use in your reading, analyzing, and writing processes?

2. Which Habits of Mind do you believe are most difficult for your students? What could you incorporate into your lessons to develop these Habits of Mind more thoroughly?

3. What are ways you can externalize, model, or scaffold and make apparent the Habits of Mind that students are learning?

References

Adams, C. (2015, May). GED revisions spur bumpy year for equivalency exams. *Education Week, 34*(29), 9. https://www.edweek.org/ew/articles/2015/05/01/more-rigorous-ged-spurs-jitters-competition.html

Bean, J.C. (2011). *Engaging ideas: The professor's guide to integrating writing, critical thinking, and active learning in the classroom.* San Francisco: Jossey-Bass.

Bean, J.C., Chappell, V., & Gillam, A. (2011). *Reading rhetorically* (3rd ed.) New York: Longman.

Braine, G. (1989). Writing in science and technology: An analysis of assignments from ten undergraduate courses. *English for Specific Purposes 8,* 3–15.

Bruffee, K.A. (1993). *Collaborative learning: Higher education, interdependence, and the authority of knowledge.* Baltimore, MD: Johns Hopkins University Press.

Carson, J. (2001). A task analysis of reading and writing in academic contexts. In D. Belcher & A. Hirvela (Eds.), *Linking literacies: Perspectives on L2 reading-writing connections* (pp. 246–270). Ann Arbor: University of Michigan Press.

Chandrasegaran, A., & Schaetzel, K. (2004). *Think your way to effective writing.* Singapore: Pearson Education.

Coon, D. A., & Jacobsen, N. (2014). *Community college writing programs: Defining success for the immigrant student population.* Washington, DC: Center for Applied Linguistics.

Council of Writing Program Administrators, National Council of Teachers of English, & National Writing Project. (2011). *Framework for success in postsecondary writing.* http://wpacouncil.org/files/framework-for-success-postsecondary-writing.pdf

Cumming, A. (1997). Assessing writing. In C. Clapham & D. Corson (Eds.), *Encyclopedia of language and education: Language testing and assessment* (pp. 51–63). Dordrecht, The Netherlands: Kluwer.

Elbow, P. (1973). *Writing without teachers.* New York: Oxford University Press.

Elbow, P. (1986). *Embracing contraries: Explorations in learning and teaching.* New York: Oxford University Press.

Ericsson, P. F. (2005). Celebrating through interrogation: Considering the outcomes statement through theoretical lenses. In S. Harrington, K. Rhodes, R.O. Fischer, & R. Malenczyk (Eds.) *The outcomes book debate and consensus after the WPA Outcomes Statement* (pp. 104–117). Logan: Utah State University Press.

Faught. B. (2006, November). A history of the exam. *Maclean's, 119*(45), 53.

Fernández, R., Peyton, J. K., & Schaetzel, K. (2017, Summer). A survey of writing instruction in adult ESL programs: Are teaching practices meeting adult learner needs? *Journal of Research and Practice for Adult Literacy, Secondary, and Basic Education, 6*(2), 5–20.

Flower, L., & Hayes, J.R. (1981). A cognitive process theory of writing. *College Composition and Communication, 32*(4), 365–387.

GED Testing Service. Sample extended response passages and prompts for classroom practice – RLA. https://ged.com/wp-content/uploads/extended_response_classroom_practice.pdf

Grabe, W. P., & Stoller, F. L. (2013). *Teaching and researching: Reading* (2nd ed.). Routledge.

Hirvela, A. (2016). *Connecting reading & writing in second language writing instruction* (2nd ed.). Ann Arbor: University of Michigan Press.

Horowitz, D. (1986). What professors actually require: Academic tasks for the ESL classroom. *TESOL Quarterly, 20*(3), 445–462.

Johnson, K. (2013). Beyond standards: Disciplinary and national perspectives on habits of mind. *College Composition and Communication, 64*(3), 517–541.

Koda, K. (2005). *Insights into second language reading: A cross-linguistic approach.* New York: Cambridge University Press.

Lumley, T. (2005). *Assessing second language writing: The rater's perspective.* Frankfurt, Germany: Peter Lang.

Plakans, L. (2008). Comparing composing processes in write-only and reading-to-write test tasks. *Assessing Writing, 13*, 111–129.

Ramage, J.D., Bean, J.C., & Johnson, J. (2009). *The Allyn and Bacon guide to writing* (5th ed.). New York: Longman.

Ramage, J.D., Bean, J.C., & Johnson, J. (2011). *Writing arguments: A rhetoric with readings.* Boston: Pearson Education.

Stoynoff, S., & Chapelle, C.A. (2005). *ESOL tests and testing.* Alexandria, VA: Teachers of English to Speakers of Other Languages.

Weigle, S. (2004). Integrating reading and writing in a competency test for non-native speakers of English. *Assessing Writing, 9,* 27–55.

Zinth, J. (2015). GED, HiSET and TASC Test: A comparison of high school equivalency assessments. *Education Trends.* Denver: Education Commission of the States. https://www.ecs.org/ged-hiset-and-tasc-a-comparison-of-high-school-equivalency-assessments/

Chapter 10

Teaching Writing in an Age of Standards

Gilda Rubio-Festa,
North Carolina Community College System

Opening Questions

1. How can standards-based instruction ensure that adult English language learners can compete for 21st century jobs?

2. How can standards-based instruction inform writing instruction to accelerate adult learners' progress to post-secondary education and into the job market?

3. How can writing activities be aligned with English language proficiency standards to develop writing skills that transfer to academic contexts?

Whether in North America or Europe, adult English language programs aim to improve the economic mobility and job preparedness of adults learning English. Research by the Organization for Economic Cooperation and Development (OECD) indicates that the key for integration into the labor pool is learning the language of the host country (OECD, 2014). Ensuring that these adult learners acquire English language skills that will equip them for the 21st century workforce requires designing instruction that facilitates English language acquisition and builds content-specific knowledge necessary to enter vocational or occupational training (see discussion in Chapter 2).

In the United States, adult education programs have recently been tasked not only with teaching English to immigrant students but also with preparing them for post-secondary education and training opportunities that help address the nation's labor shortages (Carnevale, Smith, & Strohl, 2014). According to the Washington Student Achievement Council (2015), U.S. employers in key industry sectors—business, management, and sales and service occupations—claim the greatest need for workers in middle-skill jobs, which require some form of post-secondary education (p. 11). Many states have chosen to address this skills gap by investing in education for the immigrant workforce (National Skills Coalition, 2017).

To meet labor demands and projected job growth, the federal government overhauled its public workforce development system in 2014 by passing the Workforce Innovation and Opportunity Act (WIOA). The legislation supports the use of instructional models that prepare adults, including those learning English, for transition to college and careers. Under Title II of WIOA—also known as the Adult Education and Family Literacy Act (AEFLA), a major funder of state adult education programs—instruction must be aligned with state-adopted national standards, which refers to the College and Career Readiness Standards (CCRS) for Adult Education (U.S. Department of Education, 2013, 2017). For teachers, aligning instruction to the standards requires in-depth knowledge of the standards and support to develop lessons aligned with them. This is particularly challenging in adult education programs, where 80 percent of teachers work part time (National Council of State Directors of Adult Education, 2016).

This chapter provides an overview of standards-based education in the United States, which has sought to create a coherent approach to instruction and assessment and to measure outcomes. Standards-based reforms have responded to the need for students to be college and career ready as they leave secondary education. This goal is linked to having a workforce that meets national demands and is globally competitive. Next, the chapter explores the impact of standards-based instruction in federally funded U.S. adult English language programs on learning and outcomes by requiring a focus on preparing adult learners to develop the skills needed for high school equivalency credentials and for transitioning to college and advancing in careers. Finally, to illustrate how standards can be used by adult ESL teachers in the United States and in programs in other countries, a teaching and learning scenario is presented that uses the English Language Proficiency (ELP) Standards as a guide for developing the writing skills that adult learners need.

■ Standards-Based Education in the United States

Standards-based education (SBE) refers to educational reforms that seek to improve student achievement by connecting essential components of the education system to a common set of goals and observable results (Buttram & Waters, 1997). In practice, the shift in focus from inputs to outputs created by SBE requires that teachers connect learning activities with assessments to demonstrate what a learner is able to do as a result of instruction. Standards-based instructional planning, therefore, involves backward design, starting with end goals and developing lesson plans and activities accordingly.

The standards-based education reform movement in the United States (Buttram & Waters, 1997) was bolstered by a highly publicized and controversial 1983 report, *A Nation at Risk* (National Commission on Excellence in Education), which argued that the U.S. education system was in a state of decline and that the future of the nation was at stake (Marzano & Kendall, 1998). The report gave several recommendations for improving the education system, including the need for more rigor, new academic standards, and greater accountability for student performance. In the years following its publication, private businesses and corporations also became invested in the state of the nation's education system. Some employers began to address gaps in employees' basic skills by offering their own courses in reading, writing, and math, while others lobbied for increases in the government's educational spending. Still others provided grant funding to support school and teacher innovation. At the same time, individual states began increasing academic standards, raising graduation requirements, and creating policies to increase student engagement (PBS Online, 2002). Of these efforts, creating standards was thought to be important in promoting educational equity. Because standards inform curricula and lesson development, students, no matter where they study, are instructed on and expected to meet the same standards. By leveling the playing field, standards are critical in countering the decline predicted in *A Nation at Risk*.

By 2000, most states had started to develop their own academic standards, but disparities between the educational outcomes of the nation's growing minority and majority student populations needed to be addressed more directly. The 2001 No Child Left Behind Act (NCLB) emphasized improving student achievement and closing achievement gaps by holding schools responsible for meeting proficiency standards (U.S. Commission on Civil Rights, 2004). Recognizing the unique needs of English language learners (described in Short, 2000), NCLB held states accountable for developing the English proficiency of students learning English, so that they could develop the English proficiency levels needed to make progress in essential content areas and succeed in academic contexts and the workplace (Bailey, Butler, & Sato, 2005).

NCLB was criticized in the education community for its over-reliance on standardized testing at the expense of student learning (Kolodziej, 2011; McDonnell, 2005). Some believed that it "unfairly held schools responsible for resolving educational problems that have their roots elsewhere, in broader social ills like poverty" (McGuinn, 2016, p. 393). Attempting a new strategy, the federal government rolled back its role in K–12 education in 2015 and provided financial incentives for state reforms, including the adoption of the Common Core State Standards (CCSS), which had been developed by a nonpartisan team of educators and policymakers.

As with other standards, the main goal of the CCSS was to support student college and career readiness. With respect to English literacy, the authors of the English Language Arts Standards (a component of the CCSS with a focus on learning English) clarified their intention:

> The skills and knowledge captured in the ELA/literacy standards are designed to prepare students for life outside the classroom. They include critical-thinking skills and the ability to closely and attentively read texts in a way that will help them understand and enjoy complex works of literature. Students will learn to use cogent reasoning and evidence collection skills that are essential for success in college, career, and life. The standards also lay out a vision of what it means to be a literate person who is prepared for success in the 21st century. (Common Core State Standards Initiative, 2018)

These standards help solidify what to include in ESL adult education curricula to prepare adult learners for work and further education.

The CCSS reflect the official mission of the U.S. Department of Education (2017): to "promote student achievement and preparation for global competitiveness by fostering educational excellence and ensuring equal access." In practice, the Department of Education's role has tended to be one of ensuring and providing funding for equal access to free, high-quality education for all students and of supporting the improvement of state and local systems through financial incentives and dissemination of research (Thomas & Brady, 2005). In adult education, systemic reforms, such as a new CCSS-aligned high school equivalency exam (see discussion in Chapter 9), and funding formulas focus on student progress toward college-and-career readiness, and the CCSS have been adapted and continue to guide instruction.

■ Standards-Based Instruction in Adult Education

Standards such as the Comprehensive Adult Student Assessment System (CASAS) and Equipped for the Future (EFF) content standards have long been a reference point for adult education programs (Cunningham Flores, 2005). As the field has shifted beyond a focus on life skills and sought to better align curricula with post-secondary and career readiness, the guidance provided by these standards did not seem sufficient. In 2003, the Office of Vocational and Adult Education (OVAE) funded a project to assist states in the development of content standards and implementation of standards-based instruction, with the goal of improving accountability and academic outcomes (U.S. Department of Education, 2004).

The next major initiative to support standards-based instruction was the development of the College and Career Readiness Standards for Adult Education (U.S. Department of Education, 2013). These standards clearly define what adult education students should be able to do to succeed in academic settings and job training and for full civic participation. They are based on the Common Core State Standards (CCSS), which, for example, require that teachers select texts that include academic language and develop activities for academic engagement so that texts and activities serve the dual purpose of building knowledge and improving academic literacy.

To address English language learners' needs, the U.S. Department of Education's Office of Career, Technical, and Adult Education (OCTAE, formerly OVAE) disseminated the English Language Proficiency Standards for Adult Education (2016). The ELP Standards support the development of academic language to prepare adults learning English for college and careers, and they outline the language demands needed to access or meet the CCR Standards. In summary, these standards outline the need and suggest a process for developing the English language skills needed to build knowledge across academic areas and within workplace contexts.

■ Aligning the ELP Standards with Writing Instruction

The ELP Standards are based on principles that reflect current views of language development and instruction (U.S. Department of Education, 2016). To ensure that adults learning English are prepared for academic and workforce success, instruction needs to focus on making content accessible. The ELP standards (1) acknowledge that instruction needs to respect and account for adult learners' diverse life experiences, work skills, and motivation and (2) ensure that adults learning English have the same opportunities that native English-speaking students in the program have to prepare for transitions to college and the workforce. The standards include specific reference to the "key instructional advances" found in the English Language Arts Standards. For example, they emphasize regular opportunities to work with academic texts so that students have exposure to and practice with vocabulary used across disciplines. This includes developing instructional strategies involving reading and writing informational and academic texts, combining information from multiple texts (Grabe & Zhang, 2013), and working with "sequenced texts to build knowledge about a topic" (U.S. Department of Education, Office of Vocational and Adult Education, 2013). The principles underlying the standards encourage instruction that gives students time to think about and connect with the content of and have adequate practice with selected texts. Instruction needs to "slow down for learning, thinking, and language" (Daro, 2012, p. viii).

The ELP Standards describe the English language skills that adults learning English need to master to have access to and succeed in academic and workplace contexts. They are organized to support adult learners from beginning to advanced levels with ten anchor standards, a general set of skills that students need to know for college and career readiness, organized into two groups. Standards 1–7 describe reading, writing, listening, speaking, and integrated skills that learners need to be able to access and succeed in as they receive instruction that is aligned to academic content standards. Standards 8–10 describe the language structures that learners also need to be able to use to participate in instruction aligned with the standards. Each anchor standard is supported by five level descriptors. The level descriptors guide instruction, so that it can be planned for all levels of English proficiency. The anchor standards, those generally needed for college and career readiness (English Language Proficiency Standards, p. 74) are shown in Figure 10.1.

The ELP Anchor Standards for adult education present writing in an integrated fashion, along with other language skills and content

Figure 10.1   Learner Skills and Language Modalities in Anchor English Language Proficiency Standards for Adult Education, 2016

ELP Standard	Learner Skills	Modalities
1	Learners can use listening and reading skills to understand and engage with oral presentations or texts.	Receptive skills
2	Learners can use all skills to exchange information, present analysis, or to respond to questions.	Interaction of receptive and productive skills
3	Learners can use writing and speaking skills to respond to texts.	Productive skills
4	Learners can use writing and speaking skills to support evidence-based arguments.	Productive skills
5	Learners can use all skills to research, evaluate information, and organize findings.	Interaction of receptive and productive skills
6	Learners use all skills to identify and critique a point of view.	Interaction of receptive and productive skills
7	Learners can use a range of speaking and writing skills to match task, purpose, and audience.	Productive skills
8	Learners can apply appropriate strategies to infer the meaning of words and phrases in oral presentations and literary and information texts.	Receptive skills
9	Learners can produce clear and coherent level-appropriate speech and text.	Linguistic structures
10	Learners can communicate orally and in writing using standard English conventions.	Linguistic structures

material. They focus on balancing receptive and productive skills so that teachers will support the development both of students' ability to understand and produce oral and written language (p. 15). These standards are broken down further into specific reading, writing, speaking, listening, and language standards. The ELP Anchor Standards for Writing are shown in Figure 10.2.

We have added CCR Writing Standards 4 and 10 from the CCR Anchor Standards for Writing in the CCSS (National Governors Association Center for Best Practices, 2010) for the sake of coherence. The language of CCR Anchor Standards 4 appears under the broader ELP Standards for Adult Education (ELP Standard 9); the language of CCR Anchor Standard for Writing 10 in the CCSS, however, does not appear in the ELP Standards for Adult Education. We have included it because it reflects sound instructional writing practices—such as process writing, reading-to-write, content-based instruction, collaborative writing, and multimodal writing—supported by the contributors to this volume. The next section provides an example for developing a standards-based unit of study.

◼ Classroom Scenario: Developing a Standards-Based Instructional Unit in an Adult Education Program

This classroom scenario shows how an instructor or a program can use the ELP Standards to develop the academic writing skills that adults need to succeed in post-secondary instruction and the workplace, and how aligning writing instruction to the standards gives coherence to a writing curriculum so that adult learners, who often have limited time to attend classes, are able to reach their goals.

Elizabeth teaches in a federally and state-funded adult education program that serves more than 1,000 English language learners a year. It is in an urban location and offers five levels of instruction. To meet funding requirements, the program must report students' progress and meet certain benchmarks. Another requirement is that instruction

Figure 10.2   College and Career Readiness (CCR) Anchor Standards for Writing from ELP Standards for Adult Education and Common Core State Standards (National Governors Association Center for Best Practices, 2010)

CCR Anchor Writing Standard	Writing Skills	Instructional Categories
1	Write arguments to support claims in an analysis of substantive topics or texts, using valid reasoning and relevant and sufficient evidence.	Text types and purposes
2	Write informative/explanatory texts to examine and convey complex ideas and information clearly and accurately through the effective selection, organization, and analysis of content. [This includes the narration of historical events, scientific procedures/experiments, or technical processes.]	
3	Write narratives to develop real or imagined experiences or events using effective technique, well-chosen details, and well-structured event sequences.	
4	Produce clear and coherent writing in which the development, organization, and style are appropriate to task, purpose, and audience.	Production and distribution of writing
5	Develop and strengthen writing as needed by planning, revising, editing, rewriting, or trying a new approach.	
6	Use technology, including the internet, to produce and publish writing and to interact and collaborate with others.	
7	Conduct short as well as more sustained research projects based on focused questions, demonstrating understanding of the subject under investigation.	Research to build and present knowledge
8	Gather relevant information from multiple print and digital sources, assess the credibility and accuracy of each source, and integrate the information while avoiding plagiarism.	
9	Draw evidence from literary or informational texts to support analysis, reflection, and research.	
10	Write routinely over extended time frames (time for research, reflection, and revision) and shorter time frames (a single sitting or a day or two) for a range of tasks, purposes, and audiences.	Range of writing

must be aligned with the state's academic content standards. When students are enrolled, they must set career goals and know the types and levels of education required to achieve those goals. To support the transition to post-secondary education, the program offers a high-intermediate ESL writing class. The overall goal of the class is to improve students' academic language skills, so that they can transition into a credit-bearing career pathways program (Withington et al., 2012). The class uses a textbook that focuses on language forms and grammar. This term, Elizabeth will align her instruction with the ELP Standards to ensure that her instruction will give students practice with the academic writing and reading that is expected. Elizabeth's goal is to help students improve their language skills and vocabulary around career clusters while they develop writing skills that include using evidence from texts. Next, she selects the standard that focuses on writing—in this case, Standard 3 (shown in Figure 10.3)—and reviews the level descriptors to select the level that is most appropriate for the class's proficiency.

In this example, Elizabeth selects ELP Standard 3 and Level Descriptor 4. She organizes her lesson into a four-week unit, which allows class time for sustained writing practice and in-depth study of content. Building in class time for writing practice serves adult education students who face multiple barriers to regular attendance, such as lack of affordable childcare or an inflexible work schedule. Elizabeth uses a content-based approach, in which students learn about different careers and then write about their experiences in exploring career choices. (See Chapter 2 for a discussion of content-based instruction.) Using this approach helps Elizabeth incorporate the key instructional strategies of exposing students to content-rich text, providing regular practice with text complexity, and developing reading and writing skills that require referring to a text that has been read. Elizabeth operationalizes the standard by creating unit objectives, skill objectives, writing tasks, and assessments. She also surveys her students to identify careers that are of most interest to them, a recommended practice for adult learners: "Because adults need to know why they are learning something, effective teachers explain their reasons for teaching specific skills" (Teaching Excellence in Adult Literacy, 2011, p. 1).

Figure 10.3 English Language Proficiency Standards for Adult Education, Standard 3 Level 1–5 Descriptors (U.S. Department of Education, 2016)

ELP Standard 3	Level 1	Level 2	Level 3	Level 4	Level 5
An ELL can...	By the end of English language proficiency level one, an ELL can...	By the end of English language proficiency level two, an ELL can...with support	By the end of English language proficiency level three, an ELL can...with support	By the end of English language proficiency level four, an ELL can...	By the end of English language proficiency level five, an ELL can...
speak and write about level-appropriate complex literary and informational texts and topics.	◘ communicate information and feelings about familiar texts, topics, and experiences.	◘ deliver short oral presentations ◘ compose simple written narratives and informational texts about familiar texts, topics, experiences, and events.	◘ deliver short oral presentations ◘ compose written informational texts ◘ develop the topic with a few details about familiar texts, topics, and events.	◘ deliver oral presentations ◘ compose written informational texts ◘ develop the topic with some relevant details, concepts, examples, and information ◘ integrate graphics or multimedia when useful about a variety of texts, topics, or events.	◘ deliver oral presentations ◘ compose written informational texts ◘ fully develop the topic with some relevant details, concepts, examples, and information ◘ integrate graphics or multimedia when useful about a variety of texts, topics, or events.

Next, Elizabeth collects and analyzes texts that will be used to build students' knowledge of the topic. She uses authentic texts, such as instruction manuals, brochures, and training guides, to create problem-solving tasks (Ellis, 2003) that require authentic responses. Adhering to the ELP principles, she plans for the pre-teaching of vocabulary and other supports that she will need to provide so that learners can complete the tasks successfully. She creates writing tasks and sequences them so that learners can follow the thread to construct meaning related to their life experiences and goals (Teaching Excellence in Adult Literacy, 2011). She builds in time for students to go through the writing process from planning to drafting to revising to publishing. Elizabeth's planning process and the four-week unit plan are shown in Figure 10.4. In this scenario, Elizabeth aligned her instruction with the ELP Standards to develop the writing skills

Figure 10.4   Elizabeth's Unit Aligned with the ELP Standards

Unit Lesson Plan – 4 Weeks Selecting Your Career Path ELP Standard 3, Level Descriptor 4	
ELP Standard: Anchor 3. An ELL can speak and write about level-appropriate complex literary and informational texts and topics. **Level Descriptor 4.** An ELL can compose written information texts and develop the topic with some relevant details, concepts, examples, and information about a variety of texts, topics, and events.	
1. Develop Assessment	**Notes**
■ Learners will describe the writing process orally. ■ Learners will apply the writing process by producing an informational report on career exploration.	Elizabeth's learning outcomes—what she wants learners to be able to do by the end of the unit—target cognitive as well as writing skills. She wants her students not only to demonstrate the basic cognitive ability to describe a process but also to develop the higher-level cognitive ability to apply this skill.
2. Write Unit Objectives	**Notes**
■ Content Objectives: Learners will select a career using objective criteria that include education, wages, key job knowledge and abilities, and a career path. ■ Language Objectives: a) Learners will use transition words to demonstrate the relationship between ideas and to subordinate one idea to another; b) Learners will be able to use career- related vocabulary words to complete a career inventory assessment.	Elizabeth develops her learning objectives for the unit using a content-based approach, which requires both content and language objectives.
3. Select Materials	**Notes**
■ Locate various informational texts on career exploration for intensive reading to develop comprehension skills. ■ Provide longer-length material for extensive reading and a career-related video to build background knowledge and receptive skills (Carrell & Carson, 1997; Day & Bamford, 2002).	Connecting reading to writing, Elizabeth selects texts with different formats. She includes news articles, industry websites, journal articles, and textbooks. She will also help students select a text for extensive reading. She will give 10 minutes of class time for this activity.
4. Develop Pre-Teaching Activities	**Notes**
■ Identify a list of vocabulary, highlighting "career" type vocabulary. ■ Select common grammatical features, transition words, and phrases from the readings and other source materials. ■ Use graphic organizers to teach the writing process.	Elizabeth will scaffold learning in the unit by pre-teaching vocabulary and introducing strategies for self-directed vocabulary study (Decarrico, 2001).

Figure 10.4 (Continued)   Elizabeth's Unit Aligned with the ELP
Standards

5. Select and Sequence Tasks	Notes

▣ Introduce Career Clusters: Career Clusters Career One Stop, U.S. Department of Labor (videos about different careers) https://www. careeronestop.org/videos/careervideos/ career-videos.aspx
▣ Assign a Quick-Write: Give students five minutes to write about occupations viewed in the video.
▣ Have Students Read/Write: Students to read a *New York Times* article on middle skill jobs.
▣ Lead a Guided Composition Activity: Students write a paragraph that explains middle-skill jobs in the U.S. labor market, as presented in the article.
▣ Write a Longer Piece:
 • Students read a *Wall Street Journal* article to learn about job fairs.
 • Students cluster ideas, gathering information from the article.
 • Students write a three-paragraph informational essay about why job fairs are useful (what information they provide about jobs)
 • They follow this process:
  1. Outline
  2. Draft
  3. Writing conference
  4. Revise
  5. Publish
	Elizabeth develops activities and sequences them so that learners build background knowledge. She uses multiple sources of information, including federal websites, videos, and news articles. To help learners focus on purpose, organization, facts, and examples, she scaffolds reading activities with a series of questions. Finally, she guides learners in constructing a paragraph that they can use to reinforce content and vocabulary.

essential for post-secondary and workplace success. The first step was to become familiar with the standards' purpose, rationale, content, and organization. A foundation in her planning was to incorporate key instructional strategies, such as using information-rich and increasingly complex texts as the basis for reading and writing and sequencing activities that provide enough support so that students experience success with the tasks. Elizabeth used a content-based approach, so that activities were contextualized around careers. She used authentic materials, such as a career video, and provided supporting activities so learners could engage meaningfully with the material.

This unit took learners through the writing process, a skill that they can transfer to academic and workplace settings. It provided them with valuable knowledge about different careers, a topic that learners need to make important life decisions. Using the ELP Standards as a guide provided a clear scope for work that allowed her, as the teacher, and the students to understand what the class will be doing, why they will be doing it, and the expectations for success.

■ Concluding Thoughts

Standards have been part of education reform in the United States for many decades. The U.S. Department of Education's Office of Career, Technical and Adult Education has a history of supporting development and implementation of standards that emphasize results and connect the teaching and learning processes, professional development, and assessments. With a set of common expectations for what students should know and be able to do at each level, instruction is developed in line with clear goals, affording all students opportunities for success. The CCR Standards have set out clearly the knowledge and skills required for college and career readiness. The ELP Standards provide an outline of the academic language needed so that learners can meet the CCR Standards and a framework of instructional strategies that engage learners in academic literacy tasks similar to those required in academic and workplace contexts. These standards provide a coherent approach to developing a curriculum or units focused on writing, a skill often neglected in adult education programs (Fernández, Peyton, & Schaetzel, 2017). For many adult learners with limited time to attend classes, standards-based instruction yields benefits in the least amount of time by allowing instruction that is focused on language development and content-specific knowledge at the same time.

This chapter provides the rationale for and a demonstration of a unit that aligns instruction with the ELP Standards. The classroom scenario and unit plan illustrate how an instructor can unpack the ELP Standards to create meaningful instruction that incorporates reading and writing and supports college and workplace readiness. English language learners, who represent about 40 percent of the students served in federally and state-funded adult education programs, need the college and career readiness skills that are requisite to participating fully in the 21st century economy (U.S. Department of Education, 2016).

Implementation of standards-based instruction in adult education programs improves the academic rigor of instruction and can accelerate adult learners' transitions to post-secondary programs and the workplace. However, broad support from policymakers, administrators, professional development staff, and teachers is crucial for sustainability. It is especially important for funding to be allocated to a professional development system that ensures that both full-time and part-time teachers can participate. Finally, we need more research to understand best practices for instruction aligned to these ELP Standards, so that programs have research-based models that can be replicated.

Questions for Reflection and Application

1. The goal of the ELP Standards for reading and writing instruction is to prepare students for access to and success in post-secondary education. Adult English language learners, however, have immediate needs to use literacy skills to meet the demands of their lives. How can we help adult learners understand and transfer these academic writing skills to other areas of their lives, such as workplace communication, or in their roles as parents and community members?

2. Teachers using standards-based instruction need to have the tools, strategies, and knowledge of methods and approaches to teach reading and writing well, aligned with the standards. What beliefs and methods do you tend to draw from in planning instruction, and how will this affect your work in shifting to standards-aligned instruction?

3. The instruction of English in adult education programs needs to shift its focus to developing language skills and knowledge, so that students can access and engage in content learning across disciplines. This shift requires training and continuous professional development. What can program administrators do to ensure that teachers have support and engagement as they adopt new practices?

References

Bailey, A., Butler, F., & Sato, E. (2005). *Standards-to-standards linkage under Title III: Exploring common language demands in ELD and science standards.* Los Angeles: Center for the Study of Evaluation.

Buttram, J., & Waters, T. (1997). Improving America's schools through standards-based education. Introduction. *NASSP Bulletin, 81*(590), 1–6. https://eric.ed.gov/?id=EJ550491

Carnevale, P. M., Smith, N., & Strohl, J. (2014). *Recovery: Job growth and education requirements through 2020.* https://cew.georgetown.edu/cew-reports/recovery-job-growth-and-education-requirements-through-2020

Carrell, P. L., & Carson, J. G. (1997). Extensive and intensive reading in an EAP setting. *English for Specific Purposes, 16*(1), 47–60.

Common Core State Standards Initiative. (2018). *English language arts standards, anchor standards, college and career readiness anchor standards for writing.* http://www.corestandards.org/ELA-Literacy/CCRA/W

Cunningham Flores, M. (2005). *Content standards in adult education.* Washington, DC: Center for Applied Linguistics. http://www.cal.org/caela/esl_resources/bibliographies/constanbib.html

Daro, P. (2012). *Challenges and opportunities for language learning in the context of Common Core State Standards and Next Generation Science Standards.* Proceedings from Understanding Language: Language, Literacy, and Learning in the Content Areas. Stanford, CA: Stanford University. http://ell.stanford.edu/sites/default/files/Conference%20Summary_0.pdf

Day, R., & Bamford, J. (2002). Top ten principles for teaching extensive reading. *Reading in a Foreign Language, 14*(2), 136–141.

Decarrico, J. S. (2001). Vocabulary learning and teaching. *Teaching English as a Second or Foreign Language, 3*, 285–299.

Ellis, R. (2003). *Task-based language learning and teaching.* New York: Oxford University Press.

Fernández, R., Peyton, J. K., & Schaetzel, K. (2017). A survey of writing instruction in adult ESL programs: Are teaching practices meeting adult learner needs? *Journal of Research and Practice for Adult Literacy, Secondary, and Basic Education, 6*(2), 5–20.

Grabe, W., & Zhang, C. (2013). Reading and writing together: A critical component of English for academic purposes teaching and learning. *TESOL Journal, 4*(1), 9–24. https://www.rand.org/content/dam/rand/pubs/reprints/2009/RAND_RP1384.pdf

Kolodziej, T. (2011). The benefits and detriments of the No Child Left Behind Act. *ESSAI, 9*(1), 21.

Lyons, L. (2014, October 29). *Teachers favor Common Core Standards, not the testing.* Gallup Organization. https://news.gallup.com/poll/178997/teachers-favor-common-core-standards-not-testing.aspx

Marzano, R. J., & Kendall, J. S. (1998). *Implementing standards-based education.* Washington DC: National Education Association.

McDonnell, L. M. (2005). No Child Left Behind and the federal role in education: Evolution or revolution? *Peabody Journal of Education, 80*(2), 19–38.

McGuinn, P. (2016, July). From No Child Left behind to the Every Student Succeeds Act: Federalism and the education legacy of the Obama Administration. *Publius: The Journal of Federalism, 46*(3), 392–415.

National Commission on Excellence in Education. (1983). *A nation at risk: The imperative for educational reform.* Washington, DC: U.S. Department of Education. https://www.edreform.com/wp-content/uploads/2013/02/A_Nation_At_Risk_1983.pdf

National Council of State Directors of Adult Education. (2016). *The blue book.* Washington, DC: NCSDAE. http://www.naepdc.org

National Governors Association Center for Best Practices. (2010). *Common Core State Standards for English/Language Arts—College and Career Readiness Anchor Standards for Writing.* Washington, DC: Council of Chief State School Officers. http://www.corestandards.org/ELA-Literacy/CCRA/W

National Skills Coalition. (2017). *Middle skills job fact sheets.* Washington, DC: Author. https://nationalskillscoalition.org/state-policy/fact-sheets

OECD. (2014, December). How can migrants' skills be put to use? *Migration Policy Debates, 3.* http://www.oecd.org/els/mig/migration-policy-debates-3.pdf

PBS Online. (2002). Are we there yet? *Frontline.* https://www.pbs.org/wgbh/pages/frontline/shows/schools/standards/bp.html

Reynolds, K. M. (2017). Strategic curriculum planning: Standards and objectives in content-based instruction. In M. A. Snow & D. M. Brinton (Eds.), *The content-based classroom: New perspectives on integrating language and content* (2nd ed., pp. 67–78). Ann Arbor: University of Michigan Press.

Schmidt, W. H., Houang, R. T., & Shakrani, S. (2009). *International lessons about national standards.* Washington, DC: The Thomas B. Fordham Institute.

Short, D. J. (2000). *The ESL standards: Bridging the academic gap for English language learners.* ERIC Digest. Washington DC: Center for Applied Linguistics. http://www.cal.org/content/search?SearchText=The+ESL+Standards

Snow, M. A., & Brinton, D. M. (Eds.) (2017). *The content-based classroom: New perspectives on integrating language and content* (2nd ed.). Ann Arbor: University of Michigan Press.

Teaching Excellence in Adult Literacy (TEAL). (2011). *Adult learning theories: Fact Sheet No. 11.* Washington, DC: Author. https://lincs.ed.gov/state-resources/federal-initiatives/teal/guide/adultlearning

Thomas, J. Y., & Brady, K. P. (2005). Chapter 3: The Elementary and Secondary Education Act at 40: Equity, accountability, and the evolving federal role in public education. *Review of Research in Education, 29*(1), 51-67. https://www.researchgate.net/publication/250185409_Chapter_3_The_Elementary_and_Secondary_Education_Act_at_40_Equity_Accountability_and_the_Evolving_Federal_Role_in_Public_Education

U.S. Commission on Civil Rights, Office of the General Council. (2004). *Closing the achievement gap: The impact of standards-based education reform on student performance.* Washington, DC: Author. http://www.worldcat.org/title/closing-the-achievement-gap-the-impact-of-standards-based-education-reform-on-student-performance-draft-report-for-commissioners-review/oclc/55978829

U.S. Department of Education. (2017). *The federal role in education.* Washington, DC: Author. https://www2.ed.gov/about/overview/fed/role.html.

U.S. Department of Education. Office of Vocational and Adult Education. (2004). *Adult education content standards warehouse.* Washington, DC: Author. https://www2.ed.gov/rschstat/eval/sectech/factsheet/standards/2004.html.

U.S. Department of Education. Office of Career, Technical and Adult Education. (2013). *College and career readiness standards for adult education.* Washington, DC: Author. http://lincs.ed.gov/publications/pdf/CCRStandardsAdultEd.pdf

U.S. Department of Education. Office of Career, Technical and Adult Education. (2016). *English language proficiency standards for adult education.* Washington, DC: American Institutes for Research. https://lincs.ed.gov/publications/pdf/elp-standards-adult-ed.pdf

U.S. Department of Education. Office of Career, Technical and Adult Education. (2017). *Federal initiatives: Adult education and literacy.* Washington, DC: Author. https://www2.ed.gov/about/offices/list/ovae/pi/AdultEd/national-activities.html

Washington Student Achievement Council. (2015). *A skilled and educated workforce: 2015 update.* Olympia: State Board for Community and Technical Colleges and Workforce Training and Education Coordinating Board. http://wtb.wa.gov/Documents/SkilledandEducatedWorkforce2015.pdf

Withington, C., Hammond, C., Mobley, C., Stipanovic, N., Sharp, J. L., String-field, S., & Drew Jr, S. F. (2012). Implementing a statewide mandated career pathways/programs of study school reform model: Select findings from a multisite case study. *International Journal of Educational Reform, 21*(2), 138–158.

ADDITIONAL RESOURCES

- LiteracyWork International. ESOL Transition 2011.

  This document (http://literacywork.com/Literacywork.com/Welcome.html) provides information and resources for teachers focusing on college and career readiness for adults learning English

- Literacy Information and Communication System (LINCS).

  Funded by the U.S. Department of Education, Office of Career, Technical, and Adult Education (OCTAE), LINCS (https://lincs.ed.gov/state-resources) has a wealth of resources and tools for adult education instruction.

Epilogue:
Higher Expectations and
How to Meet Them

JoAnn (Jodi) Crandall,
University of Maryland, Baltimore County

This collection is a welcome addition to professional development texts for teachers and administrators in adult education, community college, or university programs who are preparing English learners to acquire the writing skills needed to be successful in academic, job-training, or workplace settings and to transition to college and career entry or advancement. The volume is also very timely, with the higher expectations placed on adult educators and learners by the College and Career Readiness Standards for Adult Education (U.S. Department of Education, 2013), the English Language Proficiency Standards for Adult Education (U.S. Department of Education, 2016), and the high school equivalency examinations aligned with these standards. The writing demands in these exams—the General Educational Development exam (GED), the High School Equivalency Test (HiSET), and the Test Assessing Secondary Completion (TASC)—as Schaetzel (Chapter 9) explains, require learners to respond to a prompt and write an argumentative essay after reading two texts within 30–60 minutes. Added expectations include the twenty-first century skills of critical thinking, communication, collaboration, and creativity, key skills for adults for post-secondary education and employment, especially in middle-skill jobs, which are most likely to provide a sustainable living wage (Trilling & Fadel, 2009). As Peyton, Schaetzel, and Fernández explain in the Introduction, "The communicative demands of the twenty-first century workplace have led to a fundamental shift in the focus of adult education," requiring "high-level language skills, critical-thinking skills, computer literacy, and confidence" (p. 1). All of these higher-level skills are addressed in multiple ways in this collection.

■ A Structure for Needed Professional Development

Because these standards are relatively new, program managers and teachers may have had limited professional development on how to adapt their instruction to meet these much higher expectations, including those related to academic and professional writing. This collection is an excellent source for understanding the intent of the standards (especially as they apply to writing) and some ways to design and provide instruction aligned with them. Several authors describe activities that align with the standards, culminating in Chapter 10, where Rubio-Festa illustrates the process of using the standards as a starting point and then, through backward design, developing a four-week unit to prepare learners in a high-intermediate ESL writing class to transition to a credit-bearing career pathways program.

The editors have structured the text around "ten instructional approaches that have emerged from the research related to college and career readiness and standards that guide instruction" (Introduction, p. 11). The authors of these ten practices in teaching adult English learners are not only very knowledgeable about the research in their respective areas (including adult ESL, SLA, composition studies, writing-to-learn, reading, and educational and cognitive psychology) but also experienced teachers and curriculum developers who effectively translate that research into relevant instructional strategies that culminate in coherent lesson plans that are useful for immediate use by teachers in their classes and as models for the development of new lessons. Opening questions at the beginning of each chapter stimulate thought and guide the reading, and concluding reflection and application questions encourage reflection on teaching in light of the approaches and activities described. A list of print and media resources is also provided at the end of most of the chapters.

Within the chapters are examples of a number of different approaches to teaching writing to adult English learners (e.g., language experience, CBI, project- or problem-based learning) as well as a range of activities (e.g., quickwrites, dictogloss, jigsaw reading and listening, role plays, note-taking on a film or lecture, dialogue journals, graphic organizers, sentence- and paragraph-starters, interviews, surveys, internet research, oral or media presentations, as well as focus-on-form activities) at all levels of English proficiency, many of which are then integrated into the lesson plans in the chapter.

Through the structure of both the volume and the individual chapters, the editors have offered an excellent outline for professional development activities in a range of contexts (through study circles, workshops, or lesson study) as well as self-directed professional development, with recognition of the limited time for professional development available to adult educators, 80 percent of whom work part-time (National Council of State Directors of Adult Education, 2016, cited by Rubio-Festa) and often at more than one institution. The structure also makes it a potential textbook for teacher preparation courses in MA TESOL programs. I would have welcomed this text when I was teaching graduate courses in Teaching Advanced ESL Reading and Writing or Teaching Adult ESL.

A New Emphasis on Writing, Academic Content, and Computer Skills

As many of the contributors note, writing has been a neglected skill in classes for adult English learners, where the focus has been on oral communication and reading. This is not unique to adult education or adult ESL. For a variety of reasons—large classes, limited time, lack of confidence in one's own writing, and limited preparation for teaching writing—writing is a neglected skill in most ESL and EFL programs. It is not surprising, then, that the survey of and follow-up interviews with adult ESL instructors and program managers conducted by the volume editors (Fernández, Peyton, & Schaetzel, 2017;

Peyton & Schaetzel, 2016) found that, while they understood the need to prepare their learners to write "argumentative, technical, and informative texts" (p. 7), many felt challenged in teaching academic writing and needed professional development. The lack of attention to writing is also partially the result of the emphasis on listening and reading in standardized assessments and the time required to validly and reliably evaluate writing (and speaking).

Writing, when taught, has often been limited to initial literacy or very basic informational or personal writing (filling in forms, writing emails or simple descriptive or narrative paragraphs), rather than the more challenging academic writing. However, as several contributors demonstrate, it is possible to effectively connect oral and written communication to build academic and professional writing skills. Egan and Parrish (Chapter 8) illustrate through four sample lessons how oral skills can serve as a bridge to writing for learners at varied levels of English proficiency in a range of academic, career, and community civic contexts.

It is also possible, as Fernández (Chapter 1) explains, to turn the traditional emphasis on reading and oral skills in adult ESL classes to prioritizing writing. She demonstrates this through a number of activities and then integrates these into a writing-centered learning unit that can support reading (writing-for-reading) as well as speaking (writing-to-speak or speaking-to-write) and, at the same time, build learners' content knowledge, through writing-to-learn. Schaetzel (Chapter 9), in focusing on skills required to unlock the prompts in high school equivalency tests, also illustrates the value of teaching reading-to-write.

Many of the lessons in the collection follow a CBI model that draws on academic, career, or community content or contexts, demonstrating ways in which teachers and programs can help learners meet a major goal of adult education under the new standards: to build academic and workplace knowledge and skills "to succeed in academic settings and job training and for full civic participation" (Rubio-Festa, p. 239).

Brinton and Griner (Chapter 2) illustrate, in a unit on the Lewis and Clark Expedition, how academic content (an American history topic that is likely to be of interest to immigrants and refugees) and authentic materials (letters, journal entries, photos, biographies, and videos) can be used to build students' overall communication skills, including writing a persuasive personal application letter, a problem-solution paper, and a journal entry.

Wong's two-hour, low-beginning lesson for literacy-level learners (Chapter 7) introduces occupations and work schedules, noting that "English literacy is a skill that is best developed in a meaningful context that allows students to see connections between writing and meaning and between their tasks in the classroom and their lives outside it" (p. 185).

Included in the expected academic and workplace skills are those related to technology. Satin and Quann (Chapter 5) illustrate the role of technology in helping learners meet writing standards through a project that involves researching jobs online, gathering information from multiple print and media sources, assessing the credibility of these sources, and collaborating to develop the final presentation, which may be done through PowerPoint or Prezi.

◼ Writing as a Process and the Need for Scaffolding

Traditionally, writing has been taught from a product perspective: a writer completes a writing task of three or five paragraphs, which is then assessed. However, as Reynolds (Chapter 3) indicates, that is not how people actually write or how we should be teaching writing. He points out: "We frequently discover what we want or need to write while we are writing; we negotiate content and form with other people; and we might have multiple drafts . . . before we arrive at a document on which we are willing to put our name" (p. 75). Writing is more appropriately viewed and taught as a process, and Reynolds provides suggestions to help adult English learners understand and negotiate the various steps of the writing process.

Important in that process is the scaffolding and feedback provided by teachers or peers. Peyton (Chapter 4) discusses the role of graphic organizers (KWL charts and Venn diagrams) in helping learners develop informational, comparative, or argumentative writing. She also describes the value of dialogue journals in providing gradual writing support, helping to reduce writer anxiety and increasing writer confidence (while also mirroring the increasing collaboration in real-world writing, an important twenty-first century skill). When undertaken through email, WhatsApp, or other digital tools, dialogue journals can also develop computer communication skills.

Ferris (Chapter 6) also notes the importance of scaffolding throughout the writing process, focusing on effective feedback that "empowers" learners, rather than "demoralizing" them. She provides an extensive list of "effective, efficient, and empowering" ways for teachers to respond to developing writers, including with written commentary and one-on-one writing conferences (online or face-to-face). She also offers guidance on the focus of feedback at all stages of the writing process.

■ Teaching Learners with Limited Formal Education or Literacy

Adult English learners share their lack of preparation for college- and career-ready writing with their English-speaking peers, many of whom take developmental writing courses upon entering the community college. However, for those who are learning academic writing in another language, the challenge is obviously greater. And, as Wong (Chapter 7) and other contributors note, while writing may be difficult for any adult English learner, it is particularly challenging for those with limited formal education and/or literacy in their first language. They may have strong oral skills but limited experience with written language (both in their first language and in English), or they may have limited skills in both. While large programs may have special literacy-level ESL classes, smaller programs are likely to integrate learners needing literacy instruction with other learners in beginning classes, some of whom may be quite literate but have limited oral English skills. In addition, those with formal education may have come from an oral tradition that gives limited attention to reading and writing. This diversity makes teaching beginning classes a challenge.

While there is research and practical guidance for teaching basic writing to adult English learners with limited prior formal education or literacy, much less has been provided for teaching the types of literacy skills needed "as a precursor to academic and professional writing" (Wong, Chapter 7, p. 164). Wong provides examples of effective strategies for bridging to this more challenging writing, as well as a thematic, standards-based lesson introducing occupations and work schedules "that promotes writing from the beginning." As Wong indicates, the need for appropriate adult ESL literacy-level classes is great: 40 percent of adult immigrants (Organization of Economic Cooperation and Development, 2013) and 58 percent of refugee adults have a low level of literacy (Richwine, 2017).

■ Concluding Thoughts

As this collection makes clear, writing can no longer be a neglected skill in classes for adult English learners, and the types of writing taught can no longer be limited to personal or narrative three- or five-paragraph essays or basic writing tasks such as form-filling or sentence completion since, ultimately, English learners in adult education programs will need to take and pass one of the high school equivalency exams and be prepared for college and careers. The challenges to both teachers and learners are great, but this collection of carefully selected activities and lesson plans provides a number of avenues for meeting them. Thankfully, as well, the writers of these chapters are themselves excellent writers, offering their chapters as models of clear academic and professional writing.

References

Fernández, R., Peyton, J. K., & Schaetzel, K. (2017). A survey of writing instruction in adult ESL programs: Are teaching practices meeting adult learner needs? *Journal of Research and Practice for Adult Literacy, Secondary, and Basic Education, 6*(2), 5–20.

National Council of State Directors of Adult Education. (2016). *The blue book.* Washington, DC: Author. http://www.naepdc.org

Peyton, J. K., & Schaetzel, K. (2016). Teaching writing to adult English language learners: Lessons from the field. *Journal of Literature and Art Studies,* (6), 1407–1423.

Trilling, B., & Fadel, C. (2009). *21st century skills: Learning for life in our times.* San Francisco: Jossey-Bass.

U.S. Department of Education. Office of Vocational and Adult Education. (2013). *College and career readiness standards for adult education.* Washington, DC: Author. http://lincs.ed.gov/publications/pdf/CCRStandardsAdultEd.pdf

U.S. Department of Education. Office of Career, Technical and Adult Education. (2016). *English language proficiency standards for adult education.* Washington, DC: American Institutes for Research. https://lincs.ed.gov/publications/pdf/elp-standards-adult-ed.pdf

Contributor Bios

Donna M. Brinton works as a private educational consultant in the field of TESOL/Applied Linguistics. Previously, she was employed as Senior Lecturer at the Rossier School of Education at the University of Southern California and worked for 27 years at the University of California, Los Angeles, in a variety of positions, including Associate Director of UCLA's World Languages and Cultures, Lecturer in Applied Linguistics, and Academic Coordinator of the UCLA ESL Service Courses. She is the co-author/co-editor of several professional texts, including *Content-Based Second Language Instruction, The Content-Based Classroom, New Ways in Content-Based Instruction, New Ways in ESP, Heritage Language Education: A New Field Emerging, Teaching Pronunciation, The Linguistic Structure of Modern English*, and the 4th edition of *Teaching English as a Second or Foreign Language*. Additionally, for twelve years she co-edited *The CATESOL Journal*. Donna has published several English language textbooks, numerous articles, and online content-based lessons for EFL learners. Most recently, she guest-edited an issue of *The CATESOL Journal* on research-based pronunciation teaching (with John Levis and Ana Wu). She has conducted short-term international teacher training in Asia, Central Asia, Africa, the Pacific Rim, the Middle East, and the Americas.

JoAnn (Jodi) Crandall is Emerita Professor of Education at the University of Maryland, Baltimore County, where she co-directed the MA TESOL Program and established and directed the interdisciplinary PhD Program in Language, Literacy and Culture. Prior to that, she was Vice President of the Center for Applied Linguistics, where she directed several projects for immigrant and refugee adults, including the National Clearinghouse on ESL Literacy Education. A former President of TESOL, WATESOL, and the American Association for Applied Linguistics, she has served on numerous adult ESL advisory boards focused on teacher education, professional development, and instruction. She is the co-author of *Passing the Torch: Strategies for Innovation in Community College ESL* (2007), *Adult ESL Teacher Credentialing* *and Certification* (2008), and *Health Care Career Pathways for Adult English Language Learners* (2011). She has provided professional development across the United States and in more than 40 countries and recently co-edited *Global Perspectives on Teacher Education and Professional Development in TESOL* (2016) and *Global Perspectives on Language Education Policies* (2017). She has also designed and taught ESL composition and advanced ESL writing courses for lawyers, judges, among others. She holds a PhD in sociolinguistics from Georgetown University.

Patsy Egan directs ATLAS, the ABE Teaching & Learning Advancement System, www.atlasABE.org. ATLAS, housed at Hamline University in St. Paul, provides professional development for Minnesota's Adult Basic Education workforce. As ATLAS Director, Patsy collaborates with Minnesota Department of Education staff on multiple projects focused on identifying, planning, designing, and evaluating the training and professional development needs of ABE/ESL practitioners across the state. Some of these activities include cohorts, workshops, and communities of practice around implementation of the College and Career Readiness Standards, adult career pathways, evidence-based reading instruction, contextualized career-focused instruction, and numeracy development. Patsy's research interests focus on language and literacy development and teacher education for adult learners. She is a frequent national and international conference presenter, particularly in the area of low-literacy adult ESL. Recent projects include a role as a subject matter expert on the OCTAE *ESL Pro* project, where she authored the Companion Learning Resource on *Meeting the Language Needs of Today's Adult English Language Learner* in 2016. Patsy was also involved in the OCTAE-sponsored initiative for the English Language Proficiency Standards, released in 2016.

Rebeca Fernández is Associate Professor of Writing and Educational Studies at Davidson College, where she teaches courses in first-year composition and educational linguistics and provides individualized writing support to multilingual students. She holds a doctorate in Language and Literacy from the Harvard Graduate School of Education. Early in her career, she worked in K–12 bilingual education, taught preschool Spanish, and conducted reading research on bilingual school-aged children. Afterward, she worked as an adult ESL and ABE/GED instructor at Central Piedmont Community College, where she taught all educational functioning levels and developed contextualized, content-based, and English for Specific Purposes courses for students and an online professional development course for faculty. Currently, she is collaborating with several colleagues on second language writing projects. She is a co-investigator on a longitudinal, multicohort research study on the writing development of Chinese L2 college writers. Along with Joy Kreeft Peyton and Kirsten Schaetzel, she has been conducting research, co-publishing, and developing professional development on adult ESL writing. Her recent publications include "A Survey of Writing Instruction in Adult ESL Programs: Are Teaching Practices Meeting Adult Learner Needs?" (with Peyton and Schaetzel, 2017) and "Artifacts and Their Agents: Translingual Perspectives on Composing Processes and Outputs" (with Campbell & Koo, in press).

Dana Ferris is Professor and Director of the University Writing Program at the University of California at Davis. She has been in the field of TESOL/second language writing for 35 years and has trained teachers, directed writing and graduate programs, conducted research, and published books and other materials for teachers. One of her primary areas of research has been on response to student writing, including the specialized topic of written corrective feedback or error correction. Her books on this topic include *Response to Student Writing* (2003); *Treatment of Error in Second Language Student Writing* (2nd ed., 2011), and *Written Corrective Feedback in Second Language Acquisition and Writing* (with John Bitchener, 2012). She has also published articles on her own primary research on response to writing in *TESOL Quarterly, Journal of Second Language Writing, Studies in Second Language Acquisition, TESOL Journal, CATESOL Journal, Research in the Teaching of English,* and *Writing and Pedagogy.* She was the founding editor-in-chief of the *Journal of Response to Writing* and is currently co-editor of the *Journal of Second Language Writing.* She received her PhD in Applied Linguistics from the University of Southern California.

Barry D. Griner is a Master Lecturer at the American Language Institute at the University of Southern California, where he teaches ESL courses to matriculated international students. He received a BS in Mathematics Education before spending ten years teaching EFL in Hiroshima, Japan (seven as Head Teacher). After returning to the United States, he earned an MA in Applied Linguistics and TESL at UCLA, doing research on the acquisition of the morphophonotactics of Japanese past tense. Barry's more than 30 years of teaching experience also includes two years teaching writing at the Centre for English Language Communication, National University of Singapore, as well as program evaluation/development and teacher training as an Academic Specialist for the U.S. State Department in Uzbekistan and Armenia. He is a contributing author to *Teaching Pronunciation: A Course Book and Reference Guide* (2nd edition, 2010).

Betsy Parrish, professor at Hamline University, has worked as an ESL/EFL teacher, teacher educator, writer, and consultant for more than 30 years. She has worked with learners and language teachers in the United States, Bangladesh, France, India, Russia, and Vietnam. She is a frequent presenter at state, national, and international conferences on adult education issues, including academic and career readiness, pronunciation, teacher development, and learner-centered teaching practices. She wrote *Teaching Adult ESL: A Practical Introduction,* and she was on the development team of a 12-part video series for adult ESL educators, *Teaching ESL to Adults: Classroom Approaches in Action* (2012). As a subject matter expert on the LINCS ESL Pro project, through the American Institutes for Research, she developed the online professional development module and Issue Brief on *Meeting the Language Needs of Today's Adult English Language Learner.* She has been involved in the OCTAE-sponsored initiative for the new English Language Proficiency Standards. She also provides support to local organizations and companies on working sensitively with linguistically diverse employees and clients.

Joy Kreeft Peyton is a Senior Fellow at the Center for Applied Linguistics, in Washington, DC, where she served as Vice President for 16 years. She holds a PhD in Sociolinguistics from Georgetown

University. She has more than 35 years of experience working in the field of languages, linguistics, and culture in education. Her work includes working with teachers and program leaders in K–12 and adult education settings in the United States and other countries (including Ethiopia, The Gambia, and Nepal) to improve their instructional practice and study the implementation and outcomes of research-based practice. Her work includes implementing and studying approaches to writing that facilitate engagement and learning and promote academic and professional success. She is a Senior Advisor for the EU-SPEAK project (Newcastle University), whose mission is to enhance the knowledge and skills of teachers of adult immigrants who have limited education and literacy in their native language. She is co-editor of *Understanding Adults Learning to Read for the First Time in a New Language: Multiple Perspectives* (2019) and co-author of a Wikipedia article on dialogue journal writing, a wonderful way to give language learners opportunities to interact, in writing, with more proficient writers: https://en.wikipedia.org/wiki/Dialogue_journal.

Steve Quann is an instructional design consultant. He has a Master's in Education and a graduate certificate in Instructional Technology Design. The majority of his career has been dedicated to preparing students to enter the workforce or transition to college, as a high school teacher, ESL instructor at Massasoit Community College, and Senior Technical Advisor at World Education Inc., where he provided face-to-face and online professional development for English language teachers for almost 20 years. He led the development of Words2Learn, a vocabulary-building app for students learning English. Present projects include the design and development of e-learning courses funded by the U.S. Office of Migrant Education and USAID. He has co-authored two books on integrating technology into English language instruction, both published by the University of Michigan Press: *Learning Computers, Speaking English: Cooperative Activities for Learning English and Basic Word Processing* and *Project Care: Health Care Case Studies, Projects and Multimedia for English Language Learners.* He was principal reviewer for *Integrating Digital Literacy into English Language Instruction: Companion Learning Resource* (2015).

Dudley Reynolds is a past President of the TESOL International Association and a Teaching Professor of English at Carnegie Mellon University in Qatar, where he teaches first-year writing and serves as Co-Area Head of the Arts and Sciences program. He holds a PhD in Linguistics from Indiana University. Across his career, he has taught in an elementary school in Egypt, the intensive English program at Indiana University, and the Master's in Applied English Linguistics program at the University of Houston. His primary research focuses on the development, assessment, and teaching of second language reading and writing. He is the author of *One on One with Second Language Writers: A Guide for Writing Tutors, Teachers, and Consultants* (2009) and *Assessing Writing, Assessing Learning* (2010), as well as numerous articles and book chapters. He is a frequent speaker at language teacher association conferences around the world.

Gilda Rubio-Festa is State Director of Adult Education in North Carolina and Associate Vice President of College and Career Readiness for the North Carolina Community College System, where she manages the Title II Adult Education and Family Literacy Act program. A specialist in teaching English language learners, she has assumed multiple roles in the field of adult education in the past 30 years, including that of instructor, administrator, teacher trainer, and curriculum developer. She co-developed one of the first online adult ESL teacher training programs specifically for adult education. She has presented at several TESOL conferences and served as Chair of the Adult Education Interest Section for TESOL, 2011–2012. She coauthored *Life Beyond the Language Classroom: Creating a Technical Career ESL Program Through Community Partnerships* (2009) for the TESOL Classroom Practice Series' Authenticity in the Classroom and Beyond. She earned an MA in TESOL from Columbia University, Teachers College.

Diana Satin is the Training and Technical Assistance Coordinator at English for New Bostonians, where she provides staff in ESOL programs with professional development on strengthening students' technology and language skills so they can reach their academic and vocational goals. She earned a Master's in Intercultural Relations with a specialization in teaching ESOL from Lesley University. She has been in the adult education field since 1994, as a classroom and blended learning teacher, professional development provider, curriculum developer, and author. Her publications include *Project Care: Health Care Case Studies, Multimedia, and Projects for Practicing English* (with Quann, 2007), and *Learning Computers, Speaking English* (with Quann, 2000). She has authored numerous curricula and professional development resources for World Education, the National Center for Study of Adult Learning and Literacy, LINCS, and ProLiteracy. As a professional developer, Diana has been facilitator and peer mentor of the Technology Integration Project for the New England Literacy Resource Center and has created and facilitated statewide and national workshops for LINCS and World Education. Diana is a partner on the EdTech Center @ World Education team, helping to conceptualize and promote new projects and approaches for uses of technology in adult basic education.

Kirsten Schaetzel is the English Language Specialist at Emory University School of Law, where she works with graduate students to develop and enhance their academic reading and writing skills. She holds a PhD in Applied Linguistics from Boston University. She has worked in the field of ESL for more than 30 years, both in the United States and overseas (Bangladesh, Macau, Singapore, and Ukraine). She has taught academic writing skills at work places, community colleges, and universities. She has also trained teachers at the National Institute of Education, in Singapore, and at the Center for Adult English Language Acquisition (CAELA) at the Center for Applied Linguistics, in Washington, DC. A decade ago, she began working with international law students to improve and enhance their academic and legal English skills. Her research interests include academic writing, discussion skills for academic settings, ESL teacher training, and characteristics of teacher-readers. Recent publications include "A Survey of Writing Instruction in Adult ESL Programs: Are Teaching Practices Meeting Adult Learner Needs?" (with Fernández

& Peyton, 2017), "Teaching Writing to Adult Learners: Lessons from the Field" (with Peyton, 2016), and "A Features-Based Approach for Teaching Singapore English" (with Low & Lim, 2010).

Betsy Lindeman Wong has worked in adult ESL programs for more than 20 years as an instructor, site coordinator, curriculum developer, and teacher trainer. Currently an Intensive English Program instructor in Northern Virginia Community College's American Culture and Language Institute, she has taught ESL in academic and workplace settings as well as in community education and family literacy programs. She has also served as a State Department English Language Teaching Fellow in France. Her publications include digital learning modules for Burlington English; an integrated-skill ESL textbook (*Project Success 1*, 2014) and teacher's guide (*Future English for Results 5: Teacher's Edition and Lesson Planner*, 2009); and the family literacy curriculum for Fairfax County, Virginia (https://eric.ed.gov/?id=ED482884). She has also written articles for *Scholastic Teacher* and *Educational Leadership* magazines, with practical solutions for reaching out to immigrant parents. She holds a Master's degree in ESL from Hamline University and a Master's degree in French and graduate certificate in TESOL, both from American University. For her Master's in ESL thesis, she developed a critical-thinking curriculum for IEP reading instruction (http://digitalcommons.hamline.edu/hse_all/1116/), aimed at meeting the needs of Saudi college students in U.S. academic preparation programs.

Index